THE SOUNDS OF *LATINIDAD*

SOCIAL TRANSFORMATIONS IN
AMERICAN ANTHROPOLOGY
General Editor: Ida Susser

The Sounds of Latinidad: *Immigrants Making Music
and Creating Culture in a Southern City*
Samuel K. Byrd

The Sounds of *Latinidad*

Immigrants Making Music and Creating Culture in a Southern City

Samuel K. Byrd

NEW YORK UNIVERSITY PRESS

New York and London

NEW YORK UNIVERSITY PRESS
New York and London
www.nyupress.org

References to Internet websites (URLs) were accurate at the time of writing. Neither the author nor New York University Press is responsible for URLs that may have expired or changed since the manuscript was prepared.

Library of Congress Cataloging-in-Publication Data
Byrd, Samuel Kyle.
The sounds of latinidad : immigrants making music and creating culture in a southern city / Samuel K. Byrd.
pages cm. — (Social transformations in American anthropology)
Includes bibliographical references and index.
ISBN 978-1-4798-5940-5 (cl : alk. paper) — ISBN 978-1-4798-6042-5 (pb : alk. paper)
1. Music—Social aspects—North Carolina—Charlotte. 2. Latin Americans—
North Carolina—Charlotte—Music—History and criticism. 3. Hispanic Americans—
North Carolina—Charlotte—Music—History and criticism. I. Title.
ML3917.U6B97   2015
780.89'68075676—dc23   2015000478

New York University Press books are printed on acid-free paper, and their binding materials are chosen for strength and durability. We strive to use environmentally responsible suppliers and materials to the greatest extent possible in publishing our books.

Manufactured in the United States of America

10 9 8 7 6 5 4 3 2 1

Also available as an ebook

CONTENTS

PREFACE

When I began preliminary field research in Charlotte, North Carolina, in June 2008, I knew no one and virtually nothing about Charlotte's Latin music scene. Recent protests in cities across the United States around immigration reform had piqued my interest in understanding the politics of immigration. As an anthropologist studying urban issues, I was intrigued by census data and journalistic reports about the demographic and cultural transformation occurring in many southern cities, particularly in Charlotte, which experienced exponential growth in its immigrant population from 1990 to 2000 and dramatic continued growth the decade after. And as a southerner, I witnessed anecdotal shifts when visiting family back home in Athens and Atlanta, Georgia—new Mexican restaurants, taco trucks at the flea market, Spanish-language radio stations, ethnic groceries, and so on.

My personal and research background also involved music—I had conducted research on music of the U.S.-Mexico border and New Orleans—but I had little expectation of making music the center of my study in Charlotte. However, much to my surprise, I encountered a thriving Latin music scene and many musicians who were excited about the potential of this study and welcoming to a visiting ethnographer. As an amateur musician who plays trumpet and guitar in my spare time, I was able to bring my musical training and sensibilities to many fruitful discussions about music—and even to join in playing music (although, I'm afraid, not very skillfully) during rehearsals. As I pursued participant observation, several people were intrigued enough with my project to not just answer my questions, but to constantly keep me informed on the inner workings of their bands and music-making process. Many saw my project as another form of promotion, part and parcel with the process of interactions with club owners, festival organizers, and radio staff to get their band's music out in front of the public. Although several musicians were difficult to interview because of their busy schedules, no one outright rejected my request for an interview or desire to observe the goings-on backstage.

In my research, I was greatly aided by my affiliation with the Latin American Coalition. I began volunteering there in preparation for the 2009 Festival Latinoamericano with the thought that through this festival I would meet local musicians and see how a local music festival was put on. It turned out that the event manager there, Tony Arreaza, is also a guitar player and concert promoter who has numerous connections in the music scene in Charlotte. Tony quickly connected me with several prominent local groups. After the festival, I continued working at the Latin American Coalition as a part-time event planner and apprentice to Tony. Thus, I was able to participate in and document the planning of several concerts and festivals, including the 2010 Festival Latinoamericano.

Over time I selected several bands to follow closely, along with numerous other groups that I kept in peripheral view. I attended performances of each band, taking pictures, chatting with band and audience members during breaks in the music, and observing bands as they performed live. I interviewed musicians from each group, asking them about the band's history, influences, style, and internal dynamics. I observed rehearsals in practice spaces and watched as two bands recorded albums and demos. I also witnessed several bandleaders as they booked gigs for their band, observing their interactions with club managers, restaurant owners, and festival organizers (including myself).

While I concentrated on documenting local musicians, I had several opportunities to watch national and international bands, such as Los Amigos Invisibles, Los Aterciopelados, and Los Tucanes de Tijuana, perform as they toured through Charlotte. Often, a local group would play as the opening act, and I compared the performances and musician and audience interaction at venues of local and nonlocal groups. By attending concerts on multiple occasions, I was able to document the ambience of clubs and restaurants and compare how different groups were received at the same venue.

I collected various primary sources concerning the Latin music scene, including newspaper articles and advertisements for concerts and events. I wrote field notes in a journal about each day's experience, recording subjective opinions and observed details. I also started a blog called *Sam's Sounds*, which presented my topical observations and analysis to the public. Online, I posted photographs and wrote synopses of concerts and festivals; the blog also served as a way to solicit feedback from musicians and audience members about my ideas. Musicians and audience members read my posts and commented online or in person on what I had written. This was a way for me to confirm whether my initial impressions of performances matched what others had seen or heard, and these posts helped spark dialogues about several themes that run throughout this book.

Photographs and visual evidence play a major role in my analysis. As I snapped photographs and collected copies of concert posters and flyers, I began to realize that visual representations helped me to understand the lives of musicians in greater detail. Whether it was the chaotic dancing of Dorian Gris's fans, the onstage antics of Bakalao Stars, or the artistry of Carlotan Rock's promotional posters, I realized that the visual and musical elements of performance were often inseparable (see Feld 1976); therefore I have included examples of photographs and posters throughout the work that substantiate my arguments.

I lived in two parts of Charlotte with a high concentration of Latina/o immigrants. First I lived for five months in the South Boulevard area; then I moved to East Charlotte for the next eight months of the project. Both locations offered proximity to Latino nightclubs and restaurants and everyday interactions with Latinos in the neighborhood, on public transportation, and in stores. Although my focus was on Latina/o musicians, I kept abreast of the political, economic, and social issues facing the Latino community in Charlotte, often attending rallies, marches, and community meetings. These issues, particularly the debate surrounding immigration reform and the continuing economic recession, were a constant concern for musicians and the rest of the community alike. Using these experiences and the knowledge gained from participating in the Latin music scene and organizing festivals in Charlotte, I am able to position Charlotte in the nexus of regional, national, and international configurations of Latin music.

ACKNOWLEDGMENTS

This book relied upon the help of numerous people. First, the field research was assisted by a summer reconnaissance grant and a writing fellowship from the City University of New York Graduate Center. I thank all the musicians, audience members, activists, and nonprofit staff in Charlotte who allowed me to document their lives. In particular, those musicians who took time to sit for formal interviews and informal conversations with me deserve recognition—Christian, Javier, Daniel, Carlos, Fred, Joswar, Gonzalo, Helder, Isaac, Juan Miguel, Sendy, Oscar, Reinaldo, Jorge, Alberto, and Jani, among others—I hope I have done your words justice. I would like to thank the Latin American Coalition and Jess George for continually finding ways to help me stay involved in the organization and its cultural programs. I thank Owen Furuseth, Janet Levy, and the University of North Carolina–Charlotte for their assistance and welcoming attitude for a scholar visiting the area. I commend the journalists Mark Kemp and Jacobo Strimling for helping me to understand how to place Charlotte's Latin music in context. *Un millón de gracias* go out to Tony and Ailen Arreaza for their unwavering support and dedication. Tony, your continued enthusiasm for this project and encyclopedic knowledge of music kept my research afloat in its darkest hours. Thanks to the Immigration Working Group and others at the CUNY Graduate Center, including Ida Susser, Marc Edelman, Don Robotham, the late Neil Smith, and Julie Skurski, who kindly read and commented on drafts of the project. Thanks to Jennifer Hammer and Constance Grady at New York University Press for their help preparing the manuscript. My advisor, Ida Susser, deserves credit for helping me to elaborate many of the ideas, and for encouraging me to pursue field research despite limited funding. Thanks to my mother, Debbie Zimmerman, for editing portions of the book. Finally, I thank Daliz Pérez-Cabezas and Yosette and Leilani Byrd-Pérez, the loves of my life.

Introduction

Over the past two decades in the United States, immigration, particularly from Latin America, has transformed both traditional centers of immigrant influxes and "new immigrant destinations" on a scale not seen since the last "great wave" of immigration in the late nineteenth and early twentieth centuries (Fry 2008; Suro and Singer 2002; Zúñiga and Hernández-León 2005). This book looks at one facet of this transformation: Latina/o immigrant musicians and their audiences in Charlotte, North Carolina, who, through their music making, engage in processes of community formation as they debate political questions relevant to their everyday lives as working musicians and residents of a globalizing city. Musicians in Charlotte, like much of the Latino immigrant population in the United States, find themselves the subject of battles over immigration policy, debates over the role of immigrants, evolving methods of policing and surveillance, and new iterations of the American racial hierarchy that have accompanied this era of globalization.

The response to the current "great wave" of immigration is a sea change that betrays the narrative of a "nation of immigrants" and reveals instead a regime of militarization, racialization, and social segregation. This regime is built upon two legal and political developments—the militarization of the U.S.-Mexico border and U.S. cities through the "War on Drugs" and the implementation of intensive surveillance and policing of immigrant communities after 9/11. Emerging in tandem with these developments is xenophobia stirred up by anti-immigrant activism and stigmatization of immigrants as a social problem. As the anthropologist Gilberto Rosas argues, these developments are part of the "borderlands condition" that inscribes "exceptionality" (drawing on Agamben's idea of "state of exception" [2003]) on immigrant bodies through everyday violence and surveillance (Rosas 2006).

Through their analyses of Latino cultural production, border studies scholars have long noted the exceptionality of law and lawlessness

1

of the U.S.-Mexico border and how regimes of racial, gender, and class exploitation help shape the political subjectivity of borderlands residents (Paredes 1958; McWilliams 1968; Montejano 1987; Peña 1985; Anzaldúa 1987; Limón 1994; Gaspar de Alba and Guzmán 2010). It is through attention to the shifting role of the state in monitoring everyday life and focus on the transgressive and transformative power of cultural production that border studies scholarship contributes to an analysis of contemporary Latino immigration to other regions of the United States, more so since the borderlands condition has "thickened" (Rosas 2006) throughout the United States with the expansion of border exceptionality to local immigration policing efforts. In effect, the border has moved north, as local and state governments have implemented policies that target undocumented immigrants and their families, such as the 287(g) program and state laws passed in Arizona, Utah, Georgia, South Carolina, and Alabama. In North Carolina, several counties, including Mecklenburg (where Charlotte is located), have signed on to the 287(g) program, and the state government has restricted undocumented immigrants' access to driver's licenses and higher education.

With these policy changes have emerged new forms of social and structural racism, expressed in the racialization of Latina/o immigrants. For example, terms like "illegal" and "Mexican" have become common in the public discourse and are belittling catchall terms that group all Latinos as undesirable despite their varied national origins, legal statuses, and language competencies (De Genova 2005). Anti-immigrant laws and policies that lead to the everyday policing of immigrant bodies has led some to call the U.S. South's new landscape Juan Crow (Lovato 2008). In essence, the U.S. South has responded to globalization by erecting a system that oppresses a new working class of immigrants by marginalizing them through racial labeling, policing, social exclusion, and delegitimization of their labor. Latina/o activists organizing to protest these conditions have mobilized mass marches and prominent actions, but face counterprotests, an entrenched class of policy makers who gain politically from targeting immigrant communities, and the failure of the federal government to construct a viable alternative to local devolution of immigration policy. The immigration reform movement has been unable to alter the increasing number of deportations, to rectify the status of the DREAM generation of undocumented students, or to exert pressure to alleviate the poor working conditions and wage theft suffered by immigrant laborers.

Charlotte's Latina/o musicians and their audiences play a vital role in defining Latino expressive culture. Moreover, their lives also reveal issues of politics, labor, community, class, division, and belonging that have become central to a globalizing region and city that are struggling to decide, as the historian David Hollinger (1993) put it, how wide the circle of "We" should be. During my research, the theme of *el sueño gris* (the gray dream) described the trajectory of the dreams and aspirations of Latino immigrants to the U.S. South. When I first came across the phrase in the liner notes of an album by the Charlotte band Dorian Gris, I immediately recognized the play on words from the Oscar Wilde novel *The Picture of Dorian Gray* (2008) and the phrase's significance for a band that plays punk and heavy metal. In addition to its dark playing style, in the time between the recording of a live performance and its release several months later as *Live at the Dark Room*, the band had switched bass players and saw decreasing numbers of fans coming to its shows. The band members' dreams of staying together as a band and building an audience seemed to be fading. But it took me several months to piece together the broader significance of the "gray dream" for Latino immigrants to Charlotte and the region. The failure of efforts to pass comprehensive immigration reform and the increasing number of state and local laws targeting immigrants began to turn the skies gray. For musicians, this climate of fear coupled with the economic recession hit hard, affecting turnout at concerts and threatening the sense of community that they had built around music making.

Examples of this graying dream appeared in personal narratives of Latino musicians during informal conversations and recorded interviews throughout the fieldwork process. These vignettes show the intense personal impact of immigration policing and the associated anti-immigrant environment; musicians' stories and experiences provide the inspiration for how this book is structured, with chapters following from the issues that they saw as central to their lives as working musicians. These stories are tempered by the uneven field upon which Latino immigrants act— some are documented, others are undocumented, some speak English, others are monolingual, a few are educated, with extensive social capital and resources, others not as much. For example, several undocumented musicians relayed to me their fear of driving on well-policed routes late at night after a performance. They would drive alternate routes through residential neighborhoods to avoid police checkpoints for DUI, not because they were over the limit from drinking, but because police could ask for papers that they did not have. Immigrant musicians who had U.S. citizenship or legal status travelled with less fear, but still reported racial discrimination and unpleasant encounters because of their appearance and accent.

In addition to incidents like these, musicians expressed dismay and frustration at the social segregation of Charlotte's music scene and their inability to "cross over" and build interracial or cross-cultural audiences. Latin bands like Bakalao Stars and Tropic Culture attempted with little success to bridge the cultural gap between English and Spanish, Latin and "American" musical styles, playing for small but loyal Latino audiences but never gathering large numbers of white or African American fans at their shows. A similar social segregation structured divisions within the Latin music scene, revealed through sharp genre divisions based on class, neighborhood, and nationality. Some bands, like the rock group Dorian Gris, worked within these divisions to build an enthusiastic audience of working-class Mexican fans, with whom they collaborated to draw up performances of stirring liveliness that have come to define a particular niche of class identity in the city. Other musicians have worked tirelessly to create genre-bending performances that question class, national, and ethnic differences within the Latino population. A local guitarist, Tony Arreaza, leads a band that blends Latin rock, pop standards, and *música tropical* to create a new pan-American canon of music. The singer Leydy Bonilla has begun to mix the styles of *merengue* and *bachata* from her native Dominican Republic with R&B and *regional mexicano* through collaborations with other musicians in Charlotte.[1]

Community Formation

Bearing witness to these developments, the analysis in this book looks at how the "graying" of immigrants' dreams has important consequences for community formation and solidarity among Latina/o musicians and their audiences in the U.S. South. I extract the implications of these political and economic developments through the music making and common circumstances of members of Charlotte's Latin music scene. For some, these changes created internal tensions, leading to bands breaking up, disillusionment with the creative process, or a sense of stagnation. Others soldiered through difficulties and attempted to move their music forward in response to challenges.

Latina/o immigrant musicians find themselves at the center of the intersection of culture and politics, often being driven to negotiate a field fraught with political consideration and contested cultural boundaries and to define a vision of what it means to be Latino/a in a globalizing city in the South. In Charlotte, musicians have played a vital part in conceptualizing a *latinidad* that acknowledges the diverse backgrounds of immigrants to the city and that engages with the context of southern urban living, from the region's history as the font of American popular culture to the current anti-immigrant political climate. Music making illuminates one aspect of how Latino immigrants claim "cultural citizenship," a process that the anthropologist Renato Rosaldo describes as "the everyday practices through which Latinas/os claim space and their right to be full members of society" (Rosaldo 1994). Following from studies of community formation through local artistry (Crehan 2012; Finnegan 2007), I argue that the work that Charlotte's musicians do is political in itself. They assert a particular form of agency with audience members when collaborating on and negotiating creative expression. This collaboration uses music as the medium through which musicians and audiences synthesize disparate elements—nationalities, class backgrounds, ages, and migration experiences—into Latino identity. As such, Latin music in Charlotte is not just a collection of sounds, but a process of defining a way to live and see the world. My research demonstrates that Latinos are creating, in the face of oppressive anti-immigrant policies, group solidarity and agency. They are recognizing themselves as having a common experience as immigrants, as musically inclined people, as speakers of a shared idiom that form a group "in itself" (Thompson 1963)—a community.

Community has been an important object of study among social scientists for some time, and an important theme for southerners' sense of belonging and place. My analysis takes guidance from theorists who have discussed the meaning of community in an age of industrialization and imperialism, from Tonnies's comparison of *Gemeinschaft* and

Gesellschaft (1887) and Marx's analysis of alienation of labor power and class formation (1976), to Durkheim's concept of collective consciousness (1997). I also take notice of the findings of early anthropologists, from Malinowski to Boas, and Evans-Pritchard to Lévi-Strauss, who saw other forms of community that did not fit neatly into Western, modernist theories. A conceptualization of community also must account for how the state encourages, regulates, prohibits, surveys, and interacts with communities. While new forms of postindustrial and postmodern community are forming in "virtual" and transnational settings, the state continues to affect how and to what extent groups formulate a sense of community and shared understandings of the world.

Musical Community

Because affiliations among the individuals I studied center on music making, I use the term "musical community" to describe this process of community formation I explored—acknowledging that community in this sense is temporal, threatened by outside forces, and often incomplete. For this book, I have defined "musical community" as a sense of belonging and shared affiliation around notions of class, ethnicity, language, style, and taste expressed through music and other creative cultural expressions. For Charlotte's Latinos, "musical community" is about asserting autonomy in the face of social and structural forces that marginalize them as surveilled subjects of immigration enforcement and racial stereotypes. I divide Charlotte's Latin music scene into three distinct musical districts that each host bands and audience members who attempt to form musical community. These areas—Eastside, Intown, and Uptown—correspond to geographic and genre differences in music making. The Eastside hosts *regional mexicano* and punk/heavy metal bands that perform for working-class Mexican and Central American immigrant audiences. The Intown area consists of Latin rock bands playing for "multicultural," often middle-class, audiences of South American immigrants and second-generation youth. The Uptown area hosts bands performing *música tropical* and Brazilian music for audiences of Caribbean and Brazilian residents of Charlotte. While there is some occasional overlap between these districts, "musical community" usually formed in very specific contexts—around one band playing in a favorite club, for example—and rarely transferred to other areas outside their neighborhoods, where bands and audience members felt uncomfortable or did not dare to venture because of immigration policing.

Within these musical communities, I observed a dialectical relationship form between musicians and audience members, with musicians performing and then responding to feedback from fans by implementing the fans' views through changes in the music. Musicians (and some nonmusicians) thus pursue the intellectual work of developing folk theories concerning the meaning of their music based on dialogue with their audiences. These individuals take on a role of "grassroots intellectual" (Forgacs 2000), outlining theories that explain the values and group identities of the band and its audience.[2] They analyze the process of music making and reflect on the significance of performances, and, through this analysis, theorize about the political significance of their music in the context of immigration, the globalizing city, and anti-immigrant politics.

Charlotte's musicians also connect to global and transnational networks. Musicians are constantly referencing and interpreting music from the global scene, at least in their genre, but often from related and unrelated popular genres, because this is what fellow musicians and fans demand of them in their work. This is why I found bands covering hit songs, introducing new instruments to their orchestration (auto-tune, keyboards, timbales), and attempting to blend and bend genre to suit the desires of their audiences. When bands open for an international touring group or share the lineup at a festival, they are grounding the visiting group's music in the local musical community by introducing it or providing local context and commentary through their own performance. Musicians point to the success of a concert, the strong bonds they forge with visiting musicians, and the hospitality they show to touring groups as evidence that Charlotte is a place where Latin music is viable.

By analyzing emerging transnational networks of Latino musicians, this book demonstrates how these networks help define a southern *latinidad* that Latino residents of Charlotte use to position themselves in opposition to but fully embedded in the local constraints of immigration enforcement and urban social segregation. The everyday act of making music, whether as a musician or audience member, entails participating in this *latinidad*; thus music becomes political because it facilitates community formation and spaces where Latino immigrants feel at home. However, interactions within the Latino population between groups of different origins can be contentious (De Genova and Ramos-Zayas 2003), and my analysis complicates simplistic versions of *latinidad*. Often, community does not form out of these differences. But at times, the Latin music scene in Charlotte does produce moments of solidarity, where band and audience join together as one body. "Musical community" formation, then, is a democratic and cosmopolitan process and helps Latino immigrants identify themselves as transnational actors.

On an even smaller scale, the personal relationships formed among musicians within bands often foster communal ties through fictive kinship. The band, particularly for young musicians who have left family back in the home country, becomes a second family. Fellow band members call each other *hermano* (brother), *'pana* (friend), or *marico* (dude), share private details of their lives, and support each other during personal hardships and setbacks.[3] Young musicians become apprentices to older, more experienced band members. There are disagreements and conflict, but musicians cherish the camaraderie and experiences they share with fellow band members. These relationships become a prism through which musicians interpret the city. As Juan Miguel Marín, drummer for La Rúa, recalls about his experience with the band, "La Rúa, for all of us, was like our first girlfriend. It was very important to our lives in Charlotte. I could not imagine my life in Charlotte without La Rúa and everything that came around what we were doing with La Rúa."[4]

Musicians' experience with the city varies, in large part based on which of Charlotte's three musical districts they perform in and how their band positions itself in terms of labor conditions, politics, genre boundaries, and moral and ethical questions. The music venue becomes a place where people debate what it means to belong in the city. Facing residential and social segregation, some musical districts, such as the Eastside, have set up venues that cater exclusively to Latinos, while other audiences, for example Uptown *salsa* enthusiasts, because of their more secure legal status and affinity with non-Latino musical forms, have chosen (and find easier paths) to participate in music venues that offer space for Latin and non-Latin music side by side. Musicians and audiences put forth a vision of their Charlotte that asks whether the city should have segregated or integrated music spaces, stress mainstream or marginal voices, and allow Spanish-speaking voices to express popular performance practices.

Charlotte as Case Study

Charlotte is a site that can be an important case study of issues around immigration, cities, and music. By studying Charlotte residents, particularly Latina/o immigrant musicians and their audiences, this book looks at the interactions between a specific place and general processes that are affecting urban life under globalization. Charlotte is compelling for several reasons. As a banking center, it embodies the trajectory of a neoliberal economic transformation that has shifted the city's economic base from textiles to finance. While globalization decimated much of the industrial base erected from the 1890s onward, it also allowed Charlotte to entice financial institutions to build headquarters in the center city. Charlotte is a "globalizing city" (Graves and Smith 2010) striving to join the ranks of other financial capitals but also to retain its southern roots. Charlotte's bankers and other corporate elites have pushed for intensive construction in the center city—building skyscrapers and attempting to create urban density that, at least on a small scale, mimics Manhattan. Neither center nor periphery, Charlotte is both enveloped in circuits of global capital flows and labor migrations and struggling to retain its unique regional, southern identity.

Charlotte's growth has been based on a permissiveness and "progressive" vision of political liberalism that often accompanies the rise of a financial sector, but this stance is in decline, or is at least being complicated by the city's implementation of anti-immigrant policies. A vast divide of class, access to rights, and race separates the city's elites from its immigrant working class. While the city's elites may celebrate the supposed global diversity of Charlotte through sponsorship of the arts, meals at Brazilian steakhouses, or promotional materials celebrating foreign companies with branch offices or factories in the metro areas, the actual global diversity of Charlotte takes place in immigrants' neighborhoods, music venues, nonprofits, and places of worship. Moreover, elites' celebration of Charlotte's global culture neglects to mention the daily grind of police stops of Latino drivers, unprosecuted wage theft, dismal housing conditions, and uncertain future for undocumented students. While they sell Charlotte by directing global circuits of capital toward Uptown and displaying the city's worldliness, Charlotte's elites have erected structural barriers that segregate and contain immigrant working-class global culture to the margins of the city. Latina/o immigrant musicians are well aware of their secondary status in this hierarchy, but also take pride in what they see as their markedly greater sense of cosmopolitanism and connection to global cultural trends, while retaining groundedness in their local, southern community. They struggle to make ends meet playing for small audiences in segregated clubs, but also take advantage of openings (at Latino cultural festivals, for example) where they can market their music to a wider audience.

Music and Politics

One research hypothesis with which I began was that musicians, as public performers of Latino culture in Charlotte and fellow immigrants, would insert political commentary into their music and be a vital part of social movement organizing for immigration reform. What I found instead was that many musicians avoided overt political statements and did not actively participate in the organized politics of immigrants' rights struggles, instead holding an ambivalent and cautious view of political engagement. Throughout this book I attempt to explain this politics of ambivalence through examinations of musicians' everyday lives and their precarious existence as working musicians, through analysis of the music-making process, and through brief overviews of the organization of the immigration reform social movement.

While musicians share a sense of vulnerability with many immigrants in their audiences and neighborhoods, I found that it is musicians' unique public role as performers that has led them to pursue a strategy of self-censorship and political avoidance. They prefer to focus their attention inward, toward their musical community. This self-censoring attitude contrasts with that of immigration reform activists and other political leaders (pastors, community organizers, students, and businesspeople) in the Latino community who lead public lives in a different, more overtly political way. Musicians are in a complex and conflicted position—of supporting the immigration reform movement in private but curtailing their public involvement in politics—which may be why there have been no protest songs to accompany the immigration marches.

Yet, I argue, Latina/o musicians and audience members do engage in a political process through their performances and everyday interactions. One Charlotte journalist called this type of interaction the "collective circle," aptly describing a style of dancing, jumping, and thrashing that occurs at heavy metal and punk concerts on Charlotte's Latino Eastside (Strimling 2010). Through performance, the music pulls people together and provides a space for working out social issues. Moreover, music making takes on a larger, representational role as musicians connect to each other and transnational networks of Latino expressive culture as a part of identity formation. Musicians use music as a medium to act as grassroots intellectuals by expressing class and ethnic identity, negotiating ethical quandaries, and staking a claim to belonging to a neighborhood, city, and region of the United States. Some of this performance reinforces tradition (for example, the continuation of music making as a male-dominated profession and patriarchal gender roles in song lyrics and performance practices), while some signals new beginnings, like collaborations that attempt to break down national and genre boundaries between *bachata* and *regional mexicano* music and forge an intra-class alliance between working-class Mexican and Dominican immigrants.

Internal discussions among musicians display not just an awareness of their vulnerability as immigrants, but a nascent consciousness about collaborating to change their working conditions as musicians. Dorian Gris, drawing on interactions between band members and working-class fans, has shifted musical direction to a harder sound that represents a collective response to harsh working conditions, immigration policing, and economic insecurity. Other bands have begun to channel the bilingual and multicultural sentiments of young, second-generation Latina/o residents, through mixtures of African American and Afro-Caribbean song forms, such as R&B, *reggaetón*, rap, *merengue*, and *bachata*. Musicians—by singing in Spanish *and* English, by constructing genealogies of musical taste that span Latin American and U.S. styles, and by promoting Charlotte as a place of cosmopolitanism and intense cultural production—are laying the groundwork for a music scene that may truly express the diversity of *latinidad* in one place.

This book challenges a number of common concepts. Many works on popular music focus on famous musicians (Keil 1966; George 1988; Rose 1994; Wald 2001; Kemp 2004; Gordon 2002). While these types of studies can reveal much about music and music making, they also reinforce the well-worn narrative of fame and reconstitute the inaccurate correlation between financial success and musical skill. This book focuses on ordinary musicians who seek but often fail to find fame, and their daily struggles to make music and make a living while being musicians. Other works focus on the music as text, analyzing song lyrics and/or notation by themselves as a way to understand a culture or social group (Zavella 2012; Paredes 1958; Edberg 2004). While this method can be useful (I have used it in the past), the ethnographic evidence presents a more striking and complete picture of the lives of Charlotte's Latina/o musicians. Therefore I use lyrics sparingly, and primarily to support points musicians have made in describing their music or to illuminate my analysis of performance. Many books about Latin music focus on one genre, laying out the history and current iterations of *bachata*, *salsa*, *banda*, or *rock en español* as separate musical forms (Pacini Hernández 1995; Washburne 2008; Simonett 2001; Zolov 1999). But in Charlotte, I found all of these genres side by side, often undergoing processes of transformation, with musicians and audiences negotiating new roles while debating the genealogies of their musical knowledge. By focusing on the everyday lives of ordinary musicians, accounting for the interplay of text and performance, and situating genres within the context of the entire Latin music scene, this book seeks a deeper understanding of musicians' lives and the process of making music. I also build upon studies that evaluate musicians as political actors engaging with structural forces, social dynamics, and personal struggles and that show how their music and creative process reflect this agency (Fox 2004; Lipsitz 1994; Erlmann 1996; Spellman 1966). By documenting the lives of musicians through ethnographic analysis, interviews, photographs, and their own narratives and discourse about music, this book documents what it means to be a Latina/o musician in Charlotte and analyzes how such musicians are central to the formulation of southern *latinidad*.

Chapter Outline

Chapter 1, "Charlotte, a Globalizing City," introduces Charlotte, North Carolina, as a city and a place where Latina/o immigrants have settled. Starting with recent studies that position Charlotte as a "globalizing city" (Graves and Smith 2010; Smith and Furuseth 2006) in a region (the U.S. South) experiencing globalization (Peacock, Watson, and Matthews 2005), it presents a brief labor history of the city and region and then focuses on the Central Avenue corridor, a thoroughfare that passes through several Latino neighborhoods and a place of concentrated ethnic businesses, including music venues. The contemporary southern U.S. city must be understood in terms of struggles over immigration and the "right to the city" that have come to the forefront of current politics, the vulnerability of immigrant populations within this setting, and the momentous economic shifts that have occurred over the past decades resulting in Charlotte's rise as a center of financial industry.

Chapter 2, "The Latin Music Scene in Charlotte," reconstructs, through oral history and personal networks observed in study, the brief history of Latino musicians in Charlotte. Relying on scholarship on music and cultural studies, it also examines the threads connecting U.S., southern, and Latin American music(s) together up to the early twenty-first century. It outlines the bands that are the focus of this book and describes their musical style.

Chapter 3, "Bands Making Musical Communities," documents how bands and their audiences engage in a process of community formation around music. Working together to create music, they establish their political agency through negotiations of genre, style, and outlook, and through performance of music. The Latin music scene in Charlotte consists of the Eastside, Intown, and Uptown districts, each loosely corresponding to a geographic area of the city. Band-made communities within these districts highlight class divisions and tensions around race and ethnicity within the Latino community and between Latinos and non-Latinos.

Having set the scene for Latin music in Charlotte, the following chapters each engage with a specific issue related to music making, labor, and immigration status among Latina/o immigrants. Chapter 4, "'Thursday Is Bakalao's Day!' Bands at Work and Play," analyzes how musicians see their work: as freelance work, a full-time profession, a leisurely hobby, or a craft. Defining and analyzing the concept of "working musician," it positions musicians' labor in the context of immigration and class-based views on training and professionalism. The vulnerability of musicians as immigrant laborers plays a vital part in how they approach music making and relate to fellow musicians. It shows how musicians deal with the norm of low-paying, contingent music jobs and strategize about how to best pursue lives as working musicians. The work experience of Latina/o musicians in Charlotte highlights how globalization has brought a new vibrancy that provides some (limited) avenues for economic mobility through capital flows and migration, but also promotes a labor regime that depends on contingent, flexible labor and facilitates a growing divide between rich and poor.

Chapter 5, "The 'Collective Circle': Music and Ambivalent Politics in Charlotte," examines how Latino immigrant musicians and audience members, through their music making, debate political questions relevant to their everyday lives as working musicians and residents of a globalizing city. My research found that musicians and their audiences negotiate their political stances through a physical and intellectual process that one Charlotte journalist called the *circular colectivo* (collective circle; Strimling 2010). The collective circle describes the circle of dancers that often form at Eastside rock concerts in Charlotte, in which dancers slam into each other in dances where jumping and shoving serve to unite band and audience in a collective music-making strategy. But the term has an additional meaning—the collective circulation of ideas through music as bands, audience members, and journalists engage in debates about the political and social importance of what they are performing, how they perform it, and its meaning in the context of a politicized immigrant presence in the U.S. South. However, musicians maintain a cautious skepticism toward public activism in the form of organized protests around immigration reform, a stance that reflects a politics of ambivalence that is evident in the subject of songs and musicians' everyday lives.

Chapter 6, "Shifting Urban Genres," examines the political history of Latin genre categories, showing how genre emerges out of the contested spaces of nationalism and ethnic identity formation in Latin America and the United States. Genre categories mark musical expressions and provide distinction between social groups (Bourdieu 1984). By providing a set of rules and common assumptions, genre boundaries help to foster musical community through a sense of belonging, but also exclude others through difference. A major part of the agency of Latino musicians and their audience is how they negotiate genre boundaries together in a dialectical process, often through direct feedback during performances but also through informal conversations and online social networking sites. This process creates grassroots intellectuals who act as leaders guiding new musical developments. By deploying and, at times, bending genre rules, musicians enact and embody the common circumstances they share with their audience; they claim ownership over a method of making music. Drawing on numerous instances in which distinct genre performances butted against one another, this chapter analyzes how musicians justified these boundaries as necessary for distinguishing between diverse strains of *latinidad*, but also a trend toward musicians collaborating across genre in an attempt to construct a pan-Latino vision of belonging to the city.

Chapter 7, "Race and the Expanding Borderlands Condition," situates Latin music in the context of new forms of social and structural racism, expressed in the racialization of Latina/o immigrants and the exceptionality of immigration enforcement seemingly exempt from civil rights law oversight. After briefly outlining the legacy of racial segregation and violence in the U.S. South, along with Latin American racial projects, it analyzes the racialized experience of Latina/o immigrants to Charlotte. It highlights three themes that came to the forefront during my research: (1) how southern *latinidad*, particularly in music, informs how Latina/o immigrants see themselves as racial subjects—from being "Mexican" to notions of whiteness and blackness within the Latino community; (2) the detrimental effects of racial profiling in immigration policing and the geography of racism in Charlotte; and (3) how Latino residents see Charlotte in the context of the U.S. South as a haven from racism and a site for creating antiracist and nonracist community in the face of anti-immigrant oppression.

Chapter 8, "The Festival: Marketing *Latinidad*," analyzes the significance of the Latino cultural festival in relation to the production of southern *latinidad*, while also examining how festivals are essential to the process through which Charlotte's Latina/o musicians forge global connections with visiting musicians and promoters. It provides a behind-the-scenes look at how Latino festivals are organized and the relationship between organizers and corporate sponsors, and it explains how these global connections allow musicians to "jump scales" (Smith 1992) and create opportunities for their bands to tour or to advance other creative projects such as filmmaking. This chapter also critically examines how festivals at times produce a distorted and inaccurate picture of *latinidad*, while paying close attention to the structural and organizational limitations that influence this presentation. I argue that Latino festivals in Charlotte are sites of contestation where different groups negotiate what it means to be Latino, Mexican, Latin American, immigrant, and American. In addition, festivals contribute to a broader process of the commercialization and marketing of Latino identity, what might be termed, after the anthropologist Arlene Dávila (2012), Latin Music, Inc. I situate Latino cultural festivals in the context of ongoing attempts to define (and sometimes redefine) Latino culture.

Chapter 9, "Musicians' Ethics and Aesthetics," demonstrates how the festival facilitates communication between Latina/o musicians across genre boundaries and between musical communities. During and after their participation in these events, musicians engage in heated intellectual debates about the best way to organize festivals and treat performers, constructing social rules that guide their sense of ethics and their judgments about the "success" of an event. These ethical sensibilities stem from musicians' training and their relationships with fellow musicians and audience members that shape what constitutes "professional" behavior. By situating musicians' labor in the nexus of cultural production and consumption practices associated with festivals, the analysis shows how working musicians face many of the same political and economic limitations that dull to gray the immigrant dream.

The conclusion teases out insights gleaned from the Latin music scene for reexamining national and regional struggles over immigration policy. It reiterates how making music constitutes a form of political action and builds community through dialectical collaboration between musicians and audience members; in addition, it analyzes what this research means for a conceptualization of the city as a cultural center and for the future of Latino music in the U.S. South.

1

Charlotte, a Globalizing City

Charlotte, North Carolina, is not a "global city." It is, however, a globalizing one.
—William Graves and Heather A. Smith (2010)

Es sólo Carlotan Rock, pero me gusta. (It's only Carlotan
Rock, but I like it.)
—Ricardo de Los Cobos (2009a)

This study is about musicians and their communities, but it is also
about a city, Charlotte, North Carolina. Why Charlotte? Often during
my time in Charlotte, people would ask me that question, wondering
why I had come to study music in the "Queen City," with the subtext
of befuddlement that it could be worthy of serious contemplation. Perhaps Charlotte (or its residents) has an inferiority complex, although
this question may stem from struggles to define what Charlotte really
is. Is it a southern city, a "progressive" city, a rising center of finance, a
city obsessed with out-competing other cities, a site of suburban sprawl,
a new urban, gentrifying, mixed-use, condominium boomtown, a
NASCAR- and football-loving sports center, a music-loving and foodie
town, a new gateway city for immigration, or the most populous city in
a swing state? Charlotte contains elements of all these descriptions; its
diversity of forms and location within a region experiencing globalizing
processes make it a city of complex and contradictory transformation.

This chapter will outline why Charlotte is an important city to consider for urban anthropology. First, I will situate Charlotte in the literature on global cities and discuss its role as a "globalizing" and "musical"
city in the U.S. South. Second, I will briefly summarize the labor history
of Charlotte and its development to the present. Third, I will discuss
the diversity of today's Charlotte, focusing on the Central Avenue corridor, a thoroughfare that passes through several Latino neighborhoods

and a place of concentrated ethnic businesses, including music venues. Fourth, I will outline the development of notions of southern *latinidad* and how Latino identity and cultural production operate in a globalizing city in the U.S. South. The contemporary southern U.S. city must be understood in terms of struggles over immigration and the "right to the city" that have come to the forefront of current politics, the vulnerability of immigrant populations within this setting, and the momentous economic shifts that have occurred over the past decades resulting in Charlotte's rise as a center of financial industry. But it also must be understood in terms of a social and cultural transformation in which newcomers try on some elements of southern identity while staking a claim to belonging as urban citizens of Charlotte.

Globalizing City

In an edited volume focusing on Charlotte, the geographers William Graves and Heather Smith summarize recent scholarship that examines how "the external forces of globalization combine with the city's internal dynamics and history to reshape local structures, landscapes, and identities of a once quintessentially southern place" (Graves and Smith 2010, 3). They stress the importance of studying the process of places *becoming* global, not just researching places that have already become global. By inserting process into the study of globalization, my analysis connects the "globalizing city" to how music as a commodity and music making are becoming global; in Charlotte's case in the same place, but in different and segregated social spheres. This is a move that questions the focus of previous studies of "global cities" that have tended to focus on prominent places like New York, London, and Tokyo, while still adhering to the main theoretical tenets that underpin an analysis of globalization and urban life in the late twentieth and early twenty-first centuries. Graves and Smith are quick to admit, as the epigraph states, that Charlotte is not a "global city"; they hold no delusions of the city's grandeur. However, they make a strong case, which I would like to piggyback on, that Charlotte is worth studying precisely because it is neither center nor periphery, that it is undergoing a chaotic process of globalizing while retaining its unique regional, southern identity.

In fact, by marketing the city's southernness, city boosters hope to benefit from the distinctiveness of place (in terms of "southern charm," low real estate prices, and the region's anti-union labor laws). Turning the chauvinism of the global city on its head, Graves and Smith conclude that "in many cases the driving question for our authors is how the global fits into the Southern and not the other way around" (3).

The literature on the "global city" has focused on several themes important to this study and the recent history of the city of Charlotte. First, global capital flows and the development of a culture of international finance have surfaced in Charlotte through the rise of two major banks and several other financial institutions that make their headquarters in the city. The Charlotte banking industry played a major part in two banking/financial innovations of the past thirty years—the rise of the automatic teller machine (ATM) and the deregulation of interstate banking that allowed the merger of smaller regional banks into conglomerates such as Bank of America (see below). Second, as the sociologist Saskia Sassen theorized, the development of a financial sector is accompanied by a parallel low-wage service sector that supports high-wage finance managers (Sassen 1988, 1991). In Charlotte, this has spurred increased migration of college-educated bankers from northern cities as well as immigration from Latin America of service workers—the janitors, restaurant employees, landscapers, construction workers, couriers, and domestics that make the city's upper-middle-class lives run smoothly. A third labor migration, of middle-class African Americans from northern cities, has provided midlevel employees for banks and government agencies. Third, a globalizing Charlotte has meant changes in the city's culture and ambience. There are pressures: from the city's elite to form a "world-class" center city; from poor residents to provide better social services, housing, and public transportation; from newcomers to create a sense of community; from established residents and environmentalists to curb the city's outward growth; and from Latino immigrants for recognition, access, and a stop to police profiling and deportations. These pressures, and the conflicts and negotiations that result, reveal that Charlotte still has an unclear identity in formation; and the basic crossroads, as already mentioned, is the intersection of global and southern cultures.

What makes a city a city? Scholarship on cities has often discussed typologies of cities that describe physical structures, zones, and architectural styles, while situating cities within the social, economic, and political structures of historical epochs (Mumford 1961; Drake and Cayton 1993; Garreau 1992; Low 1996; Sawers and Tabb 1984). Other authors have defined cities in terms of the inequality and crises that shape how urban life is made and remade (Schneider and Susser 2003; O'Connor 1973; Davis 2006; Caldeira 1999). Still others have attempted to unmask the surface reality of cities to reveal the underlying drama of daily urban life (Benjamin 1999; Harvey 2006; Jacobs 1992). My study of Charlotte builds upon these works, but also accounts for the ways a city can be a "musical city." By "musical city," I refer to how the city becomes a site for music and shapes and directs how music making occurs among its residents (Graf 2007). All cities have a cacophony of everyday sounds, yet these sounds do not always produce music. Musicians make the "musical city" not just because they make pleasant sounds—a subjective judgment for fans of particular types of music—but because they attempt to form community around music making. The "musical city" is a process that builds (and sometimes dismembers) the brick-and-mortar places, demographics, social relationships, consumption and production patterns, and popular practices that make music possible. These processes, to a degree, happen in every city, but the specificity of the Latin music scene in Charlotte emerged out of an influx of Latino immigrants, opening of bars and clubs, friendships established between musicians, learned leisure habits of dancing, drinking, listening to music, and "going out," and a need to belong to a musically framed community of peers.

Charlotte presents an important case study for understanding how immigrants interact with the city through music. The general processes of globalization happening in Charlotte have a specific impact on how Latina/o immigrants make music; for example, the diversity of immigrants from across Latin America and the recent history of immigration have meant that Charlotte's Latin music scene does not have one genre or nationality that dominates music making (unlike other centers of Latin music in the United States). Latino immigrants interact with Charlotte, but also bring their knowledge of urban life in Mexico City, Guayaquil, Santo Domingo, Caracas, and New York to bear on how they build social ties through music. They remain in constant contact with these other cities and their music scenes, while also branching out to nearby southern cities to position Charlotte in a continuum of musical cities.

In my theorization of the "musical city," I draw on the ethnomusicologist Aaron Fox's discussion of musical communities that engage in "popular practice" (Fox 2004) that are separate from the music industry's fields of production and consumption. Everyday practices of music making can be essential to establishing and maintaining class and social identity. In the U.S. South, this notion of a musical city has special meaning, whether it is New Orleans, Memphis, Nashville, or Atlanta, or "southern" cities in the North, like Chicago (Berry, Foose, and Jones 1986; Sublette 2004; Touchet and Bagneris 1998; Regis 1999; Smith 1994; Booth 1993; Helm and Davis 2000; Malone 1979; Pecknold 2007; Sarig 2007). A discussion of musical cities in the U.S. South should be paired with mention of Latin American musical cities, including Havana (Sublette 2004), Mexico City (Zolov 1999), and Rio de Janeiro (McCann 2004), and Latin American cities in the United States—Los Angeles (Simonett 2001; Loza 1993), Miami, and New York (Washburne 2008; Roberts 1979; Flores 2000).

Charlotte is a musical city (although obviously not as well-known as some others) that merges some of the attributes of southern and Latin American musical cities. Although Charlotte also hosts a thriving rock scene and has important historical ties to gospel and bluegrass music, Charlotte's Latin music scene presents the most compelling assemblage of musical acts that span genres and instrumentation. Charlotte's Latino musicians are well aware of the U.S. South's regional musical history and the part they now play in redefining its boundaries. As an article in the Spanish-language newspaper *Mi Gente* celebrating the reunion concert of the rock band La Rúa in the 2009 Carlotan Rock festival emphatically stated, channeling the Rolling Stones (1974) in Spanish, "Es sólo Carlotan Rock, pero me gusta" (It's only Carlotan Rock, but I like it) (De los Cobos 2009a).

Early History of Charlotte

Charlotte began as an outpost of European settlers on the intersection of two Native American trading paths during the mid-eighteenth century. The city was named after Queen Charlotte, the German-born wife of

King George III. After the American Revolution, gold was found nearby, and the subsequent gold rush led to an influx of prospectors and eventually the establishment of a U.S. Mint in 1837. Charlotte was mainly bypassed by the Civil War, and it was after the war, when new railroads were built, that Charlotte had its first boom as a cotton processing center (Hanchett 1996). Cotton farmers from nearby counties in North and South Carolina would bring their crop by wagon into town, where it would be shipped to the coast by rail.

The post–Civil War era, particularly after the end of the Reconstruction period, was a time of urbanization and industrialization in the U.S. South. The piedmont region of the Carolinas and Georgia, stretching from just north of Charlotte southwest to Atlanta, became home to a thriving textile industry, as northern industrialists and their southern partners realized that cheap labor costs and proximity to raw materials (namely, cotton) made for favorable conditions for industry in the region. As several scholars have noted, the establishment of mill towns in the region marked a shift in the cultural and economic trajectory for places like Charlotte (Hall et al. 1987; Cobb 1988; Pope 1942). While during slavery and after emancipation, much of the South remained dependent on agriculture and what the historian James Cobb (1988) calls "plantation industries"—namely, lumber, turpentine, mining, and other extractive pursuits—the establishment of textile mills signaled a rearrangement of labor and capital. This rearrangement corresponded with the general movement toward what Henry Grady famously coined the "New South," outlined as the diversification of the region's economy, the rise of a new political class distinct from antebellum plantation owners, and, ever hopeful, a fresh image to replace the tarnish of the disastrous Civil War and tumultuous Reconstruction period. Of course, this vision of the New South was quickly undermined, perhaps because it was in many ways complicit with the reestablishment of a system of white supremacy throughout the region. During the 1870s, the reversal of many of the political gains made by African Americans was paired with a campaign of terror to reestablish social segregation and the erosion of economic access promised to freed slaves at the end of the Civil War.

This period of "Redemption" (Woodward 1971) extended to places like Charlotte, whose poor soil and relative isolation had limited the proliferation of large slaveholding plantations. Newly built textile factories, where black men labored in limited capacity as cleaners and haulers, for less pay and usually in areas of the factory separate and apart from white workers, formulated a racial order that extended to the housing segregation of newly built company mill towns. For some southern cities like Charlotte, the New South order of racially delineated neighborhoods represented a departure from antebellum city life, where whites, free blacks, and slaves lived in close proximity (Hanchett 1996; Jones 2008).

While bustling mill towns proved strong symbols for the region's boosters to promote their New South vision, the transformation to an industrial labor force was more gradual. In-migrating workers, often from economically depressed areas of Appalachia, while working in factories often retained ties to rural farms, returning seasonally to plant or pick crops. As several scholars have documented, Appalachian migrants brought rural practices, conceptions of time, and social attitudes to the workplace and their home life, often upsetting the regimentation desired by factory owners and managers (Hall et al. 1987; Pope 1942). Whether it was "Blue Mondays," evangelical religious beliefs, or backyard vegetable gardens, these grains of sand in the machine slowed the transition to an urban, industrialized workforce (Flynt 1979; Anglin 2002; Miller 1974). By the same token, factory managers implemented regimes of discipline, timekeeping, and education campaigns to attempt to stymie behavior they saw as harmful to production and unbecoming of proper citizens (Cobb 1988; Tullos 1989).

Out of this transition to factory work emerged new social classes and political struggles. A wealthy social group, composed of textile mill owners, railroad and transportation developers, electrical power plant investors, and financiers rose to rival old agricultural and extractive industry elites who had reasserted themselves at the end of the Civil War (Woodward 1971; Doyle 1990). These new elites, made up of striving southerners and northerners gone south, held a sometimes allied and otherwise conflicted relationship with the old guard. While opposed to electoral structures that favored rural areas over cities and embarrassed by the horrific racial violence embodied in lynchings, these new elites were quick to realize advantage in the southern labor system, built upon racial and class inequalities and paternalistic relationships.

In the factories, another class of increasingly proletarianized workers emerged in the 1910s and 1920s. Work that had started off as seasonal and an endeavor for the entire family—where husband, wife, and children worked in the same factory—became year-round, more mechanized, off-limits to children (with child labor laws), and more compartmentalized. Developments such as Ford's moving assembly line and Taylor's measured management of factory floor tasks led to a more standardized and regimented textile mill, with higher productivity and less downtime for workers. These changes, coupled with stagnant wages in the face of inflation, led to labor unrest in the late 1920s.

The "Great Strike" of 1927 was the culmination of years of smaller strikes by workers in southern textile factories (Pope 1942; Miller 1974). While the Roaring Twenties signaled economic recovery for most of the nation after the post–World War I recession of 1919, factory workers (and most of the working class in the South) did not benefit from this boom economy. After slowly building strength and organizing mills, labor unions undertook a series of strikes in the late 1920s and early 1930s, perhaps the most famous being the Communist-led Loray strike in Gastonia, North Carolina, a few miles west of Charlotte (Pope 1942). Many of these strikes were met with military and police violence, and a strategy of isolation of strikers from the larger working-class community led to the breakup of strikes. Although the Roosevelt administration attempted to shore up unions in the region during the 1930s, this period of organizing and strikes marked the high tide for labor unionism in the piedmont South (Schulman 1991).

Beginning in the 1910s and continuing in the decades after, the Great Migration of African Americans from the rural U.S. South to cities in the North and Midwest had a major impact on politics, labor, and race relations (Grossman 1991; Lemann 1991). Many black sharecroppers and tenant farmers moved north to escape debt schemes and racial codes that prevented them from making a living in agriculture. Labor recruiters canvassed the South, risking the ire of white landowners and law enforcement, to entice blacks to come work in factory jobs, steel and rubber plants, and meatpacking houses. The entrance of the United States into World War I meant the enlistment of many northern factory workers in the military and the ramping up of industrial production; black southerners filled these vacancies. As large communities of African Americans settled in northern cities, neighborhoods such as Harlem in Manhattan, Bedford-Stuyvesant in Brooklyn, and Chicago's South

Side became centers of black cultural production and even today retain links to the South through a constant influx of southern migrants. The Great Depression, World War II, and the mechanization of cotton picking all contributed to the continuation of this migration, as did factors such as intensification of racial violence, including a series of lynchings in the 1920s (Wilkerson 2010).

The post–World War II South saw a continuation of segregation and a retrenchment of anti-unionism, but also increasing urbanization and industrialization. But by the late 1950s, the Civil Rights movement began to put pressure on the established racial order in the region. Winning gains in civil rights and labor law, particularly in the 1960s, African Americans began to integrate the factory floor and corporate offices, moving into jobs previously reserved for whites. Labor organizers began to reinvigorate strategies of cross-racial organizing among workers, scoring some victories, but also encountering fierce resistance from pro-business forces in the region (Miller 1974). Women workers played vital roles in many of these resurgent movements, lending a militancy and enthusiasm that helped turn momentary strikes or job actions into lasting struggles (Sacks and Remy 1984; Kingsolver 1991; Kopple 1976). City boosters in Charlotte and nearby urban areas, like Greenville-Spartanburg (South Carolina), usually led by politicians and chambers of commerce, often paired their promotion of a city's bright points with an aggressive anti-unionism, so much so that corporations less hostile to unions were dissuaded from relocating to the area (Miller 1974).

By the 1980s and 1990s, the rural South had been transformed as farmers shifted from long-dominant crops like cotton and tobacco to new mass-marketed products like Vidalia onions, Christmas trees, cucumbers, and tomatoes. Agriculture industrialized as poultry and hog producers consolidated into larger and vertically integrated corporations (Striffler 2005). New farm labor relations emerged as many African American and white residents moved to cities and were replaced by migrants from Mexico, Central America, and the Caribbean. While some labor organizing has been successful among workers in these "factory farms," the difficulties of cross-ethnic and cross–racial collaboration among workers and the contingent status of immigrant workers hamper efforts to organize for safer and better-compensated workplaces (Striffler 2005; Fink 2002; Griffith 2006).

Postwar Charlotte

By the 1950s and 1960s, Charlotte, while retaining its ties to textile mills, was in danger of losing its position as key economic center in the Carolinas to an upstart region—the Research Triangle. The Research Triangle, the geographic nomenclature of an economic development program centered in the small cities of Raleigh, Durham, and Chapel Hill, used federal, state, and private money to foster the establishment of new businesses, mainly in high-tech sectors of computing, medical science, and research offshoots of area universities. At the same time, Charlotte felt the heat from a rival city to the southwest, Atlanta, which embarked on a development strategy centered on transportation, namely, the rapid and massive expansion of its airport and its geographic position along three newly built interstate highway corridors. For a while, Charlotte had no answer to this type of post-Fordist economic development. To add insult, by the 1970s, the domestic textile industry had begun its long and devastating (for southern workers) march to free trade zones and *maquiladoras* overseas (Nash and Fernández-Kelly 2001; Fernández-Kelly 1983).

However, a change in banking law (deregulation that allowed banks to have more branches in states where they were not headquartered) proved to be the catalyst that launched a new era in Charlotte's economic history (Hood 1996). Charlotte banks, long prominent in the state because of Charlotte's link to textile mills and regional transportation networks, quickly seized opportunities to expand to nearby states. These banks also saw promise in a newly emerging technology of computerized transactions, soon to take shape in automated teller machines (ATMs), and were among the first to install the machines in their branches. Through a combination of boosterism, cheap land, tax incentives, and lower labor costs, Charlotte was able to entice other banks to relocate headquarters to the city (often after they had taken over smaller regional banks), landing two of the nation's largest banks by the 1990s—Bank of America and Wachovia.

This economic change led to a physical and political transformation as well. In Charlotte's center city, corporate office towers, high-end steakhouses, and luxury condominiums replaced empty early twentieth-century storefronts abandoned during midcentury suburbanization.

Suburban corporate campuses were situated among neighborhoods of large single-family homes, all convenient to interstate highway connectors. Politically, the money of bank executives led to a local oligarchy with a "progressive" vision of the city's future that included urban density encouraged by zoning and public transit rail lines and smarter suburban communities centered around sprawl-containing "town" centers with centralized shopping, entertainment, and corporate offices. This vision extended to social policy as well. The city encouraged a racial meritocracy tied to profit making—perhaps first coined in Atlanta, the city "too busy to hate"—but taken up by Charlotte through its (relatively quick) implementation of school busing in the late 1960s and election of the African American pro-business mayor Harvey Gantt in the 1980s. This move distanced Charlotte from cities in the deeper South that resisted civil rights measures with greater vigor. For example, Birmingham, once an industrial center, suffered in the post–Civil Rights era from its negative image stemming from violent confrontations with marchers. The "progressive" southern vision included an appreciation of cultural diversity that extended to new immigrants to Charlotte from Asia and Latin America, coupled with the realization that globalization, from the rise of Japan and China as major U.S. trading partners to the establishment of NAFTA and other free trade agreements in the Americas, had direct impacts on the financial industry.

Diverse Charlotte

In the past three decades a more diverse Charlotte has developed—a city demographically transformed by in-migration and immigration and economically tied to a global financial system. This shift also signaled the establishment of a new class and racial hierarchy that began to supersede the old order of black and white in the late 1980s, a trend that has continued to the present. White in-migrants, many from elite northern universities, filled the ranks of financial industry workers, becoming highly paid analysts, accountants, and underwriters in banking, insurance, and the home mortgage field. Joining this white-collar group were immigrants from Ireland and Britain. Middle-class African Americans, returning children and grandchildren of the Great Migration (Stack 1996), often chose to move not to rural farmland where their parents and grandparents had originated but to booming urban centers like Charlotte, where professional, highly educated blacks found employment and long-established black cultural institutions. Another group appearing in Charlotte during this period was international technology workers who arrived on H-1 visas, often from India, China, and other countries in Asia, but also from Africa, South America, and Europe.

If these three groups make up the new elite and middle class of Charlotte, another wave of newcomers joined many native-born African Americans in the working-class and impoverished sectors of the city's economy. Latino immigrants (mostly from Mexico and Central America) and Vietnamese and Laotian immigrants found jobs in construction, landscaping, domestic service, restaurants, and other service sectors. This mirrors what scholars (Sassen 1991; Florida 2003; Inda and Rosaldo 2008) have observed for globalized cities, where service workers provide vital services at low cost to undergird the efficiency and profitability of technology, banking, and finance: key sectors of the "new (global) economy."

These incoming workers have transformed residential patterns in the city as well. The inner-ring suburban areas of East Charlotte, for example, have become more densely populated as empty lots are filled in by denser apartment development, and as public transportation and pedestrian movement become more common ways of moving though the neighborhood. As the historian Tom Hanchett (2010) argues, these "salad-bowl" suburbs are also becoming more youthful, multicultural, and "Latinized" as immigrants from across Latin America, but also Southeast Asia and elsewhere, move in and replace an aging white and black population.

As U.S. Census data show, the population of Hispanic residents in Charlotte more than doubled in the decade between 2000 and 2010, from almost forty thousand to over ninety-five thousand people (U.S. Census 2010). White, African American, and Asian American populations also increased, but at a lesser rate. Latinos now make up around 7.5 percent of the city's population, according to the census (although this number may not fully account for undocumented and mobile individuals, who are often undercounted). While growth rates for the Latino population in Charlotte and North Carolina have slowed (from almost 500 percent from 1990 to 2000 to 100 percent in the last decade; see

Smith and Furuseth 2006), the Latino population now represents a significant proportion of the city's population.

With these newcomers, Charlotte also witnessed the displacement and diminishing influence of traditional economic sectors and social groups in the geography of city life. For example, one could not have the trendy NoDa (short for North Davidson) neighborhood, with its music clubs, restaurants, art galleries, and luxury loft condos, if the textile industry still thrived in the Carolinas, because the district was once a working-class mill town (the mills themselves have been renovated into loft condominiums). Gentrification aside, impoverished African Americans struggle to find affordable housing in neighborhoods where Latino and Asian immigrant families have moved in.

But perhaps the best example of this displacement comes from efforts by Charlotte residents to position themselves on issues around immigration. Starting in the late 1990s, anti-immigrant backlash began to take shape in the form of city, county, and state policies targeting immigrant communities, particularly Latino neighborhoods. Beginning in 2006, the Mecklenburg County (where Charlotte is located) sheriff Jim Pendergraph was instrumental in setting up the 287(g) program, which gives local police power to arrest and hand over undocumented immigrants to federal immigration authorities, both in Mecklenburg County and in other municipalities (who chose to participate) nationwide (Nguyen and Gill 2010). Other anti-immigrant policies, including denying undocumented immigrants access to state driver's licenses or community colleges, mirrored earlier efforts in California and other southwestern states. These policies became part of a coordinated regional and national campaign to curtail immigrants' access to social services and circumscribe any claims they might have to civil rights or local citizenship (DeParle 2011; Vidales, Day, and Powe 2009).

In response, a local movement pushing for immigration reform also arose during the 1990s. Led by immigrant groups and mainly Latina/o activists who had cut their teeth in struggles in California, New York, and Texas over similar issues, immigration reform activists found allies in business elites who recognized that the idea of a "diverse" city was favorable to attracting international business and who were fearful of negative publicity stemming from anti-immigrant rhetoric that could take a racist tone. Another ally was the nonprofit and philanthropic community, which, after a 2001 survey by the political scientist Robert Putnam (Saguaro Seminar n.d.) that ranked Charlotte near the bottom of American cities in terms of interracial trust and dialogue, organized a collaborative effort to foster more inclusive and multicultural planning processes for the city's future.[1] Immigration reform activism took the form of protest rallies over policies targeting immigrant communities, such as the 287(g) program and civil rights violations that accompanied the enforcement of immigration law by local police. Activists also registered new voters, engaged in street theater, and held numerous fora to educate community members about immigration law and enforcement policies.

Latino Corridors

Demographers describe Charlotte as having three "Latino immigrant corridors" corresponding to U.S. Census data concerning where Hispanic residents have settled (Smith and Furuseth 2006). These corridors consist of residential neighborhoods that flank commercial thoroughfares, with community institutions such as churches, nonprofit organizations, businesses, and restaurants that help solidify social ties. The three corridors are the North Tryon Street corridor, the Central Avenue corridor, and the South Boulevard corridor (Smith and Furuseth 2006). Both the North Tryon Street and Central Avenue corridors are located on the Eastside of Charlotte, an area that has the longest history of residency by Latino immigrants. The South Boulevard corridor is located on the Southside of Charlotte, in a transitional area between high-income, mostly white residential neighborhoods and low-income African American neighborhoods in Charlotte's western half. The LYNX light rail system literally marks a division "across the tracks" of racial and class segregation between these areas of the city.

Although research took me to all three areas, I selected the Central Avenue corridor as the main focus of the study, for several reasons. First, many of the main music venues frequented by bands and their audiences were located in this corridor. Second, the Latin American Coalition—a local nonprofit that provides social services for the Latino community—is located in this corridor. Its offices are located at an important hub of the Latino community in Charlotte, next to several prominent restaurants and retail stores. I used its offices as an unofficial headquarters where I interviewed musicians and took stock of important developments in the Latino community. Third, the Central Avenue corridor proved convenient because of its proximity to other locations where musical performances occurred, including the neighborhoods of Uptown, NoDa, and Plaza-Midwood. Finally, I spent most of my time in Charlotte living in the Central Avenue corridor (after spending a few months in the South Boulevard area), which deepened my understanding of what life is like there.

Central Avenue

Central Avenue starts at the intersection of Kings Drive and 7th Street on the edge of center-city Charlotte, just across Interstate 277 from Uptown. At its starting point lies Central Piedmont Community College (CPCC), symbolically important for many Latinos in Charlotte because of a recent battle over whether undocumented students would be allowed to attend community colleges in North Carolina. CPCC also represents educational opportunity for many Latino immigrants who, although highly trained and educated in their home countries, have gone there to achieve English proficiency or gain certification in their profession. For example, one musician remembers attending classes at CPCC when he barely spoke English and had just arrived in Charlotte to join his sister. He would bring his guitar with him to school and make friends playing outside between classes. Another musician recently took classes at CPCC in an attempt to complete his college degree. Other community members I spoke to have received certification in medical, accounting, notary, and other fields, often as a way to legitimize degrees they already held from their home countries that did not transfer to practice in the United States.

Moving east, Central Avenue passes through the Intown neighborhood of Plaza-Midwood. Plaza-Midwood is a gentrifying area with a mix of restored bungalows from one of the city's first suburbs and new apartment buildings filling in the interstices of abandoned lots and urban renewal teardown projects. Trendy restaurants and bars sit next to older businesses, including some of the most cherished remnants of "classic" Charlotte, such as the Penguin Diner.[2]

However, the economic recession slowed gentrification in the neighborhood. Newly built apartments featuring cutting-edge architecture and balconies with skyline views stand vacant. A major mixed-use development, Morningside Village (HipHoods 2008), with apartments, stores, and walkable "urban" streetscapes, remains unbuilt next to Veterans Park because of the economic recession. The project began as an urban renewal scheme by the Atlanta-based Post Properties, which tore down a series of 1950s row apartments that, according to longtime neighborhood residents, were a hotbed of crime and delinquency. In their place, developers left streets paved in the shape of a neighborhood with empty grass and mud flats where apartments might have stood. A large sign at the entrance promises that this development is in the planning stage and will one day be built, but no construction happened during my time in Charlotte. Instead, local residents walk their dogs in the grass while drivers use the development's imagined streets as a shortcut to avoid traffic lights on Central Avenue.

Plaza-Midwood juxtaposes both the wealth and the poverty that are created in a contemporary city. On a Friday night, while middle-class Intown residents frequent the neighborhood's latest hot spot, homeless men gather on a street corner, smoking cigarettes and asking passersby for change. In one direction off Central Avenue are immaculately maintained bungalows on tree-lined streets, in another, gated apartments that try but fail to hide the fact that they are public housing. Remnants of the neighborhood's working-class history remain, such as 1950s small detached houses still occupied by their original owners, or rented out by enterprising Vietnamese immigrants to newcomers to the city. A nondescript building on Central Avenue serves as a bar frequented by working-class gay men, while next door an "Internet café" serves as an illicit gambling club formed by elderly African American men.

Down the hill from Plaza-Midwood, the language of the business signs changes on Central Avenue. The linguistic landscape (Gorter 2004; Hill 1999; Irvine and Gal 2000) shifts to include neon placards in Vietnamese, Spanish, and Polish. Several blocks of Vietnamese businesses include fish markets, restaurants, nail salons, and groceries. Interspersed are signs in Spanish, for law firms, notary publics, and translation services. By the time one reaches Eastway Drive, the signs are almost entirely in Spanish, signaling that this is the heart of Latino Charlotte, the

Eastside. Churches advertise bilingual and Spanish-language services. Restaurants feature Mexican regional cuisines, but also the foods of El Salvador and Honduras. Corner stores advertise remittance rates and telephone cards for immigrants wanting contact back home. Grocery stores feature Latin American food: plantains, rice, corn tortillas, mangos, and chorizo. The neighborhoods of the Eastside feature 1950s suburban-style detached houses and 1970s–1980s era apartment buildings. While the apartments provide low-cost housing for recently arrived immigrants, management companies sometimes neglect upkeep for the aging buildings. In 2010, residents of one large apartment complex organized and protested against deteriorating conditions there, including lack of heat as well as mice and roach infestations. However, this organizing effort was weakened by the demise of ACORN, a national housing advocacy group that had been active in gathering evidence against delinquent apartment landlords in Charlotte.[3]

At the intersection of Sharon Amity Road and Central Avenue, one can also see the intersection of old and new Charlotte, through some of the contradictions that have formed the Eastside as it is today. In one direction stands the Eastland Mall, an abandoned hunk of concrete surrounded by acres of parking lots. One of the first indoor shopping malls built in Charlotte, it opened in 1975 with major department stores anchoring several floors of retail stores. By the late 1990s, the major stores had left for more suburban locations. A new owner attempted to refashion the mall by featuring local African American and Latino businesses in the mall. For several years, the mall remained open, even though many of its storefronts were empty. Local soccer leagues played games on its indoor court (originally an ice skating rink). By 2010, the mall was closed. Although the city government and several developers have proposed creating a more "urban" mixed-use development at the site, so far it remains abandoned (Urban Land Institute 2007; Funk, Harrison, and Jones 2010).

Across Central Avenue from the Eastland Mall, Compare Foods occupies an old supermarket that has been recently renovated and repainted bright orange. Compare Foods is a supermarket chain owned and operated by a Dominican immigrant family. With numerous locations in Charlotte, across North Carolina, and in New York and New Jersey, Compare Foods represents a success story of ethnic entrepreneurs who started small and created wealth by catering to the burgeoning consumerism of Latino immigrants in the United States. Compare Foods began as a store that provided Caribbean fruits, vegetables, and staples to Dominican, Cuban, and Puerto Rican residents of Washington Heights and New Jersey, but the owners saw a potential market in the U.S. South and moved their headquarters and concentrated their efforts in and around Charlotte. In this transition, they also recalibrated their products to provide foods that covered the diversity of Latino immigrants in Charlotte, including Mexican, Central American, and South American–style goods. The stores gained a reputation as having the cheapest prices and the best selection of foods for cooking Latin American dishes. Almost all of Charlotte's Latino residents I met shop at Compare Foods. This common consumer experience is perhaps the best example of a unifying Latino culture being created among a diverse body of immigrants; while maintaining national/regional foodways, Latino immigrants create new markets for "ethnic" or "Latin" foods.[4]

Across Sharon Amity Road from Compare Foods on Central Avenue sits the Latin American Coalition, a nonprofit organization that provides services for the Latino community in Charlotte. The Latin American Coalition was founded by the Reverend Salvador Negrín and thirty-five other community members in 1990 to provide Spanish-language services to a small but growing Latino community in Charlotte. On any given weekday, a small lobby in the organization's offices is filled with women and their young children, sometimes interspersed with a few men, waiting to be seen by staff and volunteers of the resource center. The Coalition's resource center is often the first place that community members journey to for advice or help with problems; they feel more comfortable here because of the long history of the organization's involvement in the community and because interactions here are bilingual and culturally appropriate. Interactions in the resource center can run from the simple—helping someone figure out which bus to take—to the complex—documenting and fighting wage theft. Staff members meet with clients in cramped offices and, after listening to their stories, they make phone calls, search the Internet, or ask around the office to gather the best advice for that person. At times, they refer community members to classes and programs offered by the Coalition, for example, to see a specialist regarding their immigration case. Other times, staff will refer clients to outside agencies with which the Coalition has a long-standing relationship. During the economic recession, many community members faced economic hardship and came to the Coalition's offices for help; staff would refer them to local food banks or charities.

On the second floor of the Coalition's offices, Tony Arreaza, the events manager, and his assistant (for a year, me) sit and make phone calls and e-mail potential bands, sponsors, and vendors for cultural events such as the Festival Latinoamericano. Next door, the volunteer coordinator recruits potential volunteers to work in the Coalition offices or for special events. In a large conference room, the Coalition also holds ESL and citizenship classes. Across the hall, the nonprofit has its administrative offices and immigration law center.

These three corners of Central Avenue and Sharon Amity form a kind of nexus for the Eastside Latino community. The thriving business, particularly Compare Foods, and nonprofit anchors contrast with the post-suburban decay of the Eastland Mall. The "Latinization" of the Eastside extends from the ethnic businesses on its main drag to the remodeled housing in its revitalized neighborhoods. Music is a vital force in forging community in this area, especially when it is paired with other community-making activities, such as food and alcohol consumption, dancing, festival-going, or religious worship. Music permeates the Central Avenue corridor, whether it is prominent nightclubs located a few blocks away, the cultural festivals of the Latin American Coalition, music at churches, or the radio stations just up the road.

Musical Charlotte

To convey the Latin music scene in Charlotte, I will outline the history of music recording and live performances in Charlotte during the last century. The Latin music scene builds upon the infrastructure and networks of musical production already in Charlotte, but also exists on a somewhat separate plane.

From the 1920s to the 1940s, Charlotte was a major center in the U.S. South for recording musicians and for concerts and radio broadcasts. Charlotte became a prime spot to record early country music, so-called hillbilly records, because of the migration of poor whites from Appalachia to the mill towns of the piedmont (Hanchett 1985). Country musicians would travel on a circuit throughout piedmont mill towns playing dance halls and broadcasting live on area radio stations. In August 1927, Ralph Peer of Victor began his first of many recording sessions in Charlotte. Through the 1930s, Victor/RCA recorded country musicians in Charlotte, including the Carter Family, Bill Monroe, and Jimmie Davis. Blues and gospel groups also were recorded during these sessions, as Charlotte was part of a parallel but segregated circuit of black musicians, the Chitlin' Circuit (Lauterbach 2011; Booth 1993). The heyday of musical recording faded in the 1940s, as most country recording sessions shifted to Nashville (Malone 2006; Hawkins 2007).

However, Charlotte continued to host thriving musical communities in the postwar era. Radio station WBT in Charlotte was known for its popular weekend broadcasts of live country music throughout the 1940s and early 1950s, until the advent of television and rock and roll dethroned country music (Rumble n.d.). Black gospel music continued to thrive in Charlotte, both in area churches and through recordings produced in small studios in the city. The rock band REM, from Athens, Georgia, so admired the sound produced at Reflection Sound Studios (a local gospel studio) that it recorded several albums there.[5]

Charlotte, like other southern cities, hosted many prominent rock bands during the 1960s and 1970s. This was an era of turmoil and dramatic change brought on by the Civil Rights movement, including court-ordered desegregation of schools and conservative retrenchment in the presidential campaign of George Wallace and emergence of a (white) southern Republican Party (Carter 1995; Greenhaw 1982). But a younger generation of white and black southerners was attempting to chart a new path through music. As the journalist Mark Kemp remembers, "The feeling of community that Southern rock engendered during the early 1970s was the beginning of a healing process—in me and in many southerners of my generation—that continues to this day" (Kemp 2004). Musical groups like the Allman Brothers bridged white and black musical traditions that had become separated, combining country, blues, jazz, and gospel into rock songs. While recording sessions in the 1920s and 1930s separated black and white music into "race" and "hillbilly" records to be marketed to segregated audiences, and 1950s white rock and roll artists often riffed (and ripped) off of black rhythm and blues singers without acknowledgment, southern rock musicians openly included black musicians in their bands, wrote songs commenting on racism, and formulated new, alternative ways of being southern with their audiences. Songs such as the Allman Brothers cover of Blind Willie McTell's "Statesboro Blues" (1971) and Lynyrd Skynyrd's "Ballad of Curtis Loew" (1974) celebrated the shared musical traditions of southern blacks and whites, revealing hidden narratives of interracial musical production that stretched back at least a century (Conway 1995; Smith 1997; Russell 1970).[6] Other groups that traced southern roots, such as The Band, constructed a metanarrative about southern musical traditions through their music (Helm and Davis 2000).

By the 1980s and 1990s, southern rock had been transformed by the emergence of college town music scenes in places such as Athens, Georgia, and Chapel Hill, North Carolina. Charlotte, with its suburban commuter university, UNC–Charlotte, seems to have been mainly left out of this development. However, small pockets of rock musicians did emerge in the late 1990s in Intown neighborhoods as Charlotte attracted newcomers from other cities, such as the band FireHouse. In the first decade of the twenty-first century, Charlotte witnessed a revival of its black musical communities, as African Americans from northern cities flocked southward, and local artists such as Anthony Hamilton, Jocelyn Ellis, and the *American Idol* winner Fantasia Barrino recorded hit songs.

On this tableau we place Latino musical communities in Charlotte. While many Latina/o musicians and audience members operate in a separate sphere from white and black music in Charlotte, there are some points of intersection and interaction. Many Latino rock musicians follow local bands and have conversations with fellow musicians in bars and clubs or at a rehearsal space. On its most recent album, Bakalao Stars collaborates with Ras Congo, a Jamaican immigrant reggae singer, and it recently teamed up with a local reggae group to hold a concert together at the Neighborhood Theatre. Elddy Trevino, a Mexican American musician from South Texas, moved to Charlotte in 2002 to start Loco Sound Studios, which records local *regional mexicano*, rock, *reggaetón*, and rap artists. Local clubs that once hosted rock and R&B acts are now being converted to Latin clubs in neighborhoods where Latino immigrants have settled. For example, by late 2010, an industrial warehouse space east of NoDa that during 2009 featured heavy metal and punk bands for white audiences had reopened as Calentano, a club featuring *regional mexicano* groups and occasional Latin rock concerts.

Southern *Latinidad*

The Latin music scene in Charlotte contributes much to a larger process of the development of a southern *latinidad* that draws from elements of southern, Latin American, and Latino culture(s) to help Charlotte's Latino residents define their identity. In later chapters I describe in greater detail elements of southern *latinidad* that I outline here. First, Latino immigrants to Charlotte often hold differing notions of *latinidad* from residents of long-established centers of Latino cultural production such as New York, Miami, or Los Angeles. They are quick to question the unity of any sort of pan-Latino identity based on language usage, ethnicity, or music. As recent immigrants, they are much more likely to hold onto national or even city/regional identities of the places where they are from. Thus, I met several Ecuadorian musicians who stressed not just that they were Ecuadorian (and thus spoke Spanish differently from Dominicans or Mexicans), but also that they were *guayaqui-leños* from the coast (and thus different from residents of Quito and the Ecuadorian highlands). Second, Latino immigrants feel affiliation with and at times try to incorporate elements of southern culture into their identity. As several scholars have noted, Latino migrants to the U.S. South may find the "friendliness" and "openness" of southern small towns more hospitable than other regions in which they have worked, while the climate reminds them of home (Striffler 2005; Fink 2002). In my observations, this perception of "southern hospitality" carried over in Latinos' generally positive accounts of their interactions with most white and black southerners, despite rampant residential segregation and anti-immigrant policies. Latino immigrants also sought out shared elements of southern and Latin American culture as a means to establish their sense of belonging in Charlotte as newly minted southerners. For example, a group of Venezuelan friends would gather for backyard barbecues that meshed elements of southern and Latin American grilling traditions—with pork ribs, chorizo, marinated strip steaks, and chicken. Negotiating lunch meetings with musicians often meant deciding whether to eat *carnitas* tacos at a Mexican restaurant or southern pulled pork sandwiches at a BBQ restaurant. Musicians often brought a deep appreciation for southern music—particularly the blues—with them from Latin America and deepened their knowledge with trips to local clubs like the Double Door Inn to hear blues acts. A love of base-ball brought Dominicans and Venezuelans together for debates about ballplayers, friendly Saturday afternoon softball games, and excursions to watch minor league games in Rock Hill, South Carolina, or major league games in Atlanta.

Beyond music, sports, and food, there are other factors that help explain the development of a southern *latinidad*. Contingent working conditions and a segmented labor market structure the way Latino im-migrants see themselves as workers and helps develop a sense of class solidarity among many working-class Latinos regardless of national identity. Residential segregation also contributes to the continuation of Latino cultural production separate from yet in relation to southern and U.S. mainstream culture as Latinos find limited options for recreational and leisure activities. Latino immigrants, because of immigration policy that deters circular migration and the predominance of mixed-status families, also increasingly remain for long periods in Charlotte, creat-ing a life somewhat separate from their family and friends back home (although still connected through technology and remittances). For example, one musician had a girlfriend back in his country of origin, but he could not visit her because he was undocumented and afraid he would not be able to return to Charlotte, where his brother and mother also lived. The couple chatted by phone and e-mail, but spent months living apart before finally breaking up. Finally, certain institutions, such as the Latin American Coalition, but also churches, music venues, news-papers, radio stations, and restaurants, play a vital role in helping define what a southern Latino identity is through their presentation of Latino culture and attempts to build clienteles. Latino musicians work within these institutions to build an audience and attempt to form a "musi-cal community" (see chapter 3) that serves as a source of solidarity and identity for many Latino residents of the city.

Conclusion

Charlotte is a "globalizing" city, one that is striving to reach the heights of global city-dom desired by Chamber of Commerce boosters (and many residents) through efforts to build infrastructure (roads, inter-national flights, public transportation), develop high-profile real estate (skyscrapers, luxury hotels, and condominiums), grow centers of higher learning (the constantly expanding UNC–Charlotte), and position itself economically (banking mergers, attracting new industry). But there is a cultural aspect to becoming a global city as well. In Charlotte, this includes efforts to manufacture an urban, artistic center through the creation of a "cultural campus" in downtown Charlotte housing art museums, fine arts theaters, and outdoor public art. Another campaign encourages local artistic production—through gallery crawls in trendy neighborhoods like NoDa, free concerts and festivals in the center city, and arts patronage by corporations and foundations. Through these efforts a globally aware, elite class of bankers and businesspeople have forged a fairly "progressive" vision of what they would like Charlotte to become—a global city that is cosmopolitan yet retains its southern roots.

Largely ignored in this elite conception are the creative expressions bubbling up from Charlotte's Latino community (except in the most superficial, "increasing diversity" sense). I argue that through the music scene, Latinos are staking claim to spaces and cultural tropes that position them as citizens of Charlotte the city, sometimes in opposition to and sometimes in agreement with the globalizing vision of its future. This claim to citizenship through use of the city's name is nowhere more clear than a journalist's turn of phrase, "It's only Carlotan Rock, but I like it," written in Spanish in an article celebrating the history of the grassroots rock scene fostered by the promoters of the Carlotan Rock concert series. The journalist stresses the community feeling and foresight that band members had in creating a forum for local Latin rock musicians to grow and develop. As we shall see in later chapters, Latino immigrant musicians have their own vision of what a future Charlotte might hold.

2

The Latin Music Scene in Charlotte

This chapter outlines the Latin music scene by reconstructing, through oral history and personal networks observed in study, the brief history of Latino musicians in Charlotte. I stress the diversity of the scene, especially since musicians and their genres span American, Mexican, Caribbean, and South American styles. This diversity differentiates Charlotte from traditional centers of Latino cultural production, such as New York, Miami, and Los Angeles, where one Latin American nationality or origin group predominates (although these cities have also grown more diverse in recent years). Yet these diverse genres exist in a segregated social arena, where Latinos of different nationalities and class positions affiliate themselves with a particular genre, neighborhood, and musical community, and often contrast their musical taste in opposition to other Latin music genres. Building on music and cultural studies scholarship, I examine the threads connecting U.S., southern, and Latin American music(s) together up to the early twenty-first century, while introducing the bands that are the focus of this book and describing the questions that they raise in relation to their musical style.

As many scholars have commented, the term "Latino" (and its linguistic partner, "Hispanic") is nebulous (Stavans 1995; Oboler 2006; Delgado and Stefancic 1998). While Spanish-language proficiency proved to be a key tie uniting members of Charlotte's scene, many musicians chose to sing songs written in English, and conversations between and with musicians invariably took a Spanglish form, with individuals mixing vernacular forms of English and Spanish to describe their music, instrumentation, and sound. Most bands performed in clubs that catered to Latinos and were owned and managed by ethnic entrepreneurs, but in certain cases, groups played concerts at clubs owned by non-Latinos. I have considered all of these performances for my study; the concerts at non-Latino–owned clubs reveal just as much as those at Latino clubs. Brazilian immigrants, although they speak a different language and originate from a different place, have much in common with Spanish-speaking Latino immigrants. Many U.S.-born Latinos have Latino immigrants as their families and friends; I have counted them as part of the Latin music scene even while I am careful to note differences in legal status and citizenship between these two groups. I also take into consideration a small but dedicated group of non-Latino fans of Latin music, mainly *salsa* dancers, but also some Latin rock enthusiasts who attend concerts and participate in the music scene.

There are several reasons why I use the term "Latin music" as a way to describe the music being performed. Some musicians and audience members did not identify as Latino, instead claiming their place of birth or nationality as a primary identity. They saw "Latinos" as Americanized, often referring to second- or third-generation Latinos rather than recent immigrants from Latin America like themselves. The term "Latin music" in its ambiguity straddles the border between Latino and Latin America, becoming an alternate translation of the Spanish phrase *música latina*. It is a term that is used both within the global music industry and locally in Charlotte. However, just like the genre categories I describe below, it can be at times misleading and inaccurate, and thus its usage should be taken with a grain of salt.

One defining characteristic of the Latin music scene in Charlotte is its tight-knit group of participants: social networks that have been constructed through connections from workplaces, recreational activities, churches, and other neighborhood institutions. It was rare to attend a concert of Latin music in Charlotte without running into someone I knew, even if I had not anticipated seeing anyone I had met previously. Perhaps this is a facet of the smallness of Charlotte's Latino community, even though it has grown since the 1990s. Latinos are still less than 10 percent of the city's population, numbering approximately ninety-five thousand (U.S. Census 2000, 2010).

Musicians entered into relationships of mutual assistance to find jobs, to borrow instruments and sound equipment, to provide expertise in recording and promoting their music. Musicians and audience members belonged to the same social spheres, from church congregations, work colleagues and school ties, to associations of national origin (like the local Club Dominicano) or hometowns. Musicians and restaurant and club owners relied on each other: musicians needed to promote and perform their music; the music venue needed to sell food and drinks. At face value, monetary transactions guided all of these relationships, but people rarely mentioned money as the defining aspect of these social ties. While an audience member might pay to enter the club, it is the experience of listening to music and connecting to the group onstage and fellow audience members that stands out as important. Club owners might make money from a cover charge and drinks, but creating that more ethereal comfortable atmosphere for the audience's enjoyment of music often proves to be better for business over the long run.

The Latin music scene also provides a series of places and occasions where people could see and be seen. Latinos ventured out to musical performances to see family, friends, and acquaintances, to meet and fall in love, to dress up and let loose. They also participated in the music scene in order to celebrate tradition and find out about the latest style. I have chosen the term "scene" to evoke the visual image of cinema and painting, to capture moments in a thirteen-month period in Charlotte when this book documents what happened in Latin music there.

"Scene" is a common term used to refer to social networks and moments of musical genre creation, with cues taken from the theater and dramatic arts as a way to bracket the space and temporality of musical expression. The anthropologist Erving Goffman (1959) proposed that in face-to-face interactions, individuals frame the context of their interactions and the roles they take on, much as a theatrical scene or picture frame includes some details and excludes others. But in the anthropologist Vincent Crapanzano's (2006) exploration of the difference between "objective" reality and the scene, he cautions against reducing the scene to the merely subjective, instead stressing the intersubjective, interpersonal experience of the "shadowy dimensions of social and cultural existence" (388). In my descriptions and analysis, I can "objectively" convey the reality of musicians performing and audiences cheering, describe the rituals that create a sense of community (Turner 1969), or "subjectively" convey the emotions and personal experiences of fieldwork, but the scene also exists in a third realm. Between the observed and felt, the ideal and real, the objective and subjective, are moments of mystery and magic that anyone who has experienced music understands, yet these moments are socially constructed by musicians who have a talent for evoking and gathering together the necessary elements for listeners and participants to feel these sorts of social connections. As Crapanzano notes, the scene contains an indexical process of naming and pointing out "what it is— the contextualizing element, the context, but also what it is not" (Crapanzano 2006, 399). As we shall see, the Latin music scene often performs this double move as musicians and audiences position themselves as members of one musical community and not another, as listeners to genres mark distinctions from other musical styles, as musicians assess their political role, and as they debate aesthetics and morality.

Latin Music in Charlotte

Despite the long history of Latin music in the United States and its influence on popular music (Roberts 1979; Brennan 2008; García 2006), I found little evidence of any early influence on local music production in Charlotte until the 1980s. However, it is still fruitful to consider the commonalities and parallel developments between Charlotte (and the U.S. South) and Latin America. Both experienced the postwar expansion of U.S. imperial ambitions, although in different ways. Charlotte became connected to other East Coast cities and military bases through the development of the interstate highway system, while Latin American countries were often subject to U.S. military intervention and influence (Schulman 1991; Leogrande 1998; Galeano 1997). Both Charlotte and certain areas in Latin America (such as the U.S.-Mexico border and free trade zones in Haiti, Puerto Rico, and elsewhere) witnessed the expansion of local industry from runaway shops of the northern United States, while the globalization and deregulation of the finance industry made both vulnerable to volatile shifts in the market (Kingsolver 1991; Fernández-Kelly 1983). Moreover, a new generation of youth—in Latin America, children born during military or one-party rule, and in the U.S. South a generation born during the upending of racial apartheid— played a vital role in reimagining culture and music in both places (Kemp 2004; Zolov 1999; Pacini Hernández, Fernández L'Hoeste, and Zolov 2004). Beyond these general connections, it appears that the pattern of Latin music development in Charlotte roughly follows the pattern of general Latino migration to the city, with a small settlement of initial "pioneers" in the 1980s and early 1990s, and a larger influx of immigrants coming more recently (Massey 2007; Smith and Furuseth 2006).

Latin music travelled to Charlotte with immigrants from Latin America who began arriving in the city in the 1980s. According to musicians and journalists, the first known Latino musician in town was Alex Peralta, who in the late 1980s played in a hair band in the style of Def Leppard and Bon Jovi. The group sang in English, and Peralta has since moved to Miami and become a producer of rap and R&B artists. The next documented cases of Latino musicians in Charlotte come in the mid-1990s. Tony Arreaza, just out of high school, moved to the Queen City from Venezuela to live with his sister, who had arrived several years earlier. In between English classes at a local community college, he would strum his guitar on the campus lawn. Eventually, he began playing at a dive bar on Independence Boulevard for tips, where other Latino immigrants started to gather to hear him play or join in with their own instruments.

Fred Figueroa, another Venezuelan immigrant, remembers going to hear rock bands play at clubs on the Eastside of Charlotte when he first moved to the city. In one of the bands, the guitar player had a Venezuelan flag stitched on his jeans. The guitar player, Arreaza, thought to himself, "Why is this guy [Figueroa] staring at me; who is he?" Talking after the show, they discovered their common nationality, and within a few months they had formed their own band playing covers of classic Latin rock songs.

By the late 1990s, immigration from Mexico to Charlotte had taken off, and this demographic shift began to be felt in the music scene. As Figueroa remembers,

> The Latino community when I got here was very little. You didn't see a lot of Mexican people, or any other race for that matter, and in the late nineties it was just like a big boom. You started seeing all these Mexican people and vans with ladders and paint crews going here and there, and sheet rock crews and landscaping.
>
> As far as the music scene, it's changed in the same way . . . once the Latin community came in, [they want] to be catered to, so more Spanish acts started coming in here, Tony and I started looking at opportunities to entertain that community with what we like doing, which was rock. And within the Spanish community rock is also well received; everything is not necessarily about *quebradita*[1] . . . that's usually something very

Mexican. Most of the Latin community that are not Mexican—they like rock—and that's where Tony and I came into the equation.[2]

With this influx of new immigrants corresponding to a real estate and financial industry boom in the late 1990s, Charlotte was transformed in the eyes of many Latinos, from a sleepy town where you were excited to run into someone else who spoke Spanish to a budding metropolis with new challenges of ethnic and racial tensions and new economic opportunities. Latino immigrants who had arrived just a few years earlier found they could benefit from this influx, whether by opening restaurants and stores, running radio stations and newspapers, or leading community organizations, all catering to newly arrived Latinos who had come to work in construction and the service economy. In the music scene, Tony Arreaza and Fred Figueroa joined others in forming increasingly popular bands. Some musicians branched out to become concert promoters; one even opened a recording studio. But, as Figueroa described it, Charlotte began to have two (and eventually several) parallel but largely unconnected music districts, one centered on *regional mexicano* music, the other around *rock en español*. Differences in legal status, national origin, class identity, and musical taste contributed to this split between more established and recently arrived Latino immigrants.

A seminal band in Charlotte's Latin rock scene was La Rúa. Formed in 2002 by Tony Arreaza and three Ecuadorian musicians, La Rúa became the most famous of Charlotte's Latin groups, recording two albums and having its music video, "El Chanchito" (2005), shown on MTV Latino and Mun2. Concurrent with the group's founding was the start of the annual Carlotan Rock festival, a concert that featured local and regional *rock en español* groups. Many younger musicians recall being inspired to form bands and getting their first break playing at Carlotan Rock. This Latin rock community found reinforcement and approval in a series of concerts promoted by Tony Arreaza, the La Rúa drummer Juan Miguel Marín, and his brother Herman Marín. International acts, such as Los Enanitos Verdes, Los Amigos Invisibles, Hombre G, Molotov, and Cafe Tacuba, played packed shows in Charlotte (often with local groups opening) in clubs that had never previously hosted a Latin rock group, and created a feeling that the city was a happening place for Latin music. Alas, this moment was soon over, with La Rúa disbanding in December 2006. Carlotan Rock and the big shows petered out, drawing to a standstill because of the economic recession and declining attendance in 2008–2009. Talking with musicians in 2009–2010, I got the sinking feeling that I had missed the "golden age" of Latin rock in Charlotte as several musicians told me they wished I had been there to document what was happening in 2005. One of the challenges of doing fieldwork was reconstructing this past from oral histories, newspaper articles, and reminiscences over bottles of scotch.

Meanwhile, Mexican music in Charlotte slowly came of age, as a smattering of groups formed in the mid-2000s. By 2007, the local DJ and promoter Alex Ruiz had scored a minor hit with his song "La Chica Que Conocí" (Ruiz 2007). Local *regional mexicano* groups found audiences at neighborhood dance clubs, on Spanish-language radio, and at annual festivals such as Ruiz's Carnaval de las Carolinas, where they played alongside well-known Mexican bands touring through Charlotte. Other venues in Charlotte began to cater to audiences wanting to listen to música *tropical* genres such as *bachata, merengue,* and *salsa,* drawing a diverse crowd of Dominicans, Puerto Ricans, Cubans, and Colombians.

Genre Categories

There are three main genre categories of music played by Latin groups in Charlotte—*regional mexicano, música tropical,* and Latin rock/*rock en español*—with several subgenres and adjunct styles. These categories are often used by record companies, promoters, radio DJs, and others in the music industry to describe the music; however, musicians sometimes deploy other terms, usually referring to the subgenre or style of music they play, and some invent new terms to describe their genre(s). Often, a band's name reflects its aesthetic background and shows how it positions itself in relation to (or opposition to) these commercial genre categories.[3] In the following paragraphs, I briefly cover each genre category, the bands from Charlotte that play this type of music, and the debates among musicians and scholars about these categories.

Regional mexicano refers to a set of styles that originate in rural Mexico, mainly in northern provinces and the U.S.-Mexico border region, and have an affiliation with working-class Mexican culture (Mendoza 1939; Simmons 1953; Simonett 2001; Peña 1985; Herrera-Sobek 1990;

Ragland 2009). Regional Mexican music includes subgenres such as *norteña, banda, ranchera, pasito duranguense,* and Mexican *cumbia* (also known as *onda grupera*). Although it has many stylistic similarities with *música tejana* or Tejano/Tex-Mex music, *regional mexicano* is primarily the music of Mexican immigrants to the United States and migrants to the border region, whereas Tejano is the music of Mexican Americans who have long resided in Texas and the U.S. Southwest. The types of songs performed include both up-tempo dance numbers (where audience members dance *polca, quebradito,* or *pasito*) and ballads (including both romantic ballads and *corridos*).

Regional mexicano music, with roots in earlier popular forms from Mexico, marks its beginnings in the 1960s and 1970s, when several of the more influential artists in the genre began their careers (such as Los Tigres del Norte and Ramón Ayala). During this period, performers mostly relied on updated interpretations of the *corrido*, a Mexican ballad form, to sing about themes relevant for a new generation of migrants to the United States—border crossing, difficult working conditions, undocumented immigrants' encounters with immigration authorities, and the illegal narcotics trade. By the 1970s and 1980s, a younger generation of urban migrants settling in border cities popularized a new iteration of *regional mexicano* that drew upon Colombian *cumbia* (Ragland 2009) and other pan-Caribbean styles. Often played by *sonideros* (DJs), *cumbia norteña* or *onda grupera* departed from the *corrido* form, instead relying on love songs and pan-Latino musical themes to appeal to an audience versed in multiple musical styles. In the 1990s another iteration of *regional mexicano, banda* and *tecnobanda,* rose to popularity among migrants to Southern California from northern Mexico (Simonett 2001). *Banda* originated in the northern Mexican provinces of Sinaloa and Durango in military-style brass bands; *tecnobanda* replaces many of the brass instruments with synthesized keyboard notes. Corresponding to the rise of *banda* was a resurgence of *corridos*, particularly those dealing with the lives of undocumented immigrants and the exploits of *narcotraficantes*.

Regional mexicano encompasses a wide variety of musical styles, yet is readily identifiable by its constant invocation of rural, working-class, and Mexican cultural references. The music can range from melodramatic *bolero* covers to ribald dance songs where women from the audience are invited onstage to dance in a sexually suggestive manner; from numbers that involve the audience shouting when their native province in Mexico is called out, to *narcocorridos*—stories about drug trafficking that offer criticism of government corruption and describe in grisly detail and sometimes celebrate the violence of the drug trade. Bands utilize many instruments, from the more traditional tuba, acoustic harp, and *bajo sexto* to fully synthesized instrumentation manufactured by a set of keyboards. Musicians often dress in uniform style, which usually means cowboy boots, flared pants, matching jackets, and a cowboy hat in a style that references *ranchera* and *mariachi* traditions, but can mean baggy jeans and loose T-shirts in reference to hip-hop styles. It is this variety that allows bands to specialize in music from a particular region, say, Tierra Caliente, or to position themselves with a unique performance style.

The groups that I followed that perform *regional mexicano* include Banda TecnoCaliente and Los Mentirosos. Los Mentirosos is a band from Gastonia, a suburb of Charlotte, although most of the band members originate from the Mexican state of Querétaro. They play regional Mexican music mixed with R&B vocal stylings. Banda TecnoCaliente's name, "tecno-caliente," derives from the band's particular style, which is a subset of *banda* called *tecnobanda* because of its heavy reliance on synthesized sounds produced through use of *teclados* (keyboards). Banda TecnoCaliente relies on synthesized trumpet, accordion, and other instrumental sounds manufactured by keyboards onstage while the singers harmonize. TecnoCaliente's music varies from romantic ballads to up-tempo dance numbers and even occasional collaborations with a local *merengue/bachata* singer, Leydy Bonilla.

Musicians in Charlotte had several ongoing debates concerning *regional mexicano* music. The first concerned their treatment by radio stations and prominent concert promoters in the city. Many musicians felt that the local Spanish-language radio stations offered little airplay to local artists and failed to promote their performances, even when they were booked to play at radio-produced festivals like El Grito, the Mexican Independence Day celebration. Instead, the radio stations tended to favor well-known artists from Mexico and the U.S. Southwest, neglecting to give local artists *un chance*. The second issue involves the limited geographic mobility of audience members under surveillance from the 287(g) program, which meant that musicians had to be careful about where they booked a gig, both to ensure the success of their performance and out of concern that fans might be stopped by police roadblocks. At times, however, this meant that musicians had to contend with subpar performance spaces and sound systems at Eastside clubs or poorly organized festivals.[4] The third debate centered on the future of Mexican music in Charlotte. Although Mexican immigrants make up the largest group of Latinos in Charlotte and there is a core audience of young fans in their twenties, several musicians expressed concern that *regional mexicano* styles did not appeal to other Latinos from outside Mexico and Central America and particularly to the second generation of children who have grown up bicultural, speaking Spanish to their parents but embracing other styles of Latin music (*reggaetón*, *bachata*, rock) and mainstream U.S. popular culture and music. So some bands are attempting to bring in themes and musical elements from other genres in an effort to appeal to a wider audience.

Música tropical refers to genres of popular music from the Spanish-speaking Caribbean and its associated cities of migration, namely, Miami and New York, including *salsa*, *merengue*, *bachata*, and *reggaetón* (Flores 2000; Pacini Hernández 1995; Washburne 2008; Austerlitz 1997; Manuel, Bilby, and Largey 2006). There are similarities and differences between these musical forms, but the infrequency with which musicians in Charlotte described their music as *música tropical* belies the term's salience. People more often related musical genre to national and island identity, conveying the Dominican-ness of *merengue* or equating loving *salsa* with being Puerto Rican. Yet almost everybody acknowledges the common ties that link Dominican, Puerto Rican, Cuban, Nuyorican, and even peri-Caribbean Panamanian, Venezuelan, Colombian, and Brazilian music together with common histories and shared rhythms and tropes. Aware of the tension between commonality and particularity that permeates popular Spanish Caribbean music, we can begin to describe its genres and their permutations in Charlotte.

Salsa originates from Spanish Caribbean musical forms such as Cuban *son*, *rumba*, and *guaguancó* and Puerto Rican *bomba y plena*, but was amalgamated in New York from additional popular forms such as *mambo* and boogaloo. Stylistically, *salsa* mixes African and European musical traditions, relying on West African percussive elements and vocal patterns paired with European harmonies and Spanish guitar and other stringed instruments (*trés*). This musical hybridity mirrors the complex political history of the Spanish Caribbean, demonstrating the influence (and late abolition) of plantation slavery in Cuba such that African-derived music survived in great diversity (Sublette 2004; Herskovits 1990). Another factor was the vitality of Afro-Cuban political and social organizations, which continued to struggle for civil rights and cultural autonomy throughout the independence period and U.S. occupation (Helg 1995; de la Fuente 2001).

After 1898, U.S. imperial ambitions in the region (Foner 1972; McCullough 1978) created economic shifts (liberalization, U.S. corporate takeovers of sugar plantations, construction of the Panama Canal), political developments (the status of Puerto Rico, new racial regimes, the Cuban revolution), and social transformations (migration to the United States) that contributed to the distillation of specific genres within *música tropical*. For example, without large-scale migration of Puerto Ricans to New York and transnational connections between New York and Havana during the 1940s and 1950s, we would not have the cross-cultural exchange of musicians that developed Latin jazz, *mambo*, and boogaloo in New York, a stream of music making that by the 1970s was molded into *salsa* (Sublette 2004; Roberts 1979; Flores 2000). But 1970s *salsa* also developed in the absence of Cuban influences, which had been cut off by the U.S. embargo, heavily favoring a conceptualization of the genre as Puerto Rican and Nuyorican (Washburne 2008). The dictator Rafael Trujillo promoted *merengue* as the national music of the Dominican Republic in response to what he perceived as threats to national cultural sovereignty from outside (mainly Haiti) and from working-class forms of music like *bachata* (Austerlitz 1997; Pacini Hernández 1995). *Reggaetón* traces its origins to Panamanian reggae (sung in Spanish, derived from Jamaican reggae and created by people of West Indian descent living on the isthmus) and is widely accepted as a Puerto Rican genre, yet it quickly became popularized among Nuyorican and Dominican audiences in New York.

The musicians I followed include Orquesta Mayor, Leydy Bonilla, DS The Evolution, and Bachata Flow. Orquesta Mayor is a *salsa* dance band that models itself after classic *salsa* combos like El Gran Combo de Puerto Rico and the Fania All-Stars. Although several of the musicians are Puerto Rican, the leader of the group (and trumpet player), Helder Serralde, is a Mexican immigrant trained in a conservatory in Mexico City. Leydy Bonilla is a Dominican-born *merengue* singer who has toured throughout Europe and North America. Since moving to Charlotte from New York to be close to her family, she performs with Bachata Flow, a group of musicians playing *bachata* and *merengue*, as her backup band. Leydy Bonilla sings mostly in Spanish, although she has experimented with songs in English. Bachata Flow consists of six young Dominican transplants, mostly from New York, who moved to Charlotte separately and then formed a band. Bachata Flow's style references old-school *bachata* while incorporating contemporary urban Latin popular music in its sound. DS The Evolution consists of two artists, one Dominican, the other Puerto Rican, who sing and rap over DJ-produced beats in a genre they call "urban Latino."

Among musicians in Charlotte, several key debates have emerged regarding *música tropical*. These debates centered around tensions in the music between assimilating and retaining (or reviving) cultural roots, particularly since many in this population are either U.S. citizens (Puerto Ricans) and/or long-term (often legal) residents of the mainland United States, having migrated to Charlotte from New York/New Jersey. First, to what extent are *tropical* genres defined by songs sung in Spanish? Leydy Bonilla and DS The Evolution have experimented with songs that are written and sung in English that retain the rhythmic elements and instrumentation of *bachata* and *reggaetón*, respectively. These are part of an attempt to "cross over" to an English-speaking audience, among both non-Latinos and second-generation Latinos with limited Spanish skills. Second, musicians negotiate the tension between creating new music and staying true to the traditions and rules of genre. For example, Orquesta Mayor often plays covers of classic *salsa* tunes, but with fresh arrangements written by band members, and these covers often receive an enthusiastic reception from their audience. While covering the canon of classic 1970s *salsa*, their bandleader, Helder, expresses a desire for the band to make it on the national stage by coming up with new compositions that reference this tradition but with a new twist. The idea of professionalism plays an important part in negotiating this dynamic; in addition to showing up on time and giving a good show, being "professional" means having technical prowess such as the ability to read music, arrange charts, or dissect the chord or rhythmic progressions of a song. Bachata Flow implements this professionalism in its performances and comportment by mixing long-established elements of *bachata*, such as using multiple guitars, *güiro*, and *tambor* (and not using synthesizers), with a singing style and bridges that take cues from R&B music. Band members often dress in up-to-date outfits that might be seen on young Dominican men in Washington Heights or Santo Domingo, but are not afraid to occasionally break into a performance of *perico ripiao*—an older style of *merengue* from the Cibao region of the Dominican Republic. A third debate involves the deployment of genre names in the public sphere. DS The Evolution insists that its music is not *reggaetón*, a genre it associates with crime and vice; instead, as its manager states,

> DS [The Evolution] is different; what DS plays is *urbano*, they are not *reggaetoneros*; [instead they are] *urbanos*. Why? Because they play a *cumbia*, a *bachata* . . . they play a mix of clean *reggaetón* and hip-hop, therefore, it's something different. The guys [in the band] are *jóvenes sanos* [wholesome kids]. . . . If you want to bring a *reggaetonero* now, no one is interested; when you say the word *urbano*, you have to demonstrate that it really is *urbano*— because *urbano* means you play for the street, what the street wants.[5]

Indeed, most performers of *música tropical* genres in Charlotte appear to position themselves as upwardly mobile both through an embrace of professionalism and mainstream Caribbean/Latino cultural expressions and a disassociation from the working-class *barrio* currents that also flow within the music.

The third genre category relevant to the Latin music scene in Charlotte is Latin rock. For this study, I prefer the term "Latin rock" over the more well-known phrase *rock en español* for several reasons. First, the bands included in this category at times sing songs in English, Portuguese, and Spanglish, in addition to Spanish. Second, many musicians spoke of *rock en español* as a musical movement that had emerged in the 1990s and reached its apex around a decade later, only to be superseded by a fragmentation of the genre into subcategories that are sometimes referred to as "Latin alternative" music. Third, many bands in Charlotte played a mix of rock and other genres—pop, electronica, ska, reggae, funk, heavy metal, blues, and punk. I have included them under the umbrella of Latin rock because of the outlook of their musical community, despite the diversity of the bands' styles. Of the three genre categories discussed here, these bands and their audiences go the furthest in adopting notions of pan-Latino identity that bridge nationalistic notions of identity; Latin rock acknowledges both this positioning as "Latino" and the genre's historical roots in rock music, from both the United States and Latin America.

The historical record of rock music in Latin America supports this complicated view of the genre. As the historian Eric Zolov documents (1999), rock musicians in 1960s Mexico first sang songs in English, but eventually switched to singing in Spanish (under pressure from cultural elites and government crackdowns), developing the idea of *rock en tu idioma* (rock in your language), which eventually became *rock en español*. This transition, which occurred during the heady years of student revolt and government repression in the late 1960s and early 1970s, even affected band names—Three Souls of the Mind became El Tri, one of Mexico's most famous and long-standing rock bands. But even the "rock" in *rock en español* exists as a catchall category for Latin American bands that have consistently blurred genres in their recordings and performances. Many bands from Latin America draw on folk styles from their native countries or reference other genres, such as *nueva canción*, in their performances. Los Fabulosos Cadillacs, for example, mix rock elements with ska, reggae, jazz, and funk in a style that often departs from the straight-up backbeat rhythm or singing style of rock music. Also, *rock en español* was heavily influenced by U.S. and British rock styles of the 1970s and 1980s, particularly bands such as The Cure, The Smiths, Depeche Mode, Guns N' Roses, and Metallica.

Latin rock groups that I followed include Ultimanota, Dorian Gris, Tropic Culture, Bakalao Stars, and SoulBrazil. Ultimanota plays what its bandleader calls "cheesy cocktail music" at local restaurants during Friday or Saturday dinner hour and at weddings, birthdays, and other private events. Its music includes covers of classic *boleros*, rock and pop standards from the United States and Latin America, and a few *salsa* and *merengue* numbers. Dorian Gris is a punk/heavy metal group that plays a mix of covers and original compositions, mainly in Spanish, but with an occasional rock song in English. Although its audience is mainly working-class Mexican immigrants, three of Dorian Gris's members are from Ecuador, but they have been able to adjust their style to accommodate an enthusiastic yet critical audience. Bakalao Stars is a ska/rock/reggae band started by two brothers from Colombia. The band sings in Spanish and often appears onstage in playful costumes, from Hawaiian shirts to afros and gorilla masks. Tropic Culture is a rock/funk/disco/world music group founded by a brother and sister and their cousin, all originally from Puerto Rico. SoulBrazil plays Brazilian genres such as *bossa nova*, *samba*, and MBP at local clubs and festivals.[6] Three of the members are from Brazil and the other member is a white man from the United States.

Musicians in Charlotte engage in several ongoing debates about Latin rock. First, they worry about the future of the genre locally. During 2009–2010, many groups counted fewer audience members at shows, and several bands took a break from performing or dissolved. Some wondered where the next generation of musicians was. Others lamented that a special moment had passed, with the heyday of Carlotan Rock occurring mid-decade, which was not likely to be reproduced. Second, musicians argued about the creative process and with it the direction of their bands. This debate was often not just about coming up with new material, but fundamental questions about the role of musicians as laborers and whether what they did should be considered work or play. Engaging in the creative process following the rules of rock music sometimes means deciding whether to pursue ambitions (and dedicate limited resources and time) of touring and promotion outside the local community or to adapt an attitude of nonchalance toward questions of fame. Several bands (Tropic Culture, Dorian Gris, Ultimanota) went through divisive and at times heart-wrenching iterations of this debate, while others (Bakalao Stars) adhered to a clear philosophy of not pursuing fame. Third, Latin rock bands inserted themselves into debates over what it means to be Latino in Charlotte through their music and music making. Unlike *regional mexicano* and *música tropical*, both of which have clear genealogies of national identity (or at least in *música tropical's* case, pan-Caribbean island identity), the canon of Latin rock relies on songs from artists spanning Latin America, Spain, and the underlying but continuous influence of U.S. and British rock music.[7] As we shall see, musicians drew upon a diverse repertoire of music—reinterpreting classic covers, mixing languages, juxtaposing musical styles, and borrowing riffs—to create original performances that spoke to the diversity of their audience of Latino immigrants from a variety of countries and backgrounds. Finally, the question of crossing over, of appealing to white audiences, dogged many musicians in this community. Musicians debated what efforts should be made to sing and promote their music in English and outside the Latino community, and to what extent crossing over might benefit or detract from the relaxed interactions they had established with their core audiences.

Another set of participants in Charlotte's Latin music scene are vital to understanding how the music scene works, people I like to call "musical brokers"—radio DJs, band promoters, and club and restaurant owners. In the vein of Arlene Dávila's analysis of "cultural brokers" (2001) who act as translators and go-betweens for Latino culture to the outside world, these individuals act as "musical brokers" who interpret and package musical performance and groups for distinct audiences in their venues and on-air. These individuals are highly influential in terms of choosing bands to perform and deciding how the performance is presented through advertising, location, and stage production (sound system, lighting, set time). Their efforts shape the look and sound of concerts and festivals, with beneficial or damaging results.

These musical brokers facilitate the circulation of music as a global commodity, creating what the ethnomusicologist George Lipsitz (1994) calls a "dangerous crossroads," where music that is marketed as "exotic," "authentic," or "new" is at risk of losing its connection to place and local culture, divorced from context or history. Lipsitz wonders, When does cross-cultural identification "serve escapist and irresponsible ends and when does it encourage an enhanced understanding of one's experiences and responsibilities?" (56). For Lipsitz, the answer to this question can be found in a careful examination of how this cross-cultural borrowing plays out, with attention paid to how privilege—be it "whiteness," elevated social class, or heteronormative perspective—can blind musical collaborators into essentializing other cultures while perpetuating systems of domination, and equal focus placed on how common circumstances and experiences—of oppression, racism, or marginalization—can help people separated by geography or language overcome cultural differences to create transformative collaboration.

At times, the dynamics between Charlotte's musical brokers, musicians, and audiences revealed this tension. Musical brokers, although mostly Latino, often had middle-class and commercial ideas about the best way to promote a show and perform live music. On several occasions, brokers confided that a poorly attended concert was the result of the band's inability to follow their advice about promotion or the result of musicians performing too often. Musical brokers' views on musicians (and their music) stemmed from the limitations of promotional avenues within corporate media structuring (such as a reliance on radio DJs to publicize shows) and the financial constraints of owning a small business. As we shall see, some musical brokers were more knowledgeable and respectful of particular musical styles than others, just as some were better able to deploy their social capital and connections to create the ubiquitous advertising and buzz that usually accompany a well-attended show. However, I do not want to overstate musical brokers' power as tastemakers; both musicians and audiences talked back to them. There were limits to how (much) musicians wanted to "sell" their music to wider audiences or translate their local culture in collaborative settings like festivals. Audiences pushed back, showing their displeasure with ill-conceived collaborations, long delays in stage production, or shortened sets by their favorite performers.

Conclusion

The intertwining of Latin American and U.S. popular music began before the twentieth century and continues today. Latino immigrants to Charlotte continue this process by bringing their musical tastes to the city and reformulating these proclivities by joining a band, attending a concert as a fan, or promoting music as a small business owner. While other Latin music scenes have emerged in U.S. cities, Charlotte is notable for the diversity of the musical styles being performed there and the intense debates musicians are having about the future of Latino culture. Musicians struggle to balance tradition and innovation, negotiating genre rules and audiences that cherish the music's rich history, but also want new music that speaks to their changing lives in a new land. Although it remains to be seen in what iteration the "Latin tinge" will next appear in U.S. popular music, Latina/o musicians in Charlotte are taking the lead by creating music that is distinctly southern and Latino.

The Latin music scene in Charlotte is made up of a diverse group of musicians and audience members (hailing from almost every country in Latin America) playing a number of styles. But this diversity does not create unity. Although I attempted to see as many bands playing as many genres as possible during my time there, many Charlotte musicians and audience members have a very limited understanding of what occurs outside their immediate surroundings. As I will demonstrate in chapter 3, social segregation is rife and limits the available audience, geographic mobility, and economic prospects for Charlotte's Latin bands—both within the Latino community and between Latinos and other residents of the city. The interpersonal nature of the music scene creates spaces for community formation, but because live musical performance is temporary (and not always so inspiring), any sense of group solidarity can be fleeting and fragment easily. The following chapters show how musicians attempt to deal with these limitations by recalibrating their performance styles and attitudes toward their work, by appealing to racial and ethnic identity, and by jumping scales to present their music on larger stages.

3

Bands Making Musical Communities

Musical Community

"Musical community" connotes a sense of belonging and shared affiliation around notions of class, ethnicity, language, style, and taste
expressed through music and other creative cultural expressions. Musical community, as I define it, exists at the intersection of local and mass
consumption, often serving as a point of mediation between locally
produced, "grassroots" expressions of music and nationally and globally
popular mass expressions of music. In addition to musicians' interactions with each other, audience members and other listeners to the
music engage in what the social theorist Paul Gilroy called "dialogic
rituals" (1991), where they become active participants in music- and
community-making processes. As the anthropologist Patricia Zavella
(2011) argues, these collective rituals of consumption enable Latinos (of
various backgrounds) to gain a sense of cultural citizenship that may
lead to heightened political consciousness. While Zavella found that
Mexican and Chicana/o musicians create a discursive political space
through performances that draw on themes of transnationalism and
crossing literal and figurative borders, my research found that Latina/o
musicians in Charlotte created musical community both because of and
in opposition to the stark social segregation in the city. Particular genres
became sequestered in neighborhoods and music venues, settings that in
turn shaped the modes of performance and interaction between musicians and audience members. While informed by transnational links to
Latin America, particularly through touring musicians, internal dynamics within the Latino community and between Latinos and black and
white Charlotte residents shaped the creation of musical community.

This chapter documents how bands and their audiences engage in a
process of community formation around music, keeping in mind the
impacts this process has for the greater Latino population. Working
together to create music, they establish their political agency through

negotiations of genre, style, and outlook and through performance of music. The Latin music scene in Charlotte consists of the Eastside, In-town, and Uptown districts, each loosely corresponding to a geographic area of the city. Within these districts, band-made communities high-light class divisions and tensions around race and ethnicity within the Latino community and between Latinos and non-Latinos.

"Community" is a term often used in popular depictions of and scholarship on small-scale groups, particularly groups that affiliate around a locale, identity, or activity. The anthropologist Gerald Creed cautions scholars to question what the focus on "community" and its deployment as a commonsense yet rarely defined term does, particu-larly the "sociological and ideological work" that results from using community as a concept (Creed 2006, 4). While minding this critique, I find "community" a useful term for describing and analyzing the small-scale gatherings of musicians and audiences around popular practice that I observed in Charlotte because of the shared sense of solidarity and common experience that musicians and audience members felt and expressed. However, I view "community" as accruing from a process of community formation that gives it temporality and an "imagined" di-mension, much like the nation (Anderson 2006), a process that is often uneven and incomplete. Community formation may also build upon an "archive of feelings" (Cvetkovich 2003; Zavella 2011) created through musicians' and audiences' performances and interpretations of reality, or construct "cultural memory" (Zavella 2011) that may represent critical perspectives that question power relations or provide alternative visions of how the world works. Despite this potential, in the contemporary urban setting, and particularly among populations with diverse cultural traditions, such as Latino immigrants, the formation of community is not a given.

An analysis of community must take into account the fragmentary and ad hoc nature of communities in real life and how definitions of community are particular to different historical eras and ideolo-gies. Without going into an extensive exegesis of these debates, I note that three prominent philosophical contributions to a theorization of "community"—Tonnies's comparison of *Gemeinschaft* and *Gesellschaft* (1887), Marx's analysis of alienation of labor power and class formation (1976), and Durkheim's collective consciousness (1997)—all developed from the rise of industrial capitalism and imperial projects in Europe. Early anthropologists, from Malinowski, Boas, and Evans-Pritchard to Lévi-Strauss, often saw community as timeless and rooted in non-Western kinship relations and belief systems. In the Latin American and Caribbean context (Mintz 1974; Steward 1956), anthropologists focused on the destruction of traditional forms and reconstitution of community in Spanish colonies, but also on how colonial bureaucracy, agricultural administration, and record keeping made those societies "modern" before Europe (Silverblatt 2004; Mintz 1986). This type of analysis helps us consider how the state encourages, regulates, prohibits, surveys, and interacts with communities.

In postindustrial and postmodern settings, debates about community are now centering on notions of "virtual" community formed through the Internet, social networking websites, and digital media (Boellstorff 2010). Another focus has been on how transnational migration creates communities that exist across borders through migrants' social networks and familial bonds (Smith 2005; Ong 1999; Hirsch 2003). Community, as manufactured and mediated by the capitalist market but practiced and reinterpreted by consumers and/or community members, has also become a topic of study, whether it is communities of video gamers, nature enthusiasts (Tsing 2005), ethnic groups (Comaroff and Comaroff 2009), or people attempting to exist outside or limit the purview of the market (e.g., free-cyclers, slum dwellers, subsistence farmers).

In Charlotte, for example, immigration enforcement through the 287(g) program has hampered community among Latinos because of family separation and fear stemming from state policy, but it has also created a rallying point for Latino immigrants and their allies to forge a political movement around immigration reform. The diversity of the Latino community, with immigrants from across Latin America and the Caribbean, also impedes the development of a shared sense of belonging, as Latino immigrants remain divided by questions of class, legal status, ethnicity and racial identity, and cultural expressions. These divisions, the most significant being class, shape the musical communities I outline below.

Through interactions with their audiences, bands channel sentiment and provide structure to musical communities that, within the larger Latino population in Charlotte, were often dramatically divided along class lines. As such, bands construct these communities by embodying the shared values and aesthetic of their fans and constituting a space of trust and mutual respect. This chapter examines how bands make community in the three districts of the city where Latin music is created and analyzes how band-audience interaction embodies class identity through music and performance. These three geographic districts, Eastside, Intown, and Uptown, are located in separate and largely segregated areas of Charlotte. The Eastside district consists of bands such as Banda TecnoCaliente and Los Mentirosos and their audiences—in other words, mostly listeners of *regional mexicano* music (but also Mexican rock). The Intown district includes bands such as Bakalao Stars and Tropic Culture and their fans, listeners to Latin rock and related styles. The Uptown district consists of bands such as Bachata Flow, DS The Evolution, Leydy Bonilla, and SoulBrazil and fans of *música tropical* and Brazilian music.

"Musical community" is fleeting (sometimes only lasting the length of a concert). I describe below a series of moments that highlight how bands and audiences engage in a dialectical process of defining the boundaries and direction of their music and creating solidarity and a sense of community. These communities are part of larger social networks based in the workplace, church, neighborhood, or school where Latino immigrants remake home in the United States, retain linkages to their home countries, and form transnational bonds with fellow migrants. However, I argue that musical communities form a space apart, where Latino immigrants draw on these social ties but also enter into performance that itself becomes the basis for communal bonds. Then, these communal bonds help strengthen and give direction to larger community social ties. Live performance is vitally important for creating these communal bonds, both through the performance rituals acted out during concerts and as artifacts that were often recorded (and put on YouTube), interpreted, and remembered by community members.

The "community" in this case is constituted on multiple levels. Who is included in the audience? Who is not? First, there is a stark geographic segregation corresponding to the class and racial segregation of Charlotte, highlighted below, that ties musical communities to neighborhoods (the three districts) where musicians find welcoming spaces for performance and audience members feel at home going to listen to music. Second, we must account for factors that limit who goes to see bands' live performances: age (if the concert is at a bar or nightclub), enjoyment of live music (often played at high volume and late at night), a predominance of heteronormative gender roles, the charisma of the band members, cultural and linguistic knowledge, weather, and money. Finally, there is an open dialogue between musicians and audiences that creates a fan base. Band members draw on other social networks by inviting friends to shows, but new ties are formed with prior strangers during performances when musician and listener interact. Some musical communities are more successful than others at cementing these ties and coalescing around a shared vision of what their community does and means.

Although the musical communities outlined below may appear drastically different and even oppositional in their outlooks and styles, I argue that there is one unifying facet that unites them: all play music that inspires (indeed, requires) dance and kinetic movement. If there is one thing that unifies Latin music and provides the basis for speaking of a Latin music scene in Charlotte, it is this practice. Latin popular music, despite its diversity of genres and varied geographic roots, when performed live is music for dancing. It is this aspect of active audience participation that, while not separating Latin music from other dance forms, does distance it from the relative passivity of much audience participation in mainstream popular music (and classical and jazz forms) in the United States (see Adorno 1941).

Dorian Gris

I sat by the entrance to Skandalos, an Eastside nightclub, with Carlos Crespo and his wife, Rebecca, on a chilly night in February. As a steady stream of fans entered and paid the cover charge, Crespo, the guitarist for the featured band that night, Dorian Gris, greeted each person, often by name, and gave them a copy of the band's latest EP, *Live at the Dark Room* (2009). The crowd's hairstyles (long hair, mohawks, the occasional mullet) and clothing choices (leather jackets and vests, jeans, studded belts, tennis shoes) mixed fashions from heavy metal and punk rock traditions. Soon the show started, and Crespo joined his bandmates onstage in a T-shirt reading, "No human being is illegal." After a few covers of the Doors, Los Jaguares, and Molotov, Dorian Gris launched into a set of its own songs. At first the audience stood around watching, catching up with old friends, having a few beers from the bar; but soon a long-dreadlocked figure burst into the center of the floor, headbanging enthusiastically to the opening chords of a song, and within seconds, five or six other guys joined him in a bout of energetic pushing and slamming against one another. The instigator, Greñas (Mop-head), is a local promoter of heavy metal concerts (including this one) and musician; the other dancers his friends and fellow fans of Dorian Gris. At first glance, the dancing looks violent, but everyone has a smile on his face and no fights break out. There is a delicate ballet as boyfriends on the margins of the circle of dancers shield girlfriends from errant blows and guys nursing beers give wayward dancers a shove back into the center of the floor.

Juan Espín, the lead singer of Dorian Gris, signals that he is thirsty, and somebody in the crowd goes and gets him a beer from the bar. Catcalls and whistles fill the air as Espín curses at the crowd in Mexican slang, smiling and looking sheepishly down at his feet before he signals the start of the next song. The band launches into a cover of Zurdok's "El Gallito Inglés" (1997). Tired of pacing around onstage, Espín launches himself into the crowd, and a circle of fans quickly converge on him, flailing arms and hips in every direction. He sings into the mike,

¿Quién es, quién es? (Who is it, who is it?)

And passes the mike to a fan, who screams in a guttural timbre,

Es el GALLITO INGLÉS! (It's the little English cock!)

Espín and his fans link together, arms around shoulders, and turn in a line. He drops to his knees to sing, then gives the mike over to another audience member to finish—"Es el GALLITO INGLÉS!"

These ritualized yet chaotic interactions between band and audience at Dorian Gris shows serve to break down any pretense of separation between performer and listener. The audience themselves become performers: taking the mike, singing lines from songs, jumping onstage, and forming a circle of dancers that is the focus of the concert. As Patricia Zavella (2012) explains, this type of blurring between audience and performers represents the Latino punk ethos along with a DIY (do it yourself) attitude toward promotion, musicianship, and recording. Espín relishes the audience's participation, which enhances the physical bond between band and audience: a crowd of performers embodying the music in exaggerated movement as they hurl themselves at each other. However, in contrast to Zavella's description of *punkeros* in Chicago, whose dancing at times turned violent (Zavella 2012), I never witnessed Dorian Gris's audience get out of hand. The dancers, mostly men, created and expressed their camaraderie as they mixed sweat, shaking, jumping, and occasionally putting their arms around each other's shoulders. Which is not to say that this dancing did not create divisions within the audience; a particular Latino punk heteronormative masculinity took center stage, while feminine and queer perspectives were sublimated or pushed to the margins. This differs from earlier scenes, such as East Los Angeles punk clubs of the 1970s, where Chicana *punkeras* were welcomed and able to express disruptive gender and sexual identities (Habell-Pallán 2005). At Skandalos during Dorian Gris concerts, women participate, but only momentarily; few women choose to enter the fray in front of the stage or sing into the mike. However, the same

Fans dancing at a Dorian Gris concert

nightclub occasionally hosted nights that were geared toward a queer audience, where DJs spun records of Latin pop music and gay and lesbian couples would hit the dance floor.

Dorian Gris's collective performance is also a verbal interaction. The crowd hurls friendly insults at band members between songs, and they return the favor with scatological dialogue (see Dorian Gris's "Paranoia" [2009] or El Tri's "La Raza Más Chida" [2004]). Espín relishes the exchange, and smiles every time a particularly creative phrase or jarring expletive is hurled his way. He makes sure to pause just long enough to encourage this dialogue, but not long enough to let it take over the performance before launching into another song. In this case the audience's feedback is positive, but in other cases the audience at Eastside rock shows reacted negatively, particularly if a band did not embody the same kinetic energy that Dorian Gris provides. The negative response might involve yelling barbs at the band—"Cu-le-ro! Culero!" (Asshole! Asshole!)[1]—or ironic calls for more music: "Otra! . . . Otra! . . . otra banda!" (Encore! . . . Another! . . . Another band!).

Dorian Gris's performances do not represent a fully formed class identity. Instead, the band and audience appear to be formulating their ideas of class through performances and belonging to a musical community in an urban space. They bring facets of urban street culture from Mexico City and other urban centers in Mexico to a club in Charlotte that features rock, but also other working-class Latin genres such as *regional mexicano* (on different nights or in different rooms), in a neighborhood where they work as service industry laborers and that features a heavy police presence targeting undocumented immigrants. The give-and-take between band and audience is part of a dialectical process where musical communities form class identity by working through the contradictions of their role in U.S. society and as migrants who maintain transnational links to Latin America. They use music to decipher their positionality, to arrive at an interpretation of their role as a young urban proletariat. Thus, while this account seeks to problematize class as something that is not predetermined, deterministic, or essentializing, it also will show that class identity has real contributing factors (in Charlotte's Latino community, geographic segregation, education, national origin, employment outcomes, and legal status) and actual effects (namely, the formation of different ideas of politics, leisure time, and musical style).

Members of Dorian Gris's audience demonstrate a class position through their dancing and verbal exchanges. Both are "dirty"—whether it's the sweat, feigned violence, and physicality of their dance styles or their scatological conversation with Juan Espín, the lead singer. This dirtiness corresponds to how they view and are perceived in their role as proletarian workers in restaurant kitchens, construction sites, landscaping, and custodial jobs (Holmes 2013). While association with this type of work could lead to negative stereotypes, many of the audience members I spoke with embraced the difficulty and dirtiness of their occupations. Some men viewed it as proof of their masculinity, while both men and women stressed the sacrifices they were willing to make on the job (dangerous conditions, long hours, payment scams) for their families both in the United States and abroad. While I have framed this correlation as part of the making of class identity, I must reiterate here that the audiences for all the bands featured in this chapter are mostly made up of young people, from teenagers to those in their thirties, so the ideas formulated are tied into views of youthfulness, coming of age, and hopes and dreams for the future.

¡Que Naco!

It's Sunday evening in Charlotte, and aside from the stray tailgater making his way home after watching a football game, there's not much to do. At least, one might get that impression walking around uptown Charlotte (which is what natives call downtown). But if you make your way up North Tryon Street from center city, past the looming glass skyscrapers, past the homeless shelters and used car dealerships, behind a bowling alley, a nightclub called Kalipso is just opening its doors. Every Sunday night Mexican immigrants, many celebrating the fact that Monday is their day off, gather to listen to music and to dance. Parking in a poorly lit gravel lot, you enter and get frisked by surly off-duty cops, then step onto the dance floor. A DJ plays the latest *banda* and *pasito duranguense*, couples dance, men drink can after can of Modelo Especial. Although this music and its associated performative behavior are described by middle-class Mexicans (and other Charlotte Latinos who have picked up on Mexican slang terms) as *naco* (unrefined or ghetto), for participants the music is affirming and powerful.[2] When a local band gets up on the club's tiny stage wedged into the corner of the dance floor, the crowd responds with enthusiasm. The band and audience engage in a call-and-response ritual of calling out provinces in Mexico from which they hail: "¡Viva Michaocán!" "¿Dónde está la gente de Nayarit?" Sometimes, the club has arranged for a more well-known, visiting artist to perform on their tour through the southern United States—say, Larry Hernández, Banda Recodo, or Los Tucanes de Tijuana, and the room buzzes with anticipation.[3] The artist makes them wait; radio DJs hover outside in their mobile studio hyping the event over the airwaves to get more people coming in to pack the place, and the DJ keeps the audience in motion while the featured group makes its way from a nearby hotel. Finally, the music stops, a video is projected on wall screens with the band's name, its promotional accolades, and its latest hit song. The group makes its way to the stage, through the crowd (there's no backstage at Kalipso), where fans converge to try to get a handshake, a kiss, a picture with someone famous. The band starts playing, the crowd cheers, then returns to dancing, the dancers sweating in the airless room, skillfully turning partners without stepping on neighbors' toes. Single men line the walls, searching for openings to ask women for a dance. After playing for several hours, the band begins to wind down. Last call means men double fisting cans of beer, staff cleaning mountains of trash, and altercations quickly snuffed by security guards escorting young men out of the building. Afterwards the band signs autographs, poses for pictures, and talks with radio DJs and local musicians, before venturing out on the road to the next town.

On any given Sunday night, clubs like Kalipso on Charlotte's Eastside cater to an audience of working-class Mexican immigrants. The musicians and audiences at these shows make up the first grouping of band-made musical communities in Charlotte's Latin music scene. Housed in old converted warehouses and retail stores, clubs like Kalipso, Midnight Rodeo, Skandalos, Palenque, and Backstage provide opportunities for local bands to play live music for an audience made up of recent immigrants from across Mexico. When I spoke with audience members and musicians, they insisted that these types of clubs did more; they provided a space where audience members felt "comfortable." This crowd does not attend shows at Uptown clubs or in gentrified neighborhoods like NoDa (North Davidson) or Plaza-Midwood, even if many of them work as waiters in restaurants, janitors in offices, or maids or landscapers in these areas. This geographic segregation, confining the recreational activities of Mexican immigrants to several neighborhoods in East and South Charlotte, occurred despite the fact that clubs like Kalipso often had subpar sound systems and dilapidated facilities compared to other clubs. Many community members stressed their discomfort with traveling to Uptown clubs, where they felt out of place among middle-class and non-Mexican weekend partiers. This discomfort was reinforced by fear of police checkpoints for DUI; under the 287(g) program in Charlotte-Mecklenburg County, police pulling someone over for a traffic violation could check immigration status and if undocumented, the driver could be detained and eventually deported. Even if you weren't "illegal," the sentiment in this community was that the police singled out Mexican drivers for harassment, and your chances of getting pulled over increased if you ventured outside the neighborhood.[4]

This social segregation reveals one of the ironies of globalization. Latina/o immigrants, having traveled thousands of miles to arrive in Charlotte and maintaining transnational contacts through phone and Internet connections, nevertheless fear traveling outside their neighborhoods during their leisure time. Their labor and physical bodies buttress the development of Charlotte into a globalizing city because many fill low-wage service jobs that help support the "flexible" and "creative" work of the financial sector (Sassen 1988; Harvey 1989; Florida 2003). As part and parcel of Latina/o immigrants' roles in the job market, they face policing of their bodies and impediments to their geographic mobility. As immigration scholars have long stated, the framing of immigrant labor as "illegal" and socially distinct from the mainstream enables the exploitation of immigrant workers and hinders their efforts to contest this exploitation (Inda 2006; De Genova 2002; Griswold del Castillo and de León 1996; Montejano 1987). Moreover, local implementation of the 287(g) program can be seen as part of a larger process of implementing a regime of global apartheid (Harrison 2008) that restricts movement of poor people from the global South through policing of bodies. Federal policies of border enforcement have curtailed the back-and-forth movement between countries that many immigrants, both documented and undocumented, used to engage in (Massey 2011). Immigrants with expired visas or who had migrated without documentation often discussed

Banda TecnoCaliente at the Fanta Festival on Charlotte's Eastside

their frustration with being stuck in one place. They knew it would be a big risk to return to visit family in Mexico and perhaps not be able to return to the United States. While Charlotte's undocumented Latino residents might enjoy some of the cosmopolitan taste (Appadurai 1996) developed when one leaves a parochial setting, they were denied the ease and freedom of motion that other global travelers enjoy.

Further evidence of this geographic segregation appeared during a series of festivals held in the summer of 2010. Two festivals featuring *regional mexicano* music held in an Eastside park, the Fanta Festival and El Grito celebration, attracted tens of thousands of people. Two similar events held Uptown, a soccer game featuring professional teams from Mexico and Honduras, and an indoor daylong concert with seven Mexican bands held at a community college, attracted far less robust crowds. This despite the fact that all four events were heavily promoted on the radio and publicized in newspapers, and all but the soccer game were held on Sunday afternoon.

Yet there are exceptions to this link between nationality and participation in the music of one Charlotte district. Dorian Gris is a case in
point. While the drummer is from Mexico, Carlos Crespo, the guitarist, Juan Espín, the lead singer, and Holbach Pérez, the bass player, are
all from Ecuador. The band favors Mexican and American-origin rock
songs and the vast majority of the audience are Mexican immigrants.
The Ecuadorians have actively chosen to identify with the working-class
Mexican audience that attends their shows, even though their middle-
class personal histories growing up in Ecuador might suggest another
path. Since immigrating to Charlotte, they have come to identify with
working-class Mexicans through friendships with Mexicans and their
diminished class position in the United States as precarious immigrant
workers. For Crespo, choosing to have Dorian Gris play at Skandalos
is a conscious decision that he contrasts with playing at other venues
further in town, where the band has had unpleasant experiences. In an
interview in English, Crespo recalls such an experience:

CARLOS CRESPO: Only one time, we went to play downtown, but the
    guy who promotes shows, promotes more South American rock. You
    know, because we're Ecuadorians. The people who go expect to hear,
    like, Fito Páez, Charly García, Soda Stereo . . . so we played our own
    stuff, and our covers of El Tri, Molotov.[5] I always told the guys, we
    are what we are; we don't have to change just because we play another
    gig . . . so people left.
SB: People left?
CARLOS: Yeah! Actually I really didn't care, because thirty guys from
    our usual crowd went to see us. And I was happy just to see them
    there. Greñas and his crew was there jumping. . . . There's a thing,
    like, I have to see people jumping from the stage. If I don't see jump-
    ing, then I feel like they're not having a good show. That's why I love
    playing to a Mexican crowd, more than my own South American
    crowd. South Americans are not very emotive, I mean, when they see
    a band they just *see* it. And I'm the same way.
SB: They don't get into it.
CARLOS: When I see a band, I don't go jumping. But somehow people
    in Mexico, they really do, I mean even if you go to see like Los En-

anitos Verdes, it's a very soft pop band, and they are jumping all the
time, and slam-dancing and hitting everything.

SB: Why do you think they do that?

CARLOS: I don't know. I guess it has to be something cultural. I have
no idea. Maybe they just want to liberate all these emotions, frustra-
tions . . . but they tell me that's the way it is in Mexico, so maybe it's
more like a Mexican thing. I don't know but to me it's more like they
just want to—most of our crowd, I would say 90 percent are undocumented people, and they work these miserable jobs having like eight
dollars an hour and at least—they can have fun, jump, and play.[6]

In Charlotte, there is a geographic and stylistic separation between
Mexican and South American musical communities that corresponds
to social and cultural differences they have imported from their home
countries and that have been shaped by unequal access to legal status
and different socioeconomic trajectories between these two groups once
in the United States. By embracing the musical tastes of their Mexican
fans, Crespo and his bandmates represent a countertrend of South
Americans breaching this separation of national origin. Dorian Gris's
concerts give community members a chance to engage in performative
practices central to their musical community, just as they would do at
a concert by El Tri or Molotov, but with more regular and close social
ties to the musicians. One Charlotte journalist called these performative
practices the *circular colectivo* (collective circle; Strimling 2010)—the
circle of dancers that often forms at Eastside rock concerts in Charlotte,
where dancers slam into each other and where jumping and shoving
serve to unite band and audience in a collective music-making strategy.
It was this kind of chaotic, frenetic, yet highly interactive physical performance that Dorian Gris aspired to as proof that its music succeeded.

Soundcocho

In my blog on October 3, 2010, I wrote this about the Charlotte group
Tropic Culture:[7]

I've heard Tropic Culture described as a "festival band" or jam band, the
type of group that is most in its element at fairs, festivals, and outdoor cel-

ebrations. I think this is an accurate description, if you take this label to mean that the band is a "big tent" affair, where various styles and genres exist side by side, and are imperfectly and messily mixed together. At times, Tropic Culture brings the funk of Tower of Power, the throwback disco of Jamiroquai, or the breaks common in lite, smooth and acid jazz, all with a side of tropical rhythm. When I interviewed the group this past July, they hinted that they were in the process of changing their sound. They call what they are doing a "Dance Revolution," again this is festival music, not "serious" rock you stand around contemplating (for better or worse).

Tropic Culture has always had a certain socio-political stance, in the feel-good, spread-the-love vein of listeners of Bob Marley who adhere to his pop songs and sidebar his Garveyite lyrics (War, Burnin' and Lootin'). In songs like "Eliminate the Hate" and "The Train," they advocate a pleasant social activism, never threatening or controversial. In this concert, they dedicated a song to the people of Ecuador, after a chaotic week when the Ecuadorian president was attacked by striking police. This song included the lyrics, "the revolution must begin." Without reading too much into it, we can at least say Tropic Culture wants us not to forget the troubles of the world, but at least be aware of them while we dance to their music.

From this blog entry, one can get a sense of what might be termed multicultural, Intown bands, such as Tropic Culture and Bakalao Stars, which play at music venues in the NoDa, Plaza-Midwood, and Elizabeth neighborhoods in Charlotte. I use the term "multicultural" to mean not just literally a mix of cultures (rather ubiquitous in Latin America and now in the United States), or its original meaning as part of a political push for inclusion and racial diversity (Omi and Winant 1994), but rather the term's current popular usage. Since the 1990s in popular and academic circles, "multicultural" has taken on multiple and disparate meanings corresponding loosely to left- and right-wing attempts to describe the post–Civil Rights era landscape in the United States. What began as a descriptive term to analyze the emerging diversity of schools and workplaces became codified in national policy (witness President Bill Clinton's National Conversation on Race), parallel with attacks on affirmative action, welfare reform, and the increasing imprisonment of poor black and Latino men (Doane and Bonilla-Silva 2003; Mullings 2005; Baker 2002; Morgen and Maskovsky 2003). The

idea of multiculturalism was incorporated in the language of international NGOs and United Nations agencies, affecting policy decisions in
countries with vastly different social dynamics and ethno-racial histories from the United States (Hale 2002). In this usage, multiculturalism
takes on a bland, apolitical character that in its deployment in slogans,
advertisements, and policy decisions has political repercussions, namely,
shifting discussions away from questions of lingering class and racial
inequalities (Gates 1994; PBS 1998), racially targeted violence, and citizenship. This was perhaps most prominently displayed in the pitiful plea
of Rodney King, "Can['t] we all just get along?" during the Los Angeles
riots that followed the acquittal of the police officers who beat him.

For members of the bands in question, who came of age in the late
1990s and early 2000s as immigrant children in the southern United
States, the multicultural idea (and ideal) forms an essential part of their
worldview. But this multicultural idea is of the "soft" variety that welcomes
social inclusion and cultural mixing, but falls short of explicit political
demands. They are the children of relatively successful immigrant parents who make up an emerging middle class in Charlotte. Mainly second-
generation or 1.5-generation young men, these musicians retain loose ties
with their home countries and their cultures (through periodic visits),
but mainly they have chosen to formulate an eclectic music that draws on
Latin American, U.S., Afro-Caribbean, and world music traditions.

Bakalao Stars plays rhythms and melodies that draw on Jamaican reggae and Afro-Brit ska while singing in Spanish in the mode of groups
from Colombia and Venezuela. Yet it often mixes in rock guitar riffs,
while its lead singer jumps around and falls down onstage like a pos-
sessed punk rocker. The title of its 2010 album, *Soundcocho*, a play on
the Spanish word for a hearty type of soup/stew (*sancocho*), reflects this
stylistic mixture in its music.

Bakalao Stars and Tropic Culture have dedicated fans who attend
their concerts regularly. Much of the audience consists of school classmates from high school or the local public university, where a few of the
musicians are enrolled or have graduated. Other fans are friends from
work. The bands maintain an active presence on social networking websites like Facebook, sending out event notifications with colorful posters
and e-mails detailing their next concert and encouraging everyone to attend. Bakalao Stars, in the midst of recording a new album in the fall of

Bakalao Stars promotional concert poster

2010, posted photos and video of its time in the studio. At concerts, the bands engage in a particular style of showmanship that marks this musical community apart from others. Bakalao Stars always brings a large handmade tricolor flag with "BAKALAO" and a star symbol written on it, which band members hang somewhere in the club. The Afrocentric symbolism (the flag is red, yellow, and green; basically an inverted flag of Ghana) corresponds to the band's embrace of reggae and ska, as does its collaboration with the local reggae singer Ras Congo on its recent album and during performances.

Tropic Culture, befitting its label as a "festival band," uses its musical choices as an inducement to get the crowd dancing. Unlike Dorian Gris concerts, where the audience takes the lead and seemingly spontaneously launches into action, Tropic Culture's audience rarely starts dancing until the lead singer cajoles fans to start moving. The audience has to be reminded that they can participate, that they too have a part to play in making this concert a success beyond just showing up. These two bands flirt with the line that divides a classical music/European-derived, passive spectator audience from an active, participatory, dance movement–focused audience. As such, the audience rarely engages in what could be described as a particular genre of dancing; rather, a mish-mash of styles exist side by side.

The class affiliation and outlook of the community made from these bands and their audiences are evident in the location and type of venues they choose to seek out for their performances. The majority of their concerts take place in several venues in NoDa, an Intown neighborhood near the center city. NoDa (short for North Davidson) is an old mill community that has been slowly remade as an Intown residential community with hip nightlife. Over the last two decades, the conversion of closed textile mills (Graves and Smith 2010) and working-class housing into luxury condominiums and highly sought-after historic homes signaled a process of gentrification that corresponded to the opening of coffee shops, trendy restaurants, and live music venues. Music halls such as the Evening Muse, Salvador's Deli, and the Neighborhood Theatre attract regional and national acts to play in Charlotte in intimate spaces for relatively low ticket prices. Another venue, the Visulite, in the nearby Elizabeth section, books similar acts. Following in the footsteps of bands like La Rúa and the organizers of Carlotan Rock, Tropic

Culture and Bakalao Stars have decided that this type of venue provides the best space for their style of music. Echoing the opposite sentiment from Mexican bands playing on the Eastside, several musicians told me that this community much prefers NoDa and will not travel to clubs like Skandalos to hear live music. Moreover, in their view, NoDa provides the best hope of fulfilling the ultimate goal of a band like Tropic Culture, namely, to "cross over" and reach a larger, non-Latino audience of music fans who attend shows at these venues.

Caribbean Nights

Natives of Charlotte call the center of the city—the shiny skyscrapers that house bank headquarters, the rows of steakhouses, the museums concentrated into a "cultural campus," and the hotels, bars, and nightclubs—Uptown. Uptown Charlotte is cut off from the rest of the city by a moat of highway—Interstate 277—that loops its way around the center city. It is fitting, then, that this figurative island in the middle of Charlotte would attract musicians and audiences who enjoy the music of the islands of the Spanish Caribbean and New York, genres such as *merengue, bachata, salsa,* and *reggaetón.* (While I generalize here to make a point about the geographic and social separation between band-made micro-communities, in later chapters I will delve more deeply into the significant differences between genres and musicians within this tropical grouping.) On Thursday, Friday, and Saturday nights, Uptown clubs host Latin nights, featuring DJs and occasionally live bands. Alongside and sometimes within the same club, other dance floors feature hip-hop, house and trance, and reggae music. Latinos from the Dominican Republic, Puerto Rico, Cuba, and especially New York crowd onto the dance floor to show off their skills and enjoy a night out. Joining them are white and black *salseros,* often part of a local dance studio where they have been taking *salsa* lessons and are ready to practice new spins and steps.

Of all the neighborhoods in Charlotte, Uptown alone has the density of buildings and proximity of businesses and nightlife to mimic the urban feel of a city like New York. Its *salsa* clubs loosely mimic the sense of "going out" and separation from ordinary life that New York's *salsa* clubs provide (Washburne 2008). Uptown Charlotte's affiliation with New York is no surprise, given the number of transplants from New

York working in banking and the close financial ties between the two cities. One difference is the critical importance of parking decks and garages to Uptown Charlotte's popularity. Charlotte, like other southern cities, is a car-dependent and car-happy place. This Uptown simulacrum of Manhattan attracts a community of Charlotte's Latino residents, many of whom lived in New York for years and have obtained legal status in the United States, even if originally from Santo Domingo or Havana. The attraction of Charlotte parallels a move by many *caribeños* from New York/New Jersey/Connecticut to other southern cities such as Atlanta, Orlando, and Miami. Moving for the lower real estate prices, better job opportunities, and warmer climate, these Latinos also cherish the expansion of direct Caribbean flights from airline hubs in the South (U.S. Airways in Charlotte, Delta in Atlanta). In Charlotte, Dominicans, Puerto Ricans, and Cubans all have formed small but vibrant communities based in ethnic and national solidarity and familial ties.

Perhaps the best musical example of this trend is Leydy Bonilla and the band that often plays with her, Bachata Flow. Bonilla started out performing in Santo Domingo, and then moved to New York, as many Dominican performers before her have done. At a young age, she had a modest level of success, with singles on the radio and a tour of Spain and Europe. Yet she decided to follow her parents when they moved to Charlotte rather than remain in New York alone. She continues to sing and record, but also works a day job at an insurance agency to help support her son. Bachata Flow's musicians made a similar move; separately, each of the band's members transplanted from New York to Charlotte. They had played as sidemen in different groups in New York; now in Charlotte they formed their own group and started playing in clubs.

Unlike both *regional mexicano* and Latin rock audiences, however, listeners to tropical genres like *salsa*, *merengue*, and *bachata* seem much more accustomed to dancing along with prerecorded music played by DJs. Thus, bands find their job opportunities limited to clubs whose owners prefer to feature live music on nights when they think bands will draw the largest crowds. Much more than rock groups, who often limit themselves to playing fewer concerts with the excitement of making each gig an "event," tropical bands rove from club to club and try to play as many places as possible. Bachata Flow is a case in point; on some summer weekends it played every night from Thursday to Saturday at different clubs. Although these bands have small fan bases that attend shows, it is just as likely that audience members are there to dance because they are regular attendees of the club or restaurant where the band is performing.

The audience reaction to the music of tropical bands is conversational, by which I mean there is a give-and-take of communication, both verbal and physical, that moves the performance along. For example, although Leydy Bonilla has a famous background and a striking stage presence, she always makes a point to casually ask the audience how they are enjoying the music and to thank audience members for coming out to the show. Simple gestures like these serve to lessen any (social) distance between her and the audience and involve the audience in the making of music, for example, by singing along to choruses. Beyond verbal cues between songs, the music itself provokes movement; *música tropical*, at least among Latinos, is rarely just listened to but rather is music to be danced to, usually with a partner. So the audience responds to the music by dancing, but with variations that become evident after much observation (and participation). Dancing to live music builds, that is, it often starts out with slower, more relaxed, or easier (to dance to) songs, and then intensifies with time. The band can break this intensity with a slow song or ballad, but often the point is to continue to push the dancers to maximum exertion and get as many bodies as possible out on the floor. Audience members dancing must navigate a minefield of potential pitfalls: gender imbalances leading to not enough partners, unskilled or inebriated dancers clogging up the floor, the fatigue of dancing in heels, sweat-soaked clothes, and ringing ears from bumping speakers. The band's job is to keep the music moving in such a way so that the audience forgets these worries, keeps dancing, and keeps buying drinks to convince the club owner that having a live band is worthwhile.

These bands and their audiences share a common past, of migration from the Caribbean to working-class neighborhoods in upper Manhattan and the Bronx, but in moving to Charlotte, they also share aspirations toward upward class mobility and greater assimilation with the mainstream. The bars and clubs catering to the Uptown Latin musical community reveal this tendency through their décor, dress codes, and geographic location. However, this desire to distance themselves, both literally and figuratively, from the negative aspects of northern inner-city life is tempered by a strong commitment to preserving and fostering musical and other cultural expressions from the Caribbean. For example, Punta Cana, a Dominican restaurant on nearby South Boulevard, features a traditional *perico ripiao* group on Fridays and encourages diners to sing *merengue* and *bachata* karaoke on Saturday evenings. At summer's end, the Club Dominicano de Charlotte and the Puerto Rican Cultural Society of Charlotte each hold separate picnics with home-cooked food and live music at a Southside park. Both Punta Cana and Park Road Park, where the picnics are held, are located south of Uptown in solidly upper-middle-class and mostly white neighborhoods, reinforcing community members' desires to insert themselves into the mainstream of Charlotte.

Soundscapes and Community

Anthropologists and musicologists use the term "soundscape" to describe the "contextually specific local relationship of sound and place, which impacts the cultural perceptions, beliefs, and behavior of its publics" (Schafer 1993). While the ethnomusicologist Steven Feld used the term to describe the relationship between bird and waterfall sounds and the musical aesthetics of the Kaluli people of Papua New Guinea (Feld 1990), in the urban setting such as Charlotte, soundscapes reveal contestations between and within social groups as they create commonality and difference through sound and music. As neuroscientists have pointed out (Levitin 2006), not all sounds are music, and while music has some basis in the evolution of the human brain and ears, it is also culturally constructed by what sounds and social and emotional cues children are given as their brains develop. Social and political pressures also shape soundscapes by creating narratives of the history of musical practice, or what might be called the "invention of tradition" (Hobsbawm and Ranger 1983).

As we have seen, in Charlotte the production of musical spaces coincides with local cleavages within the Latino community along lines of socioeconomic class and legal status. Yet each of these separate musical communities is closely connected to international networks of musicians and musical knowledge, keeping musicians and fans up to date with global musical trends. Thus, local Mexican musicians can open for

Los Tucanes de Tijuana, but be afraid to venture downtown. Latin rock fans can dance along to an up-tempo ska number, but dismiss Mexican dance music as *naco*. Thus, despite global connections, the musical communities of Latino Charlotte are hyper-local. This localism restricts Latinos of different backgrounds to separate musical communities, hampering efforts at pan-Latino solidarity and political action. These local constraints are also perpetuated by the gatekeepers in music venues—club owners, managers, and band promoters—who in subtle but important ways contribute to how performances run.

For example, late into a heavy metal concert that the promoter Greñas had organized, Dorian Gris took the stage at the Dark Room behind Skandalos. The date happened to be Halloween, which was fitting for the concert theme, with a band named Nataz (Satan spelled backwards) opening up. But the night also marked the end of daylight saving time, which gave the club owner one extra hour to stay open and serve drinks. Dorian Gris played for an enthusiastic crowd decked out in gothic-themed black costumes and folks in regular casual concert attire. As the concert neared closing time at 1:00 a.m. (which really felt like it was 2:00 a.m.), the crowd pleaded with the manager of the club for one more song. After hours of stopping fans from throwing beer bottles and keeping doorways clear for fire safety, he was ready to head home, but after a long pause, he finally raised his index finger up above his head to indicate that the band could play one more. The crowd was ecstatic. This back-and-forth happened two more times as Dorian Gris ended up playing three encores. When the music stopped, audience and musicians hung out for another half hour, chatting and reveling in the exhaustion of a long concert. They were a community clearly at home, and the club manager recognized the role this musical space holds in joining them together, and for creating loyal customers for the nightclub.

For bands like Tropic Culture and Bakalao Stars, Intown neighborhoods like NoDa and the music venues there provide a comfortable space that mirrors their casual and eclectic styles. These venues include coffee shops like Pura Vida, low-key bars like the Evening Muse, and a converted cinema that hosts concerts, the Neighborhood Theatre. Bakalao Stars has its practice space just down the street from these venues, so on rehearsal nights, you might find band members picking up a sandwich from the local deli or grabbing a beer at a bar.

There is also a historical reason why this community chooses NoDa for concerts. Earlier Latin rock bands like La Rúa played some of their most memorable concerts in these venues from 2002 to around 2007, while promoters of *rock en español*, like Tony Arreaza, have cultivated long-standing relationships with club owners to bring touring international groups to perform in Charlotte, usually at the Neighborhood Theatre. Current performing groups connect with that history; there is an excitement and honor that comes with opening for the Venezuelan group Los Amigos Invisibles, as Bakalao Stars did in November 2009, and then headlining a show at the same venue in December 2010. For audience members, it seems natural that their band should perform in the same neighborhood and clubs where they hang out on any given weekend. Although NoDa and other gentrifying Intown neighborhoods are essentially white public and private spaces (Hill 1999), this community of Latinos easily moves within these spaces because of their parallel backgrounds—they are mainly middle-class, educated, bilingual, and with legal status. At the same time, there is some separation; rarely will whites who are not tied into this community (for example, as girlfriends or fellow musicians) attend these groups' concerts.

For groups playing *salsa*, *merengue*, and *bachata*, Uptown clubs match the aspirations of their audience and the leisure practices associated with tropical genres, namely, dressing to the nines and engaging in social interactions through dance. Because members of this group of Latino immigrants either have U.S. citizenship at birth (Puerto Ricans) or tend to have high rates of permanent residency or naturalized citizenship (Cubans and Dominicans), they are unafraid to venture into the center city at night. At the same time, this audience has less familiarity and desire to imbricate themselves in the bohemian and gentrified lifestyles of neighborhoods like NoDa or Plaza-Midwood, where Latin rock audiences hang out. Uptown, with its shimmering office towers where a few of these highly educated, middle-class group have found jobs, holds more appeal, as do clubs in several other areas of the city, such as along South Boulevard and Ballyntyne, that also represent upward mobility for these residents of Charlotte. The adjacent clubs, bars, and nighttime entertainment allow band and audience to manufacture an experience that feels metropolitan and cosmopolitan but in a suburbanized, southern setting.

Context is vital in understanding Latin music in Charlotte. Although the sounds of *regional mexicano* may leak out through the walls of an Eastside club, the music does not have the same meaning to a non-Mexican, non-working-class listener. Even *regional mexicano* played in a concert organized by Mexican immigrant entrepreneurs but situated in a venue downtown loses meaning if the bleachers are empty because fans are afraid to venture there to hear live music. The music reflects the city's social segregation among rich, poor, blacks, whites, and even among Latinos. Second, the soundscapes and their related performance practices are about power and agency. Musicians and audience members join in making music not just as a way to express themselves or provide entertainment, but as a means to take control over a small piece of their everyday lives by constructing a space apart from immigration enforcement, insecurity, and economic and social marginalization. Third, musical community formation among Latino immigrants to the U.S. South is incomplete, as is the narrative of the southern Latino experience. It is not just that this experience is novel, having been formed over a relatively short historical period in the last thirty to forty years. The Latino experience in the Nuevo South is incomplete because of the flexible and contingent nature of immigrant labor, because of the unfinished business of racism and ethnocentrism, and because of the contradictory nature of globalization in a region that is constantly trying to both celebrate and outgrow its troubled history.

4

"Thursday Is Bakalao's Day!"

Bands at Work and Play

Music and Work

"Working musician" is an oxymoron. In U.S. society, musicians occupy a special position because their work is strongly identified with leisure and fun. As performers and entertainers, they interact with an audience during the audience's leisure time. But unlike waiters, bartenders, cooks, cleaning staff, or security guards, musicians look like they are having fun when they work. How much of this outward appearance is a genuine enjoyment of their music making and how much of it is performative affect, a mask that they wear to appeal to audiences? It is telling that the English word for what musicians do is *play*, not work. Jazz musicians have invented a metaphoric idiom to bypass this perception—a saxophone is an *ax*; an intensive practice session is called *woodshedding* (going to the woodshed); a job is a gig—and equate their profession with blue-collar occupations (Spellman 1966). Country music has also imbued its lyrics and process of music making with the trappings of working-class life (Fox 2004).

This association of music and fun is not universal. The Spanish verb *tocar* differentiates the action of strumming or striking an instrument from the other English meaning of *to play* tied to games and sports and expressed by the verb *jugar*. In the Caribbean and Latin America, musicians have traditions of playing popular music in styles that require other emotional timbres; for example, the Argentine *tango* stresses melancholy and longing, while participants in Mexican cantina music engage in melodramatic *gritos* that evoke despair and loss. Many *regional mexicano* songs, particularly *corridos* and *ranchera* song forms, continue to focus topically on experiences associated with work, with lyrics detailing crossing the border, migrating for jobs, obtaining a green card, or conflicts with bosses (Ragland 2009; Herrera-Sobek 1993). However, the Latin genres that I encountered in Charlotte most often reflected the association with fun, escape, and pleasure that have come to shape much contemporary popular music.

This chapter analyzes the ways that Latino musicians view their experience working and playing in Charlotte, building on other studies that examine the link between labor and music (Green 1972; Fox 2004; Washburne 2008; White 2008). I stress the diversity of musicians' experiences and viewpoints, while also collecting some common themes to formulate a vision of how we might think about the labor of immigrant musicians in a globalized urban workplace and better understand the connections between musicians and their fellow immigrant workers. Defining and analyzing the concept of "working musician," I position musicians' labor in the context of immigration and class-based views on training and professionalism. The vulnerability of musicians as immigrant laborers plays a vital part in how they approach music making and relate to fellow musicians. I show how musicians deal with the norm of low-paying, contingent music jobs and strategize about how to best pursue lives as working musicians. I focus on three bands, Bakalao Stars, Banda TecnoCaliente, and Ultimanota, which represent the spectrum of musicians' different attitudes and conceptions about their labor. In addition, I focus on a trio of musicians who also have become concert promoters, in order to explore another side of the music business in Charlotte. The trajectory of bands, often reflected in their attitudes about the labor of performing and living the "artist's life," also helps us to understand different notions of family and community among Latino immigrants to the U.S. South.

Being a musician, along with other creative pursuits like painting, acting, or writing fiction, is often held as the gold standard of the ideal job that allows an individual to "follow his dreams," but at the same time, musicianship is denigrated as an unworthy occupational pursuit. As the urban theorist Richard Florida argues, "following your dreams" for a new generation of recent college graduates has meant pursuing jobs in technology and finance sectors in workplaces that foster flexible hours, openness to alternative lifestyles, and novel work practices, while settling in cities where members of this "creative class" can embed themselves in the bohemian milieu of musicians and other artists (Florida 2003). While Florida argues that the symbiotic relationship between artists and an emerging "creative class" of technology workers fosters local economic growth and enhances a city's luster, I counter that this view hides the daily struggles of musicians to make ends meet. Obscured in the haze of a desirable bohemian urban lifestyle is the long-standing and persistent devaluation of artistic work. While "creative" work in the finance sector, such as speculative trading and mortgage derivatives, leads to hefty year-end bonuses (and increased financial risk for everyone), artistic creativity rarely results in fame and fortune. Instead, musicians work long hours, for little pay, and mostly as freelancers—the epitome of flexible labor. In fact, several musicians felt that their bands are treated as interchangeable pieces, competing for limited jobs and disposable if other cheaper bands are available to perform.

Charlotte's Latina/o musicians play and work on this tightrope. For many, being a musician means doing something they love or following a dream, yet when asked, they are quick to point out the anemic pay and difficult working conditions. Hidden behind the glamour of a performance is the fact that musicians spend hundreds of hours rehearsing music, expend social capital to organize and promote a concert, and put in long hours the day of a performance traveling, preparing sound equipment and lights, and breaking down the stage after the show. All of this work happens on top of musicians' day jobs, which they rely upon to pay the bills, those of their households and the band, as concerts can be a losing financial proposition. Conditions at clubs and restaurants, festivals and bars can be less than ideal: musicians dress in cramped dressing rooms or in the back seats of cars in the parking lot when dressing rooms are nonexistent; they fight dehydration while dressed in heavy polyester suits in the midday summer sun during a festival; they pull muscles lifting heavy amplifiers out of car trunks; they play in restaurants where the diners want mood music, where the owner wants them to play an extra set for the same pay, and where they must jerry-rig their own sound system; and they navigate the challenges of working in places where alcohol and drugs are readily available and seen as part of the creative process of being a musician.

From these conditions, musicians conjure up the joy and excitement of a performance. While working, they play their instruments and engage in *play* through their interaction with each other and the audience. There is a connection between the physicality of musicians' labor—the sweat, aches, and exertion of a performance—and the expressions of pleasure from audiences during live shows. But the magical moments of performances, fraught with emotional (and sexual) tensions, and linking people in human chains through dancing, singing, and music making, are constructed by the long hours that musicians put into rehearsing, perfecting their training, and organizing concerts.

This dialectic between work and play comes to define how many Charlotte musicians see their music. Some see their music as a hobby, to be pursued for leisure, while others treat music as a profession, stressing their specialized training and professionalism. Most musicians rely on their gigs to make ends meet, paying for gas with the take from a night's performance, while others have made a significant personal investment in their music in the hopes that monetary success will follow the release of the next album or the next tour. Some musicians see rehearsing and performing as a way to stay connected to fellow musicians with whom they have played for years, while a newer generation sees playing as a way to gain acceptance and respect in the Latin music scene.

Bakalao's Day

On any given Thursday night in a small room crammed full of musical instruments and sweaty musicians, Bakalao Stars rehearses. The band gathers in the NoDa neighborhood in a nondescript building that has been subdivided into practice spaces for local bands. The room is sparsely decorated, with a couple of old posters, a sagging couch, and a mini-refrigerator. One or two band members bring the cheapest beer they can find to stock up the fridge for the night. Every other conceivable space is soon occupied by musicians, as Bakalao Stars has up to eight or nine members, and their equipment. As they rehearse, members drink and joke with each other, and occasionally get into debates about the proper tempo and rhythms of songs they are preparing for an upcoming performance. If a member of another band—say, Carlos Crespo from Dorian Gris (which occupies a room down the hall)—is practicing, he might stop in to say hello and inquire how the band is doing.

Sometimes the band practices on Tuesdays, but Thursday evening is when everyone in the band knows they are expected to show up to play together as a group. This Thursday gathering often turns into a jam session, but might include a "serious" rehearsal if the band has an upcoming gig. In an interview in English, band members Christian Anzola, Javier Anzola, and Daniel Alvarado discussed the importance of Thursday rehearsals to the band's cohesion:

CHRISTIAN ANZOLA: I think that's one of the things that makes a band stay alive. If you come to band practice and you're not having a good time you might as well not be here.

DANIEL ALVARADO: Yeah.

SB: It's not worth it?

CHRISTIAN: If you come here and then you're just sitting there thinking, "Oh god, I want to go and drink a beer," maybe this is not the thing for you . . . and the thing about it is, when it comes to that, we do this as a hobby, I think none of us want to go and see Bakalao be famous or anything, but it's like a serious hobby. We do practice twice a week, it's not like you, "Oh, we got a show, and then we practice," you know.

SB: So you practice even when you don't have a show?

CHRISTIAN: Yeah!

JAVIER ANZOLA: Thursday, every Thursday no matter what.

DANIEL: It feels weird when we don't practice.

CHRISTIAN: We've been practicing Thursdays for. . . . eight years, we started doing Tuesday maybe two years ago, but Thursday's to me that's my day of music. Whenever I'm not practicing or somebody cancels on Thursday, I'm pissed, because that's my . . . I already know Thursday, I can have some beers.

SB: You have it in your head, you already know?

CHRISTIAN: Whatever I go home Friday, cool it's the weekend— Thursday it's you know—

DANIEL: Bakalao's day.

CHRISTIAN: *Yeah!*

JAVIER: It's just that time to, if you play an instrument, you know that you come in and start to play and it's just that connection between you and the instrument and you just completely forget about everything else and then there's nothing else. There's no worries, there's no bills, everything is about hit that note or hit that cymbal, or get the right riff, and you're so concentrated, you're so into it that time flies, then you hit it and you're like, "*Wow!*"

DANIEL: When we're playing shows it's kind of like a gift to ourselves for all the hard work, and we want to show off that hard work sometime, I mean not to show off, we want to share the enjoy[ment] that we have with people and we want them to have a good time. We might not be the best music players in town, but I bet if you go to a Bakalao Stars show, you're going to have a lot of fun.[1]

Bakalao Stars' view of music making as fun is an attitude shared by a number of Latina/o musicians in Charlotte. These musicians treat their music as a hobby, something to do in their spare time, not to be taken too seriously. Thursday rehearsals become ritualized as a time apart from "worries" where music becomes the central focus of their lives. Their music takes on a therapeutic and spiritual quality that corresponds to the band's identification with reggae, ska, and other Afro-Caribbean music styles. This lends their rehearsals (and interviews) a certain enthusiasm that is infectious and certainly comes across in interactions with audiences at live shows. Yet they are serious and well-organized musicians. By working hard with the attitude that this is not work, they imbue the music with a looseness and approachability that are sometimes lost by other local bands that stress being as "professional" and polished as possible. There is a realization, from age and experience, that as a band they have little chance of "making it big," so they do not kill themselves trying to become famous. While this strategy might not make for a great plotline, it helps explain the longevity of bands like Bakalao Stars, who have been playing together since 2002. Having little ambition leads to less conflict.

What do other musicians think of this type of music making? In private conversations, several musicians expressed feelings of respect and amazement that bands like Bakalao Stars were able to keep playing music for so long and as such a tight-knit group. However, fellow musicians sometimes expressed frustration at the slow evolution of these bands' music and a perceived lack of ambition on the part of bands that did not seek more of the spotlight. From the bands' perspective, these flaws are part of the communal process of making music together and performing when they want to and are ready to share new music. The attitude of Bakalao Stars means that its members must make a significant

Bakalao Stars performing in Hawaiian shirts and skirts

financial investment in the band, particularly since it is not a given that its shows will make money. At some shows, Bakalao Stars loses money because the door receipts do not cover paying the sound manager; then band members each contribute to covering costs. Its members understand that the purpose of the band is not to make money; they often work for free in order to reach a goal, such as saving money to record an upcoming album (as the band was doing in 2010, when concert profits went toward recording studio costs).

Even the band's name, Bakalao Stars, reflects its communal and laid-back style. As Javier Anzola explained,

> Bacalao is a fish that you find . . . on the *peninsula ibérica*, mostly, and it's really underground and it's really high in protein and energy. So that's why it was the *Bakalao*. We want to be underground. . . . And we want to be high in energy when—live shows and stuff like that. And *Stars* was because we were supposed to be this jamming band where everybody [participates].[2]

Anzola's "underground" statement stresses that the band holds little ambition to be famous, popular, or mainstream. The food metaphor extends to its performance style having the qualities of the fish—high in energy during its live performances. This was not the only time Bakalao Stars made reference to Caribbean and Iberian cuisine in its music. Its first two albums (2007, 2010) have drawings of fish on the album or CD cover. It performs and records numerous songs with food-related titles, such as "Mango," "Zanahoria Style" (Carrot Style), "Borrachera" (Drinking Spree), "Kokoa Brown" (Chocolate Brown), and "Ensalada" (Salad). And its second album, *Soundcocho*, is a play on *sancocho*, a Caribbean peasant soup that combines many ingredients. But the second part of its name, Stars, is just as important to its outlook as a band. Members define the band as a jamming band, where good vibes and a positive relationship with the music are highly valued. As with other collaborative groups like the Fania All-Stars, Bakalao Stars takes elements from different genres and musical traditions and mixes them together in its music.[3] Daniel Alvarado stresses that although the band was nothing serious, just a project, it has lasted over eight years. Somehow, the bandleaders have been able to transition from the initial goal of the band, which was to showcase young local musicians at a rock festival, to the long-term work of balancing their casual attitude toward music-making with the organization of concerts and recording sessions. They try not to work too hard and spoil the point of being Bakalao Stars.

TecnoCaliente

On a humid day in May, Banda TecnoCaliente is suiting up for its slot at Charlotte's annual Cinco de Mayo Fanta Festival. The sun glares off the windows of the parked cars in a grass field behind the stage; sweat glistens on the necks of the band members as they change from T-shirts to crisp white dress shirts and then don bright pink suit jackets with "Banda TecnoCaliente" embossed on the back. They take the stage, tune up their numerous keyboards, and begin playing up-tempo *banda* music. After a forty-five-minute set, with an enthusiastic crowd dancing on a soccer field, the band members exit the stage, dripping sweat, reaching for water and soda stocked on ice backstage.

TecnoCaliente is a professional band, meaning that its members have dedicated themselves on a full-time, semipermanent basis to being a band and are actively seeking larger exposure and fame within the *regional mexicano* music market. They rehearse and perform regularly and treat music making as their career. By investing significant money in uniforms, promotion (hiring a manager and a roadie), and transportation, TecnoCaliente must find regular work to stay solvent as a band; the hope is that eventually a radio hit and exposure through touring and appearances on television shows will pay off.[4] The band has converted an old Greyhound bus into a tour bus with the band's name painted on the side so members can travel together to shows (and have a private place to change and relax).

Their manager, Gonzalo Pérez, a Dominican transplant from Santo Domingo via New York, prides himself on the professionalism of the bands he promotes.[5] As Pérez explains,

> The groups have given me the support [I need to be their manager]. I'm thankful to the Mexican group [TecnoCaliente] more than others, and without offending anyone, because they have placed all of their confidence in me. They never ask me, "How much are we going to make?," only, "What time should we be there?" They don't ask anything about pay, when I [pay them] . . . that's what's left [after expenses]. That is the confidence they have in me.
>
> They are people who don't drink alcohol; it's very rare for them not to focus on music. . . . Everybody is a professional.[6]

And later in the same interview, Pérez explains how the hard work of being a musician pays off, particularly in view of the larger goal of making a hit record:

> GONZALO PÉREZ: There are many hardships you have to face, leaving your family for all this, spending nights [on the road], and at times you say, "It's not for nothing, to say, there is a goal." There is something for everyone, that makes it worthwhile and you look for it, for this the musician doesn't just seek money, the musician likes to feel good, find himself.
>
> SB: So then, what is the goal, the larger [goal for the band]?

GONZALO: Well, the trajectory is . . . that the whole world knows you, to arrive at a moment of explosion. Explosion is when you come across a [musical] theme. There are themes that change your life. For every group one single [hit song] changes their lives. Why? Because the single is a hit and the people stay with it. It changes your life emotionally, economically, morally, in every aspect it changes. I have seen this transformation because I saw it with Kinito Méndez [a *merengue* singer whom Pérez toured with as a stage manager].[7]

For Pérez and Banda TecnoCaliente, a professional work ethic and vigorous training are part of what it means to be in a band and pursue success. Professionalism means refraining from drinking alcohol or other distractions (drugs, amorous adventures) during performances and tours, but also trusting in the expertise of a band manager who is more experienced at putting on concerts and managing the band's expenses. Pérez is well aware that, while audiences might crave the magical experience of dancing and listening to music, club owners and festival organizers see *regional mexicano* groups (that are not famous) as somewhat interchangeable and thus relatively disposable as labor. In conversations, he stressed to me the importance of differentiating Banda TecnoCaliente by its actions: showing up on time, having a professional appearance and sound, eliminating the personal distractions that plague other bands. That Banda TecnoCaliente is made up of teetotalers while members of Bakalao Stars readily admit to heavy drinking as part of their rehearsals and performance points to class and identity differences between the two bands and their musical communities. When Pérez describes the professionalism and sobriety of Banda TecnoCaliente, he is positioning them not just as musicians, but as Mexican musicians who must do battle against negative stereotypes of working-class, Mexican men that associate laziness, drunkenness, and unskilled labor training with members of their musical community. Bakalao Stars, as members of a musical community made up of more assimilated 1.5 generation young adults with higher average levels of education and greater economic mobility, have less cause to construct a professional persona. In fact, their audience relishes their wild and uncontained stage presence and conflation of music, drinking, and dance with "fun."

TecnoCaliente tries to measure up not just to other local groups, but to more famous groups that tour through the U.S. South. In one instance, TecnoCaliente outshone other, better-known groups at a festival so that it became in Pérez's words, "el plato fuerte" (the main course) for that day. In this way, it became memorable—to the audience and to the event organizers who may hire the band again in the future. Pérez also promotes his bands together, so that a festival looking for bands can negotiate a better deal by choosing several bands from his stable of groups, say, contracting Banda TecnoCaliente and Bachata Flow to play the same festival.

Unlike Bakalao Stars, Banda TecnoCaliente has a larger objective of finding fame through a hit song. Band members work toward this goal with the knowledge that, if achieved, it will change their lives dramatically. Pérez describes this goal as a trajectory, a projection that ends in an explosion when a group makes it big. This teleology assumes that fame and success are inevitable, as long as the hard work and professionalism continue. An element of luck is involved as well, when one "comes across" a musical theme that enchants audiences. While the economic changes that would accompany a hit single are straightforward, it is less certain what emotional and moral changes would follow from fame. Would the band face intensified challenges from life on the road as a famous band in the form of substance abuse and temptations to marital infidelity? Would the band feel obligated to help other Charlotte Latin bands and musicians in their careers? What is clear is that Pérez, with his "professional" training for the band, is trying to prepare it for this eventuality.

Ultimanota

It's Saturday at a Cuban restaurant, A Piece of Havana, in a strip mall in the suburbs south of Charlotte. The restaurant is empty, except for the wait staff and bartender, when several members of Ultimanota arrive. The band members lug amplifiers, conga drums, speakers, and microphones in from the parking lot and begin to set up in a tight corner right in front of the bar. As the band starts to tune up, families come in, offering greetings to waitresses and band members, and grab tables facing the band. By the time the always late saxophone player arrives, Ultimanota is ready to start performing.

Ultimanota plays at A Piece of Havana on a regular basis, usually once or twice a month, during most of the year. In addition, its members sometimes find jobs playing in other restaurants, at weddings and birthday parties, and at festivals. But playing at the Cuban restaurant represents their most reliable source of work as musicians. For a night's work spanning from around 6:00 p.m. to 10:00 p.m., each band member receives seventy-five dollars. In addition, the restaurant's owner, Belkys Vargas, often provides the musicians with one free drink and some food. Their pay, however, gets eaten up by gas costs (the restaurant is ten to fifteen miles away from some of their homes) and any additional food and drink musicians consume on their breaks between sets. They also have a fixed investment in musical equipment, such as the cost of maintaining musical instruments (e.g., fixing broken guitar strings) and replacing aging parts (e.g., amplifier fuses and cords). Tallying these costs, the band members come away with little after a night's work.

What then do Ultimanota's musicians gain from playing on Saturday nights? Several members of the band are older musicians in their thirties, who, a decade earlier, were part of rock bands playing Intown clubs. The teleology of eventual fame, which Gonzalo Pérez adheres to, reached one band member only in momentary form. Tony Arreaza, Ultimanota's bandleader, was once part of the Latin rock group La Rúa. For Arreaza and other band members of his generation, Ultimanota serves as a way to keep playing music while family life and its daily obligations have limited their capacity to dedicate themselves full-time to band membership. On Saturday night, they get to escape the kids at home and have a drink with friends while playing music. For a younger musician such as the bass player, Isaac Meléndez, playing with Ultimanota gives him experience playing for live crowds and links him to the more extensive social networks of older musicians. When I inquired what Ultimanota members do with their pay from the band, I got similar responses from all. Arreaza uses the money to help pay bills. Fred Figueroa usually goes after the show to fill up the gas tank of his SUV. Oscar Huerta combines his money from Ultimanota with money earned from playing with several other local bands to supplement his income, the main source of which is working at a retail store that sells soccer gear. No band member relies solely on music making for income; each of them works other "day" jobs.

Ultimanota playing at A Piece of Havana

Ultimanota plays at A Piece of Havana at the discretion of the owner, Belkys Vargas, who often called up the band's leader, Tony Arreaza, a week or so before to request the band play a Saturday night (or sometimes Friday). However, when business was slow, particularly in winter and early spring, the band got called upon less frequently. Part of Arreaza's job as bandleader was to convince Vargas that continuing to hire Ultimanota would bring more paying customers in the door of the restaurant, thus justifying its continuing employment. This included promoting the band's gigs through Facebook and texting friends to convince them to stop by. Another tactic was getting hired by another (Intown) restaurant, Dressler's, for a series of nights, which demonstrated that the group was in demand. Arreaza started to establish a relationship of greater mutual obligation to solidify the band's role at the restaurant. Through his day job as an events manager at the Latin American Coalition, a local nonprofit, he helped Vargas promote her business by having her sell food at cultural festivals, including allowing her to be the sole Cuban restaurant selling at "Azúcar! A Caribbean Celebration," an event celebrating Spanish Caribbean culture organized by Arreaza and the Latin American Coalition.

In between sets at A Piece of Havana, Ultimanota's members sidle up to the bar. They order drinks and if someone is hungry, he asks the bartender for something that can be made quickly, so he can finish it before the next set starts. They say hello to friends and regular customers who have come out to see the band. They acknowledge the other members of this musical community and thank them for their support. Of course, they will take requests. And if diners approach him, Arreaza might give them his card and ask what kind of music they enjoy. These interactions often turn into gigs, as the band gets hired to play weddings and birthday parties.

Like Bakalao Stars, Ultimanota was organized into a band as a temporary project, in this case to play a few gigs as a cover band, which over time became semipermanent. However, Ultimanota views its performances and rehearsals differently from Bakalao Stars. Whereas Bakalao Stars stresses the creativity that comes out of rehearsals and jamming, Ultimanota rehearses much less often, mainly because band members cannot find the time every week with families and jobs. Instead, Ultimanota performs more often, and its concerts become like rehearsals in that they are a fun exercise where the band experiments with playing a new song, letting Joswar Acosta, the conga player, sing a number, or taking extended solos. While Ultimanota presents a very professional image on its website and in Tony Arreaza's relationship with restaurant owners and other clients who hire the band for private events, this professionalism is not the same touring ethic that guides Banda TecnoCaliente. Instead of rooting the band in the nightclub community, whether of Eastside Mexican clubs (TecnoCaliente) or Intown venues, Ultimanota's performances root them in the community in a different way. Its visibility at restaurants, paired with Arreaza's extensive social network, gives it access to a different crowd of middle-class Latinos who hire it to play private parties—weddings, birthdays, and other family celebrations. Thus, I witnessed the band play a Bolivian woman's fiftieth birthday celebration at an Eastside club that had been rented out for the occasion, a wedding in a Charlotte suburb, and the birthday party for a Colombian woman in the backyard of her family's Intown home.

Why do people hire Ultimanota to play private events? Beyond the initial social connection, both band and audience belong to the same age group (in their thirties and forties) and are usually the first generation of Latino immigrants who have established families and roots in Charlotte. The "cheesy cocktail music," as Arreaza describes it, appeals to listeners who want familiar songs from their early adulthood and embrace a sense of nostalgia at Ultimanota shows. Ultimanota performs new "classics," but with a twist, in effect curating an enjoyable concert that appeals to clients who, as relatively upwardly mobile, established immigrants, often attend the same concerts, frequent the same restaurants, or are members of the same church congregation.

In fact, the local church and the role that several Ultimanota musicians play in it provide an interesting point of comparison to their work with the band. Camino del Rey is an evangelical Christian church in suburban Charlotte that has a majority Latino immigrant congregation, but is led by a white American pastor who has learned Spanish and led missions to Latin America. Tony Arreaza, Joswar Acosta, and Isaac Meléndez, along with several other musicians, play in the church band on Sunday evenings. While their participation in Ultimanota is about making money, maintaining a presence in the music scene, and diversion, playing for a church audience is about showing faith and dedication to God and being part of a religious community. Their churchgoing also positions them as respectable members of a group of religious, middle-class Latino residents of Charlotte. The music played in church consists of religious hymns and popular Christian rock songs, covered by the church band during interludes between the pastor's sermon and leading of prayers. An onlooker might see these two worlds as completely separate, but membership in the church community shapes how band members act and interact as members of Ultimanota—the sense of familial obligation, as well as what constitutes proper moral and ethical behavior all stem from their relationship with this religious community.

Carlotan Rock

An important element in the lives of working musicians is the role musical brokers play in creating opportunities for performing and promoting their music. I turn to a historical example to present the vagaries of promoting shows in Latino Charlotte. Carlotan Rock is a promotion company started by three local musicians, Tony Arreaza, Herman

Marín, and Juan Miguel Marín. These musicians, realizing that the skills they utilized to promote their own shows could be put to work promoting other artists and bringing in internationally known acts, began the company in 2004. At first, the trio promoted local bands, in particular through a festival also entitled Carlotan Rock, and concerts by groups such as La Rúa, of which Arreaza and Juan Miguel Marín were members. But soon they began to bring in artists from Mexico and South America, including Los Amigos Invisibles, Molotov, Los Pericos, Hombres G, Kinky, Café Tacuba, and Los Enanitos Verdes. These bands were groups that the promoters had grown up listening to in Latin America, or had gone to see in concert in nearby southern cities, such as Atlanta. Thus, they saw it as quite a coup to get these bands to play in Charlotte, a place that bands' previous tours through the United States had skipped in favor of more established centers of Latino immigration and musical production. Many of their shows were very successful, netting profits and large crowds, and the Carlotan Rock festival became an annual event that helped promote local and regional Latin rock bands. For example, Bakalao Stars got its start at Carlotan Rock, where members formed a jamming band and then decided to continue making music together.[8]

Yet by the time I arrived in Charlotte, the trajectory of Carlotan Rock had reached its nadir. Juan Miguel and Herman Marín had both moved to other cities to pursue nonmusical careers. In 2009 the Carlotan Rock festival had to be canceled because the economic downturn meant that fewer fans were going to see shows. And while Arreaza attempted to put on a major show, bringing back Los Amigos Invisibles in November 2009, the concert was a financial bust—not enough people bought tickets, and Carlotan Rock lost money.

So how did these three recent immigrants become, at least for a few years, major players in the Latin music scene in Charlotte and conduits for international acts to enter Charlotte's Latin scene? First, I point to the relative neglect of *rock en español* and the lack of consolidation between major labels and ticket/concert companies in relation to *rock en español* at the time. Now major artists such as the Spanish rock singer Enrique Bunbury[9] have exclusive contracts to only play shows in clubs owned or affiliated with national ticket/concert companies like Ticketmaster, and so play at Charlotte's Fillmore Theater (affiliated with Ticketmaster), but in the early 2000s, Latin American rock groups playing the United

Poster for the 2008 Carlotan Rock Festival (courtesy of Carlotan Rock Productions)

States relied on local entrepreneurs like Carlotan Rock to promote their shows for local audiences. Visiting musicians rely on local promoters to connect them to an audience, particularly if it is a place where they have never previously performed. Concert promoters attempt to tie into the local musical community, which they may be a part of, by asking a local group to perform as opening act, passing out flyers for upcoming shows at clubs and bars, and using social media, such as Facebook, to publicize a show. A successful show requires preparation, as promoters must lay the groundwork for a visiting band to be well received. A musical community's taste also plays a major role in concert organization. Local bands are constantly engaging in a process of manufacturing and negotiating with their audiences a set of styles and songs, some of which come from local networks and others that arrive from abroad through radio, television, travel, and the Internet. Concert promoters, especially if they are fellow musicians tied in to this community, are well aware of these trends and look for acts that fulfill perceived desires among the musical community.

Second, Carlotan Rock's members were skilled at promoting concerts. Juan Miguel Marín, trained as a graphic designer, came up with a series of visually striking posters and flyers to promote each concert.[10] Tony Arreaza's organizational skills and social capital in the local music scene, particularly his rapport with the managers of venues like the Evening Muse, Neighborhood Theatre, and Skandalos, provided available spaces for shows. Of course, some of these skills were learned on the job; their quality and professionalism improved as Carlotan Rock gained experience. Third, Carlotan Rock had a bit of luck. Arreaza placed cold calls to artists' managers to see whether they were considering touring soon in the United States, and, if so, whether Carlotan Rock could piggyback on dates already scheduled in Atlanta, Miami, or Washington, DC, cities within driving distance on the East Coast. Contact with one band sometimes led to inroads with another group, and a successful concert encouraged bands to want to return for a repeat performance a year later.

The business of promoting concerts presented significant risk but also some rewards for the partners of Carlotan Rock. Each of them put in one-third of the total investment for a show. For an internationally known act, this might total as much as $20,000 and include a guaranteed sum paid to the band, insurance for the venue, promotional materials, sound costs (renting equipment and labor for the night of the show), and security guards. After the show, the take at the door would be used to pay expenses, and then any profits would go into a company bank account and be split three ways between them. Some of each partner's profit would of course return to go toward the guarantee for the next upcoming concert. If the partners did not have enough money on reserve for a concert, then they would use a company credit card to finance a show, trusting that the revenue coming in would cover the debt accrued in promoting and organizing the show. For several years, Carlotan Rock was moderately profitable and the partners benefited from its success. For example, Arreaza saved his money from Carlotan Rock and his work with La Rúa in a bank account reserved just for paying for his wedding, which he held in Venezuela. However, their concerts were negatively affected by immigration policing, especially when they changed the venue of the Carlotan Rock festival from Skandalos to outside the Neighborhood Theatre in 2006 and fewer people attended because of rumors of immigration raids. They changed the festival venue back to Skandalos, but a series of less than profitable concerts meant that by 2010 the company credit card had several thousand dollars of debt that the group was struggling to pay off.

Carlotan Rock provides an interesting point of comparison with the finances of several local bands. Whereas Carlotan Rock was profitable, at least at its apex, the profitability of many local bands is minimal when one examines all the costs associated with running a group of musicians throughout the year(s) and the financial structure of playing in local music venues. For example, La Rúa, arguably the best-known and most successful of Charlotte's Latin groups, played clubs where the manager would not usually pay it a guaranteed amount for its appearance, instead giving the band a percentage of the door cover charge. During festivals, it is customary for local bands not to be paid anything, or to receive a low fee of several hundred dollars, while national and international acts receive much more. Promoters justify this treatment by arguing that local groups are less famous and by presenting festivals as opportunities for local acts to promote their music and perform for larger audiences than at nightclubs. When bands do receive pay for a gig, they often have to negotiate for minimal pay in a climate where their labor is contingent and tenuous. For example, Ultimanota found it difficult to ask for more pay for its restaurant shows because of the apparent struggles of the restaurant industry during the economic recession; restaurant owners would say they were barely making ends meet and could not afford to pay the bands more money. Often restaurant owners, like Belkys Vargas of A Piece of Havana, were unsure whether they could employ the band past next week and rarely booked Ultimanota more than a few weeks in advance. On another occasion, when Ultimanota played at a suburban Mexican restaurant, the restaurant manager arbitrarily added an extra set to the band's show without raising its pay. Not only did the musicians work longer that night, but by the time they finished playing the kitchen was closed, so they did not get the free meal that was promised as part of their pay.

Band members often use the money they do earn, after paying household bills, to improve the quality of their music. Thus, La Rúa members invested an estimated $25,000 in band equipment—amplifiers, effects, microphones, and lighting—during the five-year life of the band. They also paid $250 per month for a practice space. Carlos Crespo, leader of Dorian Gris, spends significant sums on a collection of wah-wah pedals for his guitars. The elaborate suits of Banda TecnoCaliente lend the group a professional appearance, but also have to be hand-tailored at significant cost. All of these investments point to the fact that most Charlotte Latino musicians see their music as a labor of love. In addition to the social capital that is developed and employed during concerts (such as Dorian Gris's relationship with their fans or Tony Arreaza's mutually beneficial relationship with restaurant owners where Ultimanota gigs can turn into catering jobs at festivals), money capital moves through circuits between nightclub, musician, audience members, and local businesses. Bands work as freelancers, playing at venues when there is a free night available or a bandleader or promoter can gather significant enthusiasm to make a concert potentially successful. Success breeds success—a point that was brought home to me as several bands went through funks when they did not have regular concerts for several months at a time during the recession of 2009–2010. But the resilience of many groups during this difficult time highlighted how they see music as something vital to their lives. It remains to be seen whether a future economic uptick will correspond to renewed audience enthusiasm for Latin music in Charlotte. However, developments in 2011–2012 boded well, as several rock groups, including the Mexican alternative rock band Zöe, the Mexican rock/rap group Molotov, the Spanish singer Manu Chao, and the Colombian duo Aterciopelados, all played to large, enthusiastic audiences at venues in Charlotte.

Conclusion

The experience of Latino musicians working and playing in Charlotte highlights the difficulty, but also the importance, of understanding musicians' labor. The ethos of certain bands, like Bakalao Stars, and their onstage personae can make it appear as if they treat music making as "fun." However, the easygoing nature of public performance is built upon a process of community making that starts with intensive and regular rehearsals and years performing together. Other bands, such as Banda TecnoCaliente, stress the "professional" and money-making purpose of their music by tying their labor practices with a desire to have a hit record. I think the term "working musician" encapsulates the diversity of musicians' experiences and viewpoints, stressing their labor power over common divisions like amateur/professional or full-time/part-time musician. The term "working musician" also links musicians' vulnerability as laborers to the experiences of their fellow Latino immigrants, many of whom face similar labor conditions and workplace challenges. Their experience highlights both the opportunity for economic mobility that living in a globalizing city provides, and the tenuousness of this opportunity in flexible and informal labor regimes and because of a legal apparatus that delegitimizes immigrants' residency.

From the examples I have provided, what stands out is the need for musicians to assert their agency by defining the terms through which they make music. When members of Banda TecnoCaliente stress their professionalism, they are defying common stereotypes of both Mexican immigrants and musicians. Bakalao Stars and Ultimanota both see their music making as a time apart—from family obligations and from the stress of day jobs—and a space where a sense of community can be created with fellow musicians and audience members. Carlotan Rock was a way for *rock en español* enthusiasts to encourage local bands to develop their artistry and to bring in international groups who had previously bypassed Charlotte. The promoters became musical brokers, making a little money, but also forging a local Latino rock community that has had a lasting effect, even if the Carlotan Rock festival is defunct. Each example has led to the accretion of a musical legacy not just in the soundscape of the musical community, but also in the broader Latino population in Charlotte. Moreover, the experience of Charlotte's Latina/o musicians provides lessons about how Latino immigrants in the U.S. South think about work and play. Like other immigrants, musicians have to hustle to find extra income in the informal economy, often earning pay under the table and on a per diem basis. They rely on social ties with fellow migrants and word of mouth to acquire work, which can limit their economic mobility outside the Latino community. However, some musicians have developed social capital, drawing on English-language skills, experience organizing concerts, education, and length of residency in Charlotte, that helps position them as cultural brokers and tastemakers in the Latin music scene. Working as a musician involves the constant pursuit and maintenance of musical community, a difficult task in the context of immigration policing that constantly threatens social ties and through a medium that is rarely financially rewarding. Yet they succeed, at least momentarily during performances, in sparking audiences to feel a sense of belonging and solidarity. And with each other, musicians form lifelong bonds of friendship, camaraderie, and a sense of "family" that ties them together in common cause.

5

The "Collective Circle"

Music and Ambivalent Politics in Charlotte

Gracias . . . a nuestras familias y amigos por apoyarnos en
este sueño gris. Y un agradecimiento hiper-especial a la raza
que va a todos nuestros shows, sin ustedes Los Dorians no
existen.
—Dorian Gris, *Live at the Dark Room* liner notes (2009)[1]

This chapter deepens an argument I have made elsewhere (Byrd 2014)
about the ambivalent attitude of Latina/o musicians toward organized politics but also their sharp political vision in relation to their everyday lives
as working musicians, members of a musical community, and residents of
a globalizing city.[2] My research found that Latino immigrant musicians
and their audiences negotiate their political stances through a physical and
intellectual process that one Charlotte journalist called the "circular colectivo" (collective circle; Strimling 2010). As described earlier, the collective
circle describes the circle of dancers that often form at Eastside rock concerts in Charlotte where dancers slam into each other, and where jumping
and shoving serve to unite band and audience in a collective music-making
strategy. But the term has an additional meaning—the collective circulation of ideas through music as band, audience members, and journalists
engage in debates about the political and social importance of what they
are performing, how they perform it, and its meaning in the context of a
politicized immigrant presence in the U.S. South. Thus, Latina/o immigrant musicians find themselves at the center of an intersection of culture
and politics, often being driven by fellow musicians, audience members,
state institutions and policies, and professional obligations to define themselves and their music in relation to the politics of immigration.

Rather than participating in marches for immigration reform, musicians focused their energies on promoting solidarity within their local

audience and defining a sense of professional ethics. Bands' song lyrics, album liner notes, and statements during performances revealed commentaries on social issues through which musicians knowingly and unknowingly positioned themselves politically. Thus, it would be inaccurate to describe their stances as one of anti-politics (Ferguson 1994); instead, musicians have distinct notions of what constitutes formal and informal forays into the political world. Like the well-known *regional mexicano* band Los Tigres del Norte, Charlotte musicians often chronicle elements of the immigrant experience—the hardships of migration, language barriers, yearning for the homeland, generational splits between parents and children—yet they stop short of making the strong political and social commentary that distinguishes Los Tigres' oeuvre (Ragland 2009; Wald 2001; Zavella 2011).

Overall, musicians' cautious skepticism toward public activism reflects a politics of ambivalence. I argue that this ambivalence stems from the fact that musicians (and their audiences) are only partially included in the subject-making process of the state and civil society (on the local and national level). Although critical to the low-wage service sector (Sassen 1988), immigrants (particularly the undocumented) in Charlotte face circumscribed legal rights and some levels of exclusion from mainstream political and social institutions. In response, it appears that they chose to opt out of public activism and focus efforts inward in a process where musicians have emerged as mature political figures guiding local community formation through Charlotte's Latin music scene. In fact, I argue that Latino musicians act as "grassroots intellectuals" (to borrow from Gramsci's conception of "organic intellectuals"; see Forgacs 2000) who—separate from organized politics—nonetheless help audiences form political consciousness through their performance practices and interactions. Acting through specific forms of class-based knowledge, such as discourse about genre, dance styles, and performance, Latino grassroots intellectuals provide narratives that help audiences develop political awareness and group identity. These intellectual interventions play a major role in situating the music in a larger field of class, gender, and ethnic identities as music lovers debate the intricacies of style and meaning. These performances (and their attendant knowledge) are another weapon in the arsenal of the weak (Scott 1987): a means for immigrants to negotiate an anti-immigrant climate, harsh working conditions, and contingent legal status while becoming aware of their positionality in this hegemonic order.

Like other scholars studying community formation through local artistry (Crehan 2012; Finnegan 2007), I found that the collaborative process of writing, rehearsing, performing, and reworking music gave musicians and audience members a sense of agency. This mutual musical decision making, whether pursued through direct feedback at a concert (shouted comments of admiration, song requests) or revealed through online posts attached to a YouTube video on a social networking site, shows the close-knit bonds that link musicians and fans. They live in common circumstances and engage in a daily labor of defining their musical scene, a dialectical process that often involves synthesizing disparate elements—nationalities, class backgrounds, ages, and migration experiences—into creative expression. My research demonstrates that Latinos are creating, in the face of oppressive anti-immigrant policies, group solidarity and agency. They are recognizing themselves as having a common experience—as immigrants, as musically inclined people, as speakers of a shared idiom—and forming a group "in itself" (Thompson 1963), a community.

The remainder of this chapter examines the different iterations of "politics" in and around Latin music in Charlotte, engaging with several central themes that reveal the ambivalence of musicians' political positionality: (1) how songs about migration and love reveal musicians' personal politics through commentary on gender and class relations; (2) the effect of everyday policing on immigrant communities and musicians' responses to immigration enforcement policies; (3) the politics of a musical life (or how everyday music making helps constitute a sense of agency and shape the informal political stances that Latina/o musicians take; (4) the emergence of musicians as "grassroots intellectuals"; and (5) the importance of the "collective circle" as a performance style and intellectual endeavor in everyday music making.

Migration Narratives

Quite a few songs performed by Latina/o musicians in Charlotte involve commentary on the migration experience. Song themes also tend to focus on love and relationships. Although on the surface relationship songs appear to provide limited political material, my analysis shows how these songs are implicitly political through their commentary on gender relations and class difference. It is also through their representation of the migrant experience in Charlotte that these songs serve a political purpose for Charlotte musicians, because they help musical communities think through what it means to be Latino in Charlotte.

An important purpose of this type of song is to provide social commentary on the financial burdens of international migration and to relate the migrant experience to a wide audience through a narrative about romantic love. In particular, former members of La Rúa pointed to one song that they wrote that held political meaning, "El Chanchito" (The Piggybank) (2005):

Recorriendo las veredas	Walking the sidewalks
esperando encontrar,	hoping to find
Solamente una moneda	only a little change I
que me falta pa' llenar	need to fill
Mi chanchito de la suerte,	my lucky piggybank
mi cochino para ahorrar	my pig to save with,
Ya le quedan pocos días	only a few days left until
yo lo voy a	I break it open . . .
reventar . . .	
Voy a pagar en la	I'm going to pay at the
frontera	border
Pa' que cruce hasta aquí	so she can cross over
	here
Bajo un cielo con estrellas	under a sky with stars
Y una luna	and a moon
[hablado]	[spoken]
Esta es la historia de un	This is the story of a
pana,	friend
que recoge moneda por	who picks up change
las veredas.	from sidewalks
Para traerse a la pelada	going broke to bring her
Del otro lado de la	from the other side of
frontera	the border

In "El Chanchito," an immigrant man in Charlotte saves up, in his piggybank, for enough money to bring his beloved to the United States. The song's music video was one of the first shot by a Latin rock band in Charlotte and featured scenes from around the city dramatizing the story of separated lovers who are reunited.[3] The video closes with a scene of the band performing the song outside, surrounded by family and friends, an inclusion of their musical community in the portrayal of the immigrant story. The spoken section of the song also speaks to the band members' connections to the immigrant community; they are telling the (true) story of a friend and addressing a common problem of family separation that Latino immigrants face in Charlotte. In an interview in English, Juan Miguel Marín, the drummer for La Rúa, had this to say about the band's political outlook and "El Chanchito":

Back in Ecuador it was just music for fun because I loved it. I think we—with La Rúa—first we wanted to make music. I felt the songs I wrote at that time were all kind of like love stories or relationship type of stories. And in Charlotte with what we were experiencing, in terms of, "Okay, there are a lot of people that moved, like immigrants that came to Charlotte," and it's the South, and the whole bridging the Hispanic and Anglo community, the history of music as a universal language, with all those thoughts in mind, I feel like *the* one song that touches the whole immigration issue on a very light way, but when you think about it it's really true, is "El Chanchito," which is, it is a love story, it's this guy working many jobs, what happens in reality, to save money to bring the girlfriend across the border.

But aside from that, I think our main thing was to play music, and just show that yes we are from a different country but we could entertain you, we could . . . it's music and you shouldn't worry about the language or maybe if we look a little different to not come to the shows, we'll always dare people or encourage people to—"You should come check it out, it's rock in Spanish, it's music in Spanish, you'll like it"—and that's how a lot of people decided to try it and a lot of people came back.

So, it was very important to represent our culture, our country, or where we came from the best way possible. I've always been a believer of coexistence—there shouldn't be too many walls between people. I love many people from all cultures and every country so I sort of like tried to communicate that with what we were doing with La Rúa, so . . . that was the thing, but we really didn't get too heavy into politics . . . it was more about integrating people, no matter where were you from, so . . . of course we were coming from: "We're Latinos," but not heavy politics.[4]

Marín's comments point to the historicity of the moment of La Rúa's formation in 2003, a time when increased Latino immigration to Charlotte was making Latino culture more visible. After the band had performed for several months covering popular Latin rock songs, "El Chanchito" was one of La Rúa's first original songs. The band saw the song not just as a commentary on the plight of a hardworking immigrant and his girlfriend, but as a way to advocate for fellow Latinos and educate both Latinos and non-Latinos about the immigrant experience. The band sought to bridge the cultural divide between Latino and Anglo, between rock in English and Spanish, by acting as ambassadors to the English-language rock scene in Charlotte and among Latinos from different countries in Latin America. By many accounts, La Rúa was successful at this endeavor; the band attracted a diverse audience of Latinos and a small but enthusiastic following of non-Spanish-speaking fans. While there are many factors that led to this success—musical style, timing, unrelenting promotion, charisma—the underlying subtext of Juan Miguel Marín's statement is that a more overt foray into "heavy" politics would have undermined the popularity of the band. He sees "heavy" politics as positions or statements that are divisive, an outlook that would counteract his desire to coexist and bridge cultural divides. In its own way, Marín's vision of "coexistence" becomes political in a city where residential segregation limits the social interactions of Latino immigrants and white and black residents of the city. "El Chanchito" fulfills his vision nicely by stressing shared Latino and American mainstream cultural values—industriousness and family—while downplaying the structural forces that lead to labor migration and family separation.

A song by Bakalao Stars, "Pa'l Norte" (2010), presents a complementary vision to "El Chanchito" by explaining the reasons for immigration and the hardships faced by migrants both in their home countries and in the United States. Bakalao Stars considers "Pa'l Norte" one of its more political songs because it includes commentary on a pressing social issue—the plight of migrants. The lyrics tell of an immigrant's attempts to get ahead:

Estoy cansado por las calles de esa inmensa ciudad	I'm tired of the streets of this big city
La pena, la tristeza de la gente se ve	I see the shame and sadness of the people
No hay empleo, no hay estudio, ni como progresar	There are no jobs, no schools, no way to get ahead
Las penas ya me agobian el futuro se va	Troubles overwhelm me, the future is gone
Le pregunto a Papá Dios cuando se va acabar	I ask God when this would be over
Que mi tierra tan querida me voy a desterrar	I'm going to leave my beloved home
Pa' progresar	To make progress
Al Norte yo me voy, yo me voy a trabajar	Up north I'm going, I'm going to work
Porque en esta tierra no puedo progresar	Because in this place I can't get ahead
Son las cinco en la mañana me acabo a levantar	It's five in the morning, I just got up
Motivado como un diablo	motivated like the devil
Buscando trabajo pero no me da	Looking for work but nobody hires me
Porque no tengo papeles	Because I don't have papers
Le pregunto a la gente cómo llegar	I ask people how to go places
Pero no me entienden	But they don't understand me
Inglés sin barreras me voy a comprar	I'm going to buy *Inglés sin Barreras*[5]
a (con)versa esta gente	to talk with those people

"Pa'l Norte" begins by outlining the problems impoverished people living in Latin America face—unemployment, lack of schooling, and blocked access to capital or land—factors that limit their ability *pa' progresar* (to get ahead). Migration northward to the United States is seen as the most feasible solution, and life in the United States is idealized, as a place where one can make good money and throw off the chains of poverty. However, once in the United States, the migrant encounters hardship and problems (inability to find work because of lack of papers, inability to communicate because of language) that temper initial enthusiasm. Similar to "Jaula de Oro" (Golden Cage) (1988) by Los Tigres del Norte, "Pa'l Norte" warns of the irreversible effects and unintended consequences of immigration while portraying the driving structural forces and emotional desires that continue to make migration viable despite the well-known risks.

The issue of family separation has always been pressing, especially among immigrants from Mexico and Central America, who have longstanding traditions of gendered migration where young men leave their household to journey to *el norte* for work. Often men would work for several years or make annual migrations northward while mothers and wives would stay at home. However, beginning in the 1980s and increasing in the past two decades, a series of factors complicated this migration pattern (Hirsch 2003; Smith 2005; Massey 2007). First, women began to migrate for work and family reunification in the United States in greater numbers. As women in Mexico and Central America became more educated and less tied to agriculture, they migrated, often first to work in *maquiladoras* on the U.S.-Mexico border or larger cities within these countries, and then to the United States. Second, migrant labor to the United States became more permanent, particularly in the face of militarized border enforcement and harsher immigration laws, such as the 1996 Illegal Immigration Reform and Immigrant Responsibility Act (IIRIRA). Migrants who previously had pursued circular routes through the United States and returned during slow seasons to Mexico now found it harder to return each year. Many decided to stay in the United States, even if they lacked proper documentation, rather than risk a perilous border crossing through the desert. Third, life-cycle developments pressured many immigrants to remain in the United States; as young migrants who were part of a wave of immigration in the 1990s began to have children (many of whom were U.S. citizens, having been born in the United States), they put down roots in communities. Currently, the economic crisis has slowed immigration from Mexico to a standstill, and many migrants who lost jobs in the United States have returned to their country of origin (Papademetriou, Sumption, and Terrazas 2011; Passel and Cohn 2011).

In Charlotte, I saw evidence of all of these trends, but also of new challenges to family unification facing Latino immigrants. One challenge is when family members are dispersed across wide geographical distance, from the home country to the United States and other immigrant destinations. At the fiftieth birthday party for a Bolivian woman, Ultimanota was hired to play popular songs for the celebration, held in a private room at an Eastside restaurant. After its second set, the lights were dimmed and the woman's son set up a video projector. He pushed "play," and a video montage began. First, grandchildren and relatives from her hometown in Bolivia gave their blessings. Then a son in Los Angeles made an appearance and wished her happy birthday. Finally, another son in Madrid told her how much he missed her and wished that he could be there to celebrate the occasion. The lights went up, and the son in Charlotte picked up a guitar, joined the band, and began to sing her favorite song. Then the whole room joined in singing her "Happy Birthday" in Spanish, and she was presented with a cake and candles.

This video, homemade but well edited, attests to the international scope of migration from Latin America in the late twentieth and early twenty-first centuries, but also the way technology has lessened the communication gaps and social absences at important life events for dispersed families. As the Bolivian immigrant reached a milestone, it was unclear whether she would ever return permanently to her "home" in Bolivia, or would remain in Charlotte, where she has forged important familial links. She also has a transnational family, linked by technology, and not tied to one geographic place.

Political Organizing

On a chilly November evening in Charlotte, I ride with Jess George, the executive director of the Latin American Coalition, to an African American church in an Intown neighborhood just off Central Avenue. We park in the crowded gravel lot and go inside a packed chapel of St. Paul's Church. At the entrance, young Latino volunteers press stickers reading "Reform Immigration for America" on the sleeves of our jackets. Inside, the pews are full of Latino immigrants—families with young children, teenagers, and groups of twenty-something men—and a sprinkling of black and white concerned community members.

Reform Immigration for America is a national campaign for comprehensive immigration reform, represented locally through the Latin American Coalition. Tonight's meeting has been organized by Rubén Campillo, a staff member at the LAC who spends much of his time organizing local campaigns for immigration reform and coordinating local efforts with state and national efforts, such as marches in Washington, DC, and lobbying in Raleigh, the state capital. This meeting is the kickoff of an effort to recruit people for an immigration reform rally in March 2010.[6]

The first speakers of the night are several college students, who in English and Spanish tell their stories of facing limited access to college because of state laws prohibiting undocumented students from attending community college. Next, several pastors speak of the questionable ethics of discriminatory immigration laws and the separation of families through deportation. Several women, speaking in Spanish, testify about husbands and other loved ones who had been deported under the 287(g) program after being stopped by police. St. Paul's pastor, Mark Reynolds, stands up next and gives an animated sermon to his "Latino brothers" expressing the common problems facing the black and Latino communities and the solidarity he feels with the struggles of Latinos for expanded civil rights. Jess George speaks about the need to provide undocumented immigrants a path to legalization and citizenship and the important contribution of immigrants to the U.S. economy. Maudia Meléndez, a prominent community organizer and pastor, rises to speak in Spanish, telling the crowd not to despair of the seeming impossibility of their task of pushing through immigration reform; she invokes Old Testament imagery by telling the story of Moses having faith in God and trusting that he would part the Red Sea as the Jews were escaping from Egypt (see Meléndez 2010). After this rousing mini-sermon, Campillo closes out the meeting by giving the audience instructions on how to fill out postcards being passed around; by signing up with a mobile phone number, one can receive text messages with updates on how the campaign is going and when the next protest or meeting is happening.

The next few months were marked by small protests—in front of the county jail, at city parks, at city council meetings—where Latino community members gathered in public. People held up placards expressing their disapproval of the 287(g) program and waved American flags to express their desire for political inclusion in the nation.[7] Organizers worked furiously to coordinate both these smaller protests and a scheduled march in Washington, DC. In the Latin American Coalition offices, a conference room became a space where Rubén Campillo, Maudia Meléndez, and other prominent Latino community leaders pulled together a campaign in the weeks leading up to the march.

On a warm evening in March, I boarded a bus in the parking lot of the Eastland Mall, where a long line of charter buses waited to travel to Washington, DC. Groups of high school students gathered, saying goodbye to parents who could not make the trip, excited to be going to their first march. Women from a church group circled around to chant a prayer. Rubén Campillo and a group of student activists stood to one side giving a press conference under the bright lights of a TV camera set. A local Spanish-language newspaper had the most buses; it had promoted the march in its paper and given T-shirts to the participants who rode its buses. On the bus, I chatted with several people I recognized from the Coalition—clients, friends, and family members—as we had a mostly sleepless journey anticipating the next day's events.

During the march, I wandered around the National Mall. Although my purpose in attending the march was to gain a better understanding of the immigrants' rights movement and show solidarity with Latino community members from Charlotte, it so happened that music permeated the event and formed a large part of what I took away from attending. The opening convocation featured a choir singing "The Star-Spangled Banner" and several hymns in English. As groups from different states entered the National Mall, they often chanted slogans or marched in formation with small drums, while carrying banners naming their organization or state. One party even had a ragtag marching band that accompanied them down the Mall. As speaker after speaker took the stage, they often engaged the crowd with chants—"¡Sí se puede!" (Yes we can!)—being the most common. As the heat in the crowd grew stifling, I slipped behind the stage, where a group of Mexican immigrants and Mexican Americans from California were gathered around *mariachis* and folkloric dancers dressed in full regalia. The band lit into a rendition of "La Negra," a traditional song from central Mexico, and I could barely hear the vocalists over the chorus of marchers who joined in singing every word. I then made my way over to another bunch of people: Dominican immigrants who huddled around a group of percussionists playing a *tambor*, a *güiro*, and claves and improvising lyrics about the march. Rejoining the crowd, I listened to a series of speakers, each more prominent than the last—the TV personality Geraldo Rivera, officials from the NAACP and National Council of La Raza, Representative Luis Gutiérrez, Senator Bob Menendez—until on a giant TV screen a prerecorded message from President Barack Obama pledged support for immigration reform. Soon after, the gathering dispersed, and groups of participants marched back to their buses through the streets of Washington. I found people from North Carolina and walked with them. A guy walking with a guitar strapped around his shoulders launched into José Alfredo Jiménez's "El Rey" (1987) and everyone joined in. Despite the long odds against passing a bill that spring (when the U.S. Congress was preoccupied with debating health care legislation), the marchers retained their optimism and pride even as the tide that rose with the 2006 protests (which many of them participated in) appeared to turn against them in anti-immigrant laws and popular opinion.

On the bus ride home, the excitement waned as tired marchers drifted to sleep, but some expressed hope that their efforts were worthwhile. The next day's Spanish-language newspapers were flush with full-page photo montages of the march and extensive coverage of what was said and who participated.[8] The front page of a local Spanish-language newspaper, *Qué Pasa*, featured a photograph of the marchers looking at the giant video screen with President Obama speaking and asked, "¿Nos vas a cumplir? Miles le pidieron a Obama que cumpla con su promesa de campaña." (Are you going to keep your promise to us? Thousands ask Obama to keep his campaign promise.)[9] In the months after the march, small protests continued around Charlotte. I observed one gathering that took the form of performance art and public theater as a form of protest against the recently passed Arizona law SB 1070.[10] Activists dressed up as the Bill of Rights were arrested by police and put in handcuffs, only to be rescued by Lady Liberty, dressed in green robes and holding a torch. This performance was given on the sidewalk in NoDa on a Friday evening in English and Spanish, and people going to concerts, bars, and restaurants stopped to watch and were given flyers about immigration reform.

In December, activists had a hopeful moment when Senate majority leader Harry Reid attempted to attach the provisions of the DREAM Act (giving undocumented college students a path to legalization) to a military spending bill. On a Friday night, I sat with several activists watching the Senate proceedings, but the amendment eventually failed. This is how 2010 ended—an eventful but mostly fruitless year of politicking for immigration reform in Charlotte and nationwide.

Reprise

Since 2010, political efforts around immigration reform have gone through a dramatic evolution. The deflated optimism of 2010 quickly turned to frenetic organizing as activists faced a series of anti-immigrant bills introduced in legislatures in North Carolina and other southern states. Many of the activists who led these defensive efforts were students who had only recently joined the movement during marches in 2009–2010. They embarked on new strategies such as an emphasis on organizing rural immigrant communities overlooked in the 2010 campaign, circulating online petitions and videos, intensively lobbying elected officials, and engaging in high-profile acts of civil disobedience. These strategies facilitated a more grassroots approach to organizing, and a new enthusiasm helped many activists recover from the disappointment of 2010.

For the students and young people, the DREAM-ers, the 2010 marches were their first experiences organizing and participating in a mass political event and visiting Washington, DC. For them, the march acted as a rite of passage that led to further political participation.[11] Charlotte's DREAM activists became part of a larger movement among student activists in several states who have taken the risky move of proclaiming their undocumented status voluntarily in public during protests, bringing attention to their personal cases (many were brought to the United

States as babies by their parents, some are ranked at the head of their class) and the barriers facing undocumented students (limited access to college education and no federal loans).[12] In May 2011, young activists descended on the Cinco de Mayo Fanta Festival and gathered thousands of signatures for their "Drop the I Word" campaign.[13] These students represent a younger generation that is coming of age in a climate where they, their parents, and friends face the constant threat of deportation and targeting by police and government authorities. As students, they have been portrayed as a demographic "problem" that requires more resources (for ESL classes, translators, etc.) and have faced resistance to being admitted to higher education (Wainer 2006). Having grown up in the United States, they argue that because of their already strong ties of community and belonging to country and region, they have a legitimate claim to immigration reform and a path to citizenship as de facto members of the nation.

Eventually, the strategies implemented after 2010 led to a series of successful actions: from preventing the passage of numerous anti-immigrant bills in the North Carolina legislature to pressuring President Obama to implement an executive order giving temporary legal status for some undocumented youth through the Deferred Action for Childhood Arrivals (DACA) process. As Lacey Williams, the advocacy director for the Latin American Coalition, explained, DACA was a direct result of lobbying and protests organized by youth, such as the Coalition-sponsored United 4 the Dream group, and in particular a confrontation at the 2011 National Council of La Raza national conference, when students interrupted Obama's speech with chants of "¡Sí se puede!" and shouts to pass immigration reform.[14] The 2012 election became a setting for protests and sit-ins to convert DACA into a broader comprehensive immigration reform.

In 2013 the U.S. Senate passed a comprehensive immigration reform bill, but it faced an uphill battle in the House of Representatives. Many representatives from North Carolina opposed the bill. In an effort to change their mind and rally support for the Senate bill, activists from the Latin American Coalition organized a "Road to Reform" tour that traveled throughout the state targeting recalcitrant representatives' districts, particularly in rural areas. The Latin American Coalition lent its organizational infrastructure to Latina/o immigrant communities that lacked formal advocacy groups, and student activists helped local residents present their concerns through lobbying efforts at representatives' district offices. They also staged roadside rallies to raise awareness in these districts. In Washington, DC, the Latin American Coalition's executive director and development coordinator were both arrested in a street-blocking act of civil disobedience to pressure representatives to bring the Senate bill to a vote.[15] Several activists expressed cautious optimism about the prospects of reform happening, although as this book went to press no bill had been passed into law.

The immigration reform movement became more focused on issues directly affecting the immigrant community as a whole. Activism coalesced around case upon case of families separated by local and state immigration enforcement policing. Some of these families created an initiative through the Latin American Coalition called Familias Unidas to support families going through deportation and publicize their stories. For DREAM-ers, this push arose from a more collective analysis of their activism; their participation became not just for the DREAM Act, but for immigration reform for their parents. Whereas the narrative around the DREAM Act portrayed students as innocent victims of parents who had brought them to the United States illegally at a young age, now many DREAM-ers were ready to portray their parents as heroes and to state that a path to citizenship should be available for all immigrants. Both DREAM activists and families facing separation provided compelling stories that the Latin American Coalition and other groups would periodically feature in online campaigns to raise awareness and in marches in Charlotte and the state capital, Raleigh. The communications director of the Coalition, Armando Bellmas, and a graduate student at University of North Carolina–Charlotte, Hannah Levinson, decided to make a short film about several of these featured cases, and the film turned into a feature-length documentary, *From the Back of the Line* (2013). Through interviews with Latina/o immigrants facing deportation, footage of their families, and coverage of a series of immigration reform marches and street performances, the filmmakers captured what Armando called "a slice in time" of the immigration struggle in Charlotte. Despite their precarious status—many of the individuals interviewed in the film are facing deportation for minor traffic offenses like running a red light and worry about being separated from spouses and young children—the filmmakers stress the lives the film's subjects have made in the United States, as "American families just like yours or mine."[16]

Another striking element of the renewed immigration activism after 2010 has been the important role visual art has played in protests and campaigns. DREAM-ers often made cardboard cutouts of butterflies, which they colorfully decorated with glitter, paint, and fabric. The symbolism of the monarch butterfly, as an insect that migrates as part of its natural life cycle over several generations between Mexico and the United States, spoke to many young activists as a way to legitimate and beautifully represent their experiences. Through another project, OBRA Art Collective, young undocumented artists create "immigrant affirming art" to raise awareness about immigration reform (OBRA n.d.).[17] In campaigns to stop deportations, activists have designed stencils and online posters that represent families facing separation. For example, for the case of Luis Zarco, activists designed a colorful portrait that was displayed at a vigil and through online Facebook posts leading up to his court proceedings date. On September 18, 2013, an immigration judge cancelled Zarco's deportation case, allowing him to remain in Charlotte with his family and become a legal permanent resident.

So far, this integration of artistry and activism has not included widespread participation of musicians. However, several musicians, including two members of Ultimanota, performed at an April 10, 2013, march in Charlotte.[18] The songs they chose, Manu Chao's "Clandestino" (1998) and Los Tigres del Norte's "De Paisano a Paisano" (2000), demonstrated their solidarity with the marchers through the songs' themes, which touch on the humanity of immigrants regardless of status. Other artistic participation in protests has included spoken word performances and poetry readings by DREAM-ers and children whose parents are facing deportation. However, the vast majority of musicians do not participate fully in this type of overt political organizing. While some musicians conveyed their distaste or hesitancy to get involved in protests, others are just too busy, especially as they work two or three jobs, to get involved in time-consuming campaigns. When musicians do link up with immigration reform activists, it is most often as performers—singing the national anthem at a rally or allowing an organizer to announce an upcoming event between songs at a concert. While few musicians make forays into overt politics, Charlotte's political activists appear not to fully enlist musical communities as part of their campaigns, instead relying on organizing networks of the church, radio listeners and newspaper readers, and nonprofit organizations.

The Politics of Musical Life

It is in the context of political organizing and protest that we must consider the relative lack of overt political music among Latinos in Charlotte. Where are the protest songs?[19] Where is the *corrido* chronicling the plight of undocumented students or torn-apart families? In Charlotte, these don't exist, despite the history of political commentary in Latin American rock (Pacini Hernández, Fernández L'Hoeste, and Zolov 2004; Zolov 1999) or *regional mexicano* music (Ragland 2009).[20] Instead, musicians from across genres stressed to me during interviews that they seek to avoid political issues in their music. Many musicians remarked that they attempt to relay a positive message in songs, or that they provide music so that people can have fun. During a conversation, Tony Arreaza commented that he does not like to mix politics and music because he does not see music as a political arena. He recalled one incident when La Rúa was hired to play a fundraiser for a local politician and the band did not like how it felt to be so closely linked to party politics. Perhaps a better question than where are the protest songs is whether the type of public activism tied to overt political music is necessary or prudent for Latino musicians in Charlotte. Would public activism undermine the sense of aesthetic autonomy that musicians feel guides their performances and attracts their audiences? Musicians' strategies of nonparticipation highlight their ambivalence toward organized public activism, which they support philosophically and morally (at times) but hesitate to tie fast to their artistry.

Despite this political avoidance, several groups have songs with lyrics that provide political commentary, as we have seen. Other bands, in particular Dorian Gris and Tropic Culture, are fond of interspersing their songs with conversations with their audiences during live performances (see chapter 3). For example, during one concert in October 2010, Tropic Culture expressed concern over an attempted coup d'état that had occurred in Ecuador.[21] After declaring the need for democracy, the band dedicated a song sung in English to the people of Ecuador entitled "Freedom Fighters":

> Let's start a revolution, ya'll [spoken]
> It's a rare occasion when one can see
> We need education and we think it's free
> Where to stand against these odds
> It's heroic enough for us
> For all the freedoms that we share
> The revolution must be there
> For all the freedoms that we share
> The revolution must begin.

This song was part of its new album, *Dance Revolution* (2010), which represented a change of styles and instrumentation for Tropic Culture. The band's opening line, "Let's start a revolution, ya'll," is both a statement of its new creative direction (bringing in disco and funk rhythms and attempting to make its songs more danceable) and an exhortation to its audience to effect change—with a southern twang. The song's lyrics attempt to answer questions about the purpose of the band and its musical community, while leaving vague what a "revolution" to protect "the freedoms that we share" signifies. With songs such as "Eliminate the Hate" and live performances of Bob Marley and Manu Chao covers, Tropic Culture has often positioned itself as part of a progressive, left-leaning community, although it hesitates to venture beyond the "positive message" politics of multiculturalism or the loosely choreographed style of jam band music. In "Freedom Fighters," it appears, the band still struggles with these limitations, both political and creative, to define what revolutionary change means.

A song by Bakalao Stars presents another facet of Latino social commentary in Charlotte: the link between immigrants and the environment. "Verde" (2010) is a paean to the Earth and a plea to protect the environment. For the song, Bakalao Stars enlisted the help of Itaguí, the lead singer of the Miami-based band Locos por Juana, who sings and raps as a guest vocalist on the track. "Verde" paints a bleak picture of environmental destruction to a reggae beat:

Por esta aquí, tienes que pensar	You have to think about this here
Que esta tierra pronto basta ya	That this Earth will be gone soon
Si no actuamos	If we don't act
[CALL AND RESPONSE]	
Verde	Green
Que es el color de la tierra	Which is the color of the earth
Verde	Green
El árbol lleno de ramos	The tree full of branches
Verde	Green
El aire que respiramos	The air we breathe
Verde	Green
Pa' el futuro de los chamos	For the future of the youth
No se que hacer, es muy tarde ya	I don't know what to do, it's already too late
Voy este mundo llega a su final	This world is going to end
La vida vale no más que tres pesos	Life is not worth three pesos
Solo la angustia, horror, y mil lamentos	Only anxiety, horror, and a thousand cries of pain
Se acabó el gas y esto va explotarse	There's no more gas and that is going to explode
Si no actuamos nos jodemos ya	If we don't act then we will be screwed
Ya esta guerra se salío de nuestras manos	this war is out of our hands
Por dinero y por la envidia	through money and envy
Nuestra guerra atrapamos	our war has trapped us
Global Warming acaba el mundo ya	Global Warming is about to end the world
Nuestros hijos quisiéremos salvar	We want to save our children

With "Verde," Bakalao Stars positions itself as an advocate of change that it sees as necessary to prevent the destruction of the earth through global warming. In the vein of classic politically infused reggae, the band portrays this struggle as a war between forces of good and evil in which conscious individuals must become fully involved. The song's lyrics warrant several notes. Saving the earth for "el futuro de los chamos" employs a Colombian colloquialism, *chamo*, for a universal class of people, the youth of the world. "Global Warming" is inserted as an English term in a song otherwise sung entirely in Spanish, pointing to its international acceptance as a signifier for manmade climate change and the dominance of English-language media in the environmental movement. Bakalao Stars links global warming with capitalism, singing of the commoditization of labor and human bodies ("La vida no vale más que tres pesos") and rising consumption patterns in the global South ("Por dinero y por la envidia / Nuestra guerra atrapamos"). Like Tropic Culture in "Freedom Fighters," "Verde" presents a call for action with generalized recommendations of how to act, without condemning guilty behavior or providing specific recommendations on how to curtail global warming or undermine the capitalist, consumerist nexus causing the problem.[22]

Despite their limitations, songs such as "Verde" and "Freedom Fighters" are evidence of an arena where Charlotte's Latino musicians constantly and very actively engage with their audiences. Through e-mail messages, Facebook status updates, and informal conversations at shows, musicians seek and readily receive feedback from fans and other musicians in their community. Musicians chart an informal politics through these interactions, where they construct meaning through everyday practices and performance, often around notions of community and belonging. Performance at a concert becomes just the outward manifestation of a long process of intertwined debate and discussion. While few musicians work on the front lines of political activism in the immigration reform movement, they do act as creative leaders by distilling the speech patterns, attitudes, and perspectives of their musical community into a performance and recorded body of work (written songs, CDs and MP3s, online videos, etc.) that can be referenced and renegotiated over time. Moreover, the solidarity and sense of community they form through music making extend outward into the greater Latino population, fostering connections that move beyond music-specific networks and pursuing intellectual work that guides how a southern *latinidad* is being formed.

Musicians as "Grassroots Intellectuals"

In his "Prison Notebooks," Antonio Gramsci defined intellectuals as people who give a fundamental social group "homogeneity and awareness of its own function."[23] Organic intellectuals emerge from the social group to help define its direction and vision. Gramsci's conception of intellectuals and their work cannot be separated from his views on class and class formation, which focus not just on structural determinants of a group's position in society, but also the internalization of class identity in ways of thinking and acting. In Charlotte, Latina/o musicians and other participants (especially journalists) in the music scene act as "grassroots intellectuals," meaning they perform intellectual work, but outside the realm of party or organized politics (see Susser 2011a, 2011b). As "grassroots intellectuals," musicians help audiences form political consciousness through their performance practices and interactions. Their intellectual interventions play a major role in situating the music in a larger field of class, gender, and ethnic identities as music lovers debate the intricacies of style and meaning. Musicians would engage each other, journalists, and audience members in heated debates over favorite songs, the relative success of current and past performances, and the current level of excitement surrounding bands. These discussions would happen at rehearsals, before and after concerts, at the bar or outside during cigarette breaks, and on social networking websites like Facebook. In effect, these were arenas where people created a metadiscourse about music and voice.

Often these discussions attempted to position the music at hand in context, relating a band's songs to its major influences or comparing its style to that of other local bands. This intellectual step sprang from a need to position the music in context and define its directionality. The music being created in Charlotte by Latino musicians comes from their knowledge of Latin music history; in addition, band members often spoke of moving their music "in a new direction," or that they were "trying out some new songs." For example, in the late autumn of 2009, I sat in as Dorian Gris rehearsed in its practice space. The musicians were practicing covers of songs by the popular Mexican band Caifanes/Los Jaguares for a tribute show in early January. Between songs, band members discussed which songs they liked best, which ones they should let the other bands participating in the tribute concert cover, and what was the best way to cover the song without playing and singing an exact replica of the original. Over the course of the evening it became clear how important Caifanes and Los Jaguares (the band that was formed by several former Caifanes members) were in the musical development of Dorian Gris. Because Caifanes was from Mexico City and was one of the seminal bands in the development of *rock en español* in the late 1980s and early 1990s, it had a major influence on Carlos Crespo, Juan Espín, and other band members who had grown up listening to its songs. By interpreting its songs, the tribute concert became sort of an intergenerational forum as Dorian Gris's members (who vary in age but are younger than Caifanes, but older than many local fans) passed on their versions of foundational *rock en español* songs. But the tribute concert was also an opportunity for Dorian Gris to reiterate to fans, most of whom are young, working-class Mexican immigrants, the band members' ethnic and class solidarity that they perform while onstage. A few of these songs had already become standards that the band played at every show; new covers and reworked interpretations were a way to show the development of the band and renew the enthusiasm that fans felt for their performance style.

In an interview in English with the *salsa* percussionist and singer Sendy Méndez, who is a former member of Orquesta Mayor, we discussed the intellectual work that goes into being a musician and member of a musical community:

> SB: Let me ask you another question about being a musician: How does it affect personal relationships?
>
> SENDY MÉNDEZ: You know, being a musician and having a social life is really, is difficult, because musicians are a special breed of folks. Everybody that plays an instrument, they love the arts of it, you know, when they get in a room of people that are musicians, their conversation is just all around playing music and, "Have you heard the latest beat?" or "What do you think about this, this kind

of rhythm?" especially around percussionists, because a lot of the percussion that I've learned is just from watching others, you know?

SB: Just mimicking them?

SENDY: Just trying . . . I come up to them, "How do you *do* that riff?" and then, as I develop slowly, understanding the patterns of how to play it with my hands, and how it works on a music sheet, and how the different beats and the relation of the music, so, you know, I just walk up to the guy, if it's something that really interests me, or sometimes I just pull out my phone and record that, then I go back . . .

SB: And try to figure it out!

SENDY: Slow it down, and then practice it slowly and then try to incorporate it into my hits, so . . . but that topic is very exclusive. So you bring . . . into that relationship someone who is not very musically inclined, they'll get bored. And I'm a dancer too, I love to . . . before I was doing music, I was dancing. I've been in dance groups and stuff, but I love to do the *salsa, merengue* stuff, that was my very first love. You know? I love singing, but dancing was my thing. Just—I would walk *miles* and *miles* back home just to go dancing for a couple of hours and then have to walk *all* the way back.

SB: In Puerto Rico?

SENDY: In Puerto Rico, yep. Yep—in the middle of the night, band had just finished around two or three o'clock.

SB: Walking back in the dark . . .

SENDY: I wanted to dance so—unless it's somebody that is in tune with that, reaching can be difficult, now if that person is open, and likes the arts, then it makes it a little easier.

I used to have a friend, that . . . his ex-wife would tell him, "All you do is spend time with musicians," and he said, "Well, what's wrong with *that!*" [*We laugh.*] He didn't have a problem with it. He was like a fish in water.[24]

In this interview, a general question about musicians' personal relationships turned into a deeper discussion of musicians as a "special breed of folks" who spend much of their free time discussing music. Sendy stresses the importance of metadiscourse on music for forging social relationships among musicians; percussionists listen to the latest beat, ask each other technical questions, and deconstruct an intriguing rhythm. Sendy's personal quotation, "How do you *do* that riff?" highlights this process. Learning a new riff is not always simple; it is not (as I mention) just mimicking a person's actions. Sendy corrects my simplistic question by detailing the process he undertakes: recording a riff, slowing it down and listening to its component parts, practicing it slowly and then speeding it up to get it to the right tempo. Particularly for *salsa*, which often relies on African-derived polyrhythms with patterns that can shift during a song, learning percussion parts can be challenging. Because it is a dance music played before an audience that relies on steady tempo and recognizable beats to measure turns and step patterns, the percussionists play vital roles in the *orquesta*.

Sendy's experience as a teenager in Puerto Rico serves to expand the field of qualified members to dancers, who also dedicate themselves fully to studying and living the music. Earlier in the interview, Sendy had recalled his earliest musical influences, which included a group of older men in his town who would regularly perform in jam sessions on weekends and other times sat around listening to records. As Sendy hung out with this older generation or went to dance to contemporary groups performing nearby, he was receiving his musical education in both old and new styles of Caribbean music. He states that he got the "best of both worlds" during his early musical training.

While Sendy stresses the difficulty of participating in a musical community—it requires someone who understands the technical language of musicians, who is musically inclined—at the close of his response he does leave the door open for someone who is "open" and "likes the arts" to become attuned to musical life. In interviews and conversations, many musicians stressed the hardship of living as a musician and the intense technical training that brought them to the point of being a "professional" musician. This experience of "paying your dues," as blues musicians frame it, is an important entry point for membership in a musical community; musicians who have demonstrated their technical expertise and longevity are highly regarded and more readily accepted into bands (Washburne 2008). But for Charlotte's more-established musicians, it is also exciting to see younger musicians just entering the community or to talk shop with musically inclined community members who want to join the conversation after a show.

Women in Charlotte's Latino musical communities often play marginal roles. Most of the musicians are male, but besides the occasional female musician, wives, partners, and girlfriends are often accepted into the inner circle of bands and participate in discussions about music. When I would strike up conversations with these women backstage or in the audience, they would offer compliments and critiques of the band and their partners' performances. But in the male-dominated space of band life, women sometimes do not feel comfortable, or they regret the time and money that band life drains from a household. Sendy's joke about his friend's ex-wife brings this point home. For Sendy, it is obvious why a musician would want to spend all his time with other musicians. The story becomes an opportunity for Sendy to stress musical identity— "What's wrong with *that!*" For Sendy, the musical life is something that is inescapable and hard to walk away from. Even though he had recently stepped down from his percussionist duties with Orquesta Mayor, he still acts as an emcee at cultural events organized by the Latin American Coalition and frequently sits in with local *salsa* bands, continuing to participate in his musical community.

Interestingly, as musicians became familiar with my research project in Charlotte, my role as an "expert" studying Latin music and culture began to color conversations I had at concerts, rehearsals, and social gatherings. Often musicians would ask my opinion of a performance. Because I attended numerous shows, I became a feedback loop, reporting back to musicians who could not make a weeknight show because of family or work obligations; they would ask me, "How was the crowd?" "Did they play any new songs?" Inevitably, conversations would turn to music and we would compare notes on bands we liked and disliked. Throughout these conversations, I was often struck by the intellectual depth of musicians' opinions. Whether it was *salsa*, rock, or *regional mexicano*, they stressed the heavy lifting needed to formulate a great song and wonderful performance. The key elements included lots of rehearsing, good relationships among band members, and effective presentation, but most importantly musicians theorized about understanding and empathizing with the audience. Many stressed the process of cultivating an audience by staying true to their identity, evolving with them as they changed, but also including them in the process of personal development that the band members go through.

Another forum for intellectual debate about music and music making are the Spanish-language newspapers in Charlotte. A small but dedicated group of journalists follow the Latin music scene. They write articles in the papers' cultural sections previewing an upcoming concert or reviewing a new album release, for both local and international acts. This was in contrast to English-language newspapers, which rarely covered the Latin scene in Charlotte or performances by visiting Latin American artists. One Spanish-language reporter, Jacobo Strimling, a Jewish Mexican immigrant, warrants special mention. Following the music scene closely, Strimling writes reviews for *Mi Gente* that challenge readers to think critically about the music's politics and cultural meaning for immigrants living in the U.S. South. At times he will outline the genealogy of a musician's work, tracing musical influences and pop culture references that shape the work. For example, in an article previewing the tribute to Caifanes/Los Jaguares, Strimling profiled the local musician Johnny Mortera, who, with Dorian Gris and Baco, was to perform at the tribute concert. Using quotes from his interview with Mortera, he presented a short history of Caifanes, stressing the influence of the lead singer, Saul Hernández:

> Today one cannot speak of *rock en español* without mentioning Caifanes. Montera [*sic*] thinks their music is simple, without too many notes but accepts that the songs "have a muse." "Saul is a tremendous writer, together with Cerati and Beto Cuevas[25] I consider him one of the best songwriters," commented the musician from Veracruz. "With the metaphors he uses, you miss things if you only listen to the songs one or two times."[26]

Using Mortera's words, Strimling frames a discussion of the historical significance of Caifanes/Los Jaguares on Mexican society and Latin rock. The link between Mortera, a songwriter in his own right, and Saul Hernández are evident; Mortera offers his expertise by ranking the songs of Caifanes in the pantheon of Latin rock, alongside songwriters from Soda Stereo and La Ley, two other prominent bands from Latin America who made their mark in the 1980s, when Mortera was a child growing up in Veracruz, Mexico, listening to rock music on the radio. Mortera acknowledges a common critique of Caifanes's music, that its songs are simplistic and unadorned, but also focuses his analysis on the richness of the metaphoric language in Caifanes's songs, lyrics that warrant more than one or two listens to fully grasp. Accompanying the article are two photographs, one an early press shot of Caifanes with "un look ochentero muy a The Cure" (a very 1980s look à la The Cure), as Strimling terms it, the other a current photo of Mortera with spiked, long hair that references his rock idols as he looks thoughtfully into the camera lens.

In a review of the album *Circular Colectivo*, by the Mexican ska/rock band Maldita Vecindad, Strimling (2010) stressed the political significance of the band's songs and its ongoing dialogue with audiences about social issues:

> The band that has been known since its formation in 1985 for telling "*la neta*" [the simple truth], in their sixth studio album disk continues their social narrative. The public waited for lyrics that question society and critique our idiosyncrasies and it happened. . . . [Strimling describes the lyrics and sound of each song.]
>
> 25 years have passed since these Mexican rockers appeared openly as "*pachuchotes*" [ultimate *pachucos*].[27] Their rebellious blood has not tired and the songs retain the same energy. *Circular Colectivo* fulfills a life cycle. It provokes dances of peace, those that from the outside look like jumping and shoving. Circular like a symbol of unity, collective like the music that belongs to all and is for all. La Maldita Vecindad y los Hijos del Quinto Patio [band's full name] continue telling and "*ska-neando*"[28] the history of the Latin American people.

Strimling's review of Maldita Vecindad's album provides several layers of analysis. On the surface, it is a review of a new album that describes the songs included and what the listener can expect to receive with purchase. But Strimling also uses the review to present several points about the band and its political significance. The band is known for—and, as he stresses, continues to tell—the "simple truth," writing lyrics that critique the idiosyncrasies of Mexican culture and question social mores. A new album release is not just an occasion to enjoy new music, but also to take out the band's previous albums and reflect on how the "social narrative" has progressed. As Strimling outlines in his overview of the album's songs, Maldita Vecindad continues to utilize working-class language and practices, such as the language of *corridos* ("Corrido de Digna Ochoa") or street soccer ("Fut Callejero"), to evaluate the exigencies of contemporary life in Latin America in the throes of widespread corruption, neoliberal capitalism, and transnational migration. Moreover, Strimling begins to deconstruct the album's title by analyzing the meaning of the phrase *circular colectivo*. For him, the title first refers to the band members, who, after twenty-five years together, have completed a life cycle by releasing a long-awaited album as aging musicians. Second, the *circular colectivo* presents a double move: Strimling describes the circle of dancers that often form at Maldita Vecindad concerts (and at Eastside rock concerts in Charlotte), where dancers slam into each other while jumping and pushing each other in seemingly erratic and violent motions.[29] To an outsider, these motions could be disconcerting, but as Strimling explains, they are an expression of unity for those working-class *rockeros* who move within the circle. The active performance of "jumping and shoving" links audience members to the band and each other as they sweat, head-bang, rise and fall with the music. But the title also refers to the collective circulation of ideas through music, something that Strimling believes should be for all and by all, a way to engage everyone in debates about the social and political.

As a performance ritual, the collective circle shares commonalities with other Latin American and African American expressive cultural rituals. For example, in its motives, it parallels the ring dances and shouts of African and African American tradition, which "reaffirmed community, discipline, identity, and African cultural memory" (Floyd 1995). Though of a different era, the collective circle plays a similarly empowering role as a ritual of group agency and performative autonomy. Maldita Vecindad, in its songs and performance style, references Mexican, Afro-Caribbean, indigenous, and Chicano cultural tropes that, taken together, affirm Strimling's analysis of the collective circle as a revealing metaphor. The band plays a mixture of ska, rock, *cumbia*, jazz, and Mexican folk styles, with songs referencing Mexican urban working-class culture while dressed as *pachucos* to an audience with fans in Lucha Libre masks or Aztec warrior costumes. For Charlotte audiences, Strimling's analysis of Maldita Vecindad's album provides a reference point to more consciously involve themselves in the collective circle of their interactions with local bands like Dorian Gris.

The collective circle, as an example of working-class expressive culture, also embodies the carnivalesque in a similar sense that the Latino studies scholar José Limón shows for Mexican Americans in South Texas (Limón 1994). As seen at the Dorian Gris show, the ribald verbal interactions and "jumping and shoving" dance style involve a momentary overturning of the dominant discourse and physical performance of power—through rituals that to an outsider appear nonsensical and violent. Through these carnivalesque reversals, political agency seeps. But Limón's analysis complicates the idea that these types of rituals provide neat insider/outsider cultural roles by pointing to the contestations, particularly around gender, that occur on the dance floor. My analysis builds upon this viewpoint by showing how community formed through music is all too often temporary, fleeting, tenuous, and hotly debated. The collective circle may form at a concert, or it may not, and when it does, it may be at the expense of female fans, middle-class concertgoers, or fellow musicians who feel excluded. As an intellectual endeavor, collective circulation of ideas among Charlotte's music lovers may do the same; it is a social network dominated by men, by certain nationalities, and by city-dwellers.

That being said, articles by Strimling and other journalists who profile musicians in Charlotte provide a body of writing about music that embeds politics in discussions of music making. Through their meta-discourse on the Latin music scene, music journalists act as "grassroots intellectuals" who guide and critique the music within a constant feedback loop among musically astute Latino immigrants in the city. The articles and reviews on the Latin music scene are printed on the same pages as articles about deportations, police profiling, and immigration marches and editorials that argue for immigration reform, more political involvement, and economic justice for stolen wages; yet they approach these political questions from a different angle that for many, at least in the musical communities I observed, holds more weight than regular news articles. In tandem with the everyday conversations that happen at rehearsals, concerts, and bars, these articles provide a forum where debates can range from commentary on style to critiques of structural inequality.

Intellectual work, following Gramsci's conception of "organic intellectuals," should involve more and more people in an ever-widening circle of democratization that includes working-class people in the mental work of politics (Forgacs 2000). In Charlotte, Latino musicians occupy a unique role in the musical community: they encourage community members to think about the music that they make together and the role of music in forging *latinidad* in the U.S. South. As creative leaders who have sprung out of immigrant and largely working-class neighborhoods, who often work day jobs alongside their fans, they engage in a process of rumination concerning the fate of Latin music. Whether it was the participation of community members—no matter if they lacked "musical training"—or my "expert" opinion, musicians constantly seek to include a wide circle of people in their intellectual work. Musicians are quick to acknowledge the essential role of audience members in the development of their creativity. They don't just rely on fans to show up; rather, participation in the process of music making is vital. As Dorian Gris explains in the epigraph, without the support of *la raza*, the Dorians would not exist. Musicians and other intellectuals in the Latin music scene speak for and with the collective circle of fans when they write songs, publish newspaper articles, or organize shows.

Conclusion

In this chapter, I have argued that the creative endeavors of Latino musicians in a "new immigrant destination" like Charlotte present examples that broaden the definition of politics as they struggle within a limited public arena to position themselves as political actors staking a claim to belonging to the city, region, and nation. For Latino immigrant musicians in Charlotte, making music is intellectual as well as physical labor. They arrive at theories about the political position of their music through personal experiences, through conversations and debates, and by linking performance styles and song themes with the outlook of their audiences. Music making, thus, becomes a political practice that creates affiliation and solidarity within local populations devastated by immigration policing and seeking spaces of self-affirmation and group belonging through the *habitus* of collective creative expressions. My analysis demonstrates the depth and complexity of musicians' work, showing how local performances of popular music are a far cry from rote replications of a homogenizing global popular music industry. This music making also reiterates what Latino studies scholars have long attested—that the term Latino (or Hispanic) fails to fully incorporate the diversity, divisions, and differences of individuals or groups that might fall in this category in the United States (Stavans 1995; Gonzalez 2000; Dávila 2012). However, certain commonalities—language, shared immigrant experiences—have led Latino musicians to see their work as part of the process of being and becoming Latino in the U.S. South.

Charlotte's Latina/o musicians engage in intellectual work that critiques the national(istic) and party politics central to the immigration reform social movement as ineffective at resolving both the local concerns of immigrants who face daily threats of deportation and their connections to global and transnational networks of family, labor networks, and popular culture. Instead of subsuming Latin American national and local identities into an American or Latino identity (as the immigration reform movement does), Charlotte's Latina/o musicians often hold onto and rework these Latin American identities within the southern (U.S.) context in an attempt to create locally accountable expressions of genre and *latinidad*. They refuse party dogma not because they are philosophically opposed to the aims of the movement, but because as musicians they are most effective and most invested in acting politically on local (community/neighborhood) and, to some extent, transnational scales—both scales that are neglected by the federal and state foci of the immigration reform movement.

What emerges is a politics that parallels, but in a different expressive vein, the outlook of Occupy movements (Juris 2012; Razsa and Kurnik 2012) by focusing on how representative, republican democracy as it is known today alienates and frustrates ordinary (non-elite) people's ability to participate as full citizens in politics while proving ineffective at alleviating the problems caused by deregulated and unfettered capital on a global scale. The crux of the immigration reform movement—to seek changes in law and policies—fails to remedy the plight of immigrants who are subject to racial profiling, wage theft, and anti-immigrant scapegoating. Moreover, many Latinos in Charlotte bring a healthy Latin American skepticism toward organized politics and stored knowledge of the farce of participatory democracy in countries long ruled by small groups of elites.

Latin music in Charlotte, on the other hand, focuses on a politics of everyday life that has sprung from the grassroots setting of the nightclub, the festival, and the restaurant. Globally connected through transnational social networks yet locally constrained by immigration policy, musicians attempt a politics of community formation, of seeking solidarity through performance. Through making music, they become locally enabled by the claims they make to a southern *latinidad* of belonging and urban citizenship within the spaces of music venues and neighborhoods in Charlotte. Debates among musicians about the aesthetic and social significance of their music play complementary roles, helping to develop grassroots intellectualism by contextualizing onstage/backstage issues with the situation their audiences face outside the club—reflecting the ambivalence that many immigrants feel about their roles in U.S. society. By forming the collective circle during performances, Latino musicians and their audiences attempt to negate the lonely individualism of neoliberal subjecthood while affirming a more collective, if temporary, solidarity with their peers. This type of counternarrative was just one of many I heard from musicians, journalists, and music enthusiasts in Latino Charlotte that constituted a body of grassroots intellectual work. These arguments engaged with "politics" in different ways that reflected the positionality of members of a diverse music scene. The framing of La Rúa's "El Chanchito" as a migration narrative of love reflects the band members' desire to universalize the immigrant experience and reach out as "ambassadors" to white audiences. Other bands, such as Tropic Culture and Bakalao Stars, display an awareness of pressing political questions through their music—from ideas of freedom to environmentalism. Thus, music making involves not just producing sounds, but an intellectual curiosity, as Sendy relates, to learn the latest riff, and a need to compare notes about labor conditions and treatment by festival promoters. The emergence of musicians as "grassroots intellectuals" has involved people in an ever-widening circle of democratization that includes working-class people in the mental work of politics. In Charlotte, Latina/o musicians occupy a unique role in the musical community by encouraging community members to think about the music that they make together. The collective circle and similar participatory audience behaviors key to other Latin genres, such as *salsa* dancing, are practices of music making that help constitute a sense of agency and link audiences and musicians inextricably together. These practices are symbols and actions of unity in the face of everyday conditions that threaten any sense of solidarity and belonging, such as an anti-immigrant climate that undermines Latino immigrants' acceptance by mainstream society and economic structures and racial faultlines that threaten the social cohesion of contemporary urban life. The incompleteness of these political practices underscores the work that remains to be done by Charlotte's musicians.

6

Shifting Urban Genres

The construction, deconstruction, and reconstruction of
cultural sets also involve the construction and destruction
of ideologies.
—Eric Wolf (1984)

This chapter examines the political history of Latin genre categories,
showing how genre emerges out of the contested spaces of nationalism
and ethnic identity formation in Latin America and the United States,
and relates these histories to current iterations of genre in Charlotte.
Genre categories mark musical expressions and provide distinction
between social groups. By providing a set of rules and common assumptions, genre boundaries help foster musical community through a sense
of belonging, but also exclude others through difference (Bourdieu
1984; White 2008). Genres also become representational and refer-
ential, standing in for class, racial/ethnic, and national identity when
music escapes from its local context and enters the world of globalized
listeners. Whether accurate, farcical, or stereotypical, these genre representations play a role in defining Latino identity in the U.S. South,
even or perhaps especially among those who are not close listeners to
the music. A major part of the agency of Latino musicians and their
audiences is how they negotiate genre boundaries together in a dialectical process, often through direct feedback during performances but
also through informal conversations and online social networking sites.
This process creates "grassroots intellectuals" who act as leaders guiding
new musical developments by debating elements of style and musicality.
By deploying and, at times, bending genre rules, musicians enact and
embody the common circumstances they share with their audience; they
claim ownership over a method of making music and associate themselves directly with a musical style. Drawing on numerous instances
when distinct genre performances butted against one another, this

chapter analyzes how musicians justified these boundaries as necessary for distinguishing between diverse strains of *latinidad*, but also a trend toward musicians collaborating across genre in an attempt to construct a pan-Latino vision of belonging to the city.

Questioning Genre

I'm backstage at the Hardee's Latin Fest, a music festival in Virginia Beach, Virginia, in June 2010 as Leydy Bonilla prepares to go onstage and perform with Bachata Flow. I've traveled to Virginia Beach with members of several bands from Charlotte—Leydy Bonilla and Bachata Flow, Banda TecnoCaliente, SoulBrazil, and Ultimanota—who have already performed this weekend. Leydy's young son wanders around backstage, while her father and manager, Carlos, watches over the band as they set up. A large and enthusiastic crowd has gathered on the grass in front of the bandstand with views of the ocean and boardwalk. I stand with members of Ultimanota off to one side where we can see the band and the front rows of the audience. The festival's organizer and a local radio DJ together announce Leydy, and the band readies its instruments. Leydy is nowhere to be seen, but soon we hear the opening notes of Lady Gaga's "Bad Romance" (2009), a guttural, monosyllabic procession of notes sung *a capella*. Leydy emerges from the dressing room with a wireless mike, sings the chorus of the song, and enters stage right as the band breaks into a *merengue* version of the hit song. The crowd cheers and starts dancing.

What does it mean to turn a pop song sung in English into a *merengue* for an audience of fans of "Latin" music? All of the bands that journeyed to the festival in Virginia Beach that weekend have a striking ability to perform songs that embody the genre associated with their band, but they also regularly push boundaries to come up with intriguing genre explorations like Leydy Bonilla's "Bad Romance."[1] Thus, performances of genre can reference tradition, while at the same time stressing novelty or reinterpretation of style.

Genre is often attached to nationality, class, language, and ethnicity in ways that foster belonging and community. For example, *regional mexicano* music exudes Mexican national and provincial identity, including the high-pitched nasal tone of singers, instrumentation, danceable rhythm, and frequent *gritos* (shouts) and roll-calling of Mexican provinces. The genre's name itself references its rural, working-class, and *Mexican* particularity. The rules and boundaries of genre are set down by practice, by training, and by the rhythmic constraints of performance, for example, through an associated dance style. Often these rules and boundaries are defined in reference to "tradition," but it is important to remember that tradition is manufactured through social interaction, invented as a way to draw lines of distinction between genres, and morphs over time and space. These rules provide a framework within which musicians can compose and perform their music, giving direction and shape to ideas. But there is an additional element of genre, an indescribable, undefined element of musicality that several musicians labeled *feeling*, using the English word (even in Spanish conversation) to attempt to outline the touch or manner a skillful musician might use to imbue his/her music with an essence of a particular genre. *Feeling* corresponds loosely to what others have labeled "soul" or "groove" in various African-derived forms of U.S. popular music (Keil 1996; Charters 2009; Spellman 1966). Aaron Fox describes "feeling" as the principal goal of country music performance in rural Texas honky-tonks (Fox 2004, 32). Chris Washburne also describes a Hispanicization of the term among *salsa* musicians in New York who use the term *filin* to distinguish old-school *salsa dura* from the commercialized and saccharine *salsa romántica* of the 1990s (Washburne 2008, 2). The element of *feeling* connects with discussions of authenticity and what makes a song or performance adhere to genre categories, or occasionally, create new spaces for exploration of what genre means. Finally, despite what dislocation a new landscape of listening that relies on electronically downloaded music might suggest, genres grow out of a sense of place, and are often remade when transferred and translated to new locales or new audiences.

This critical view of genre raises several questions that will be explored in this chapter. First, does the proposed attachment of genre to nationality, class, and ethnicity correspond to the actual makeup of musical communities in Charlotte? Second, do the rules of genre foster or restrict creativity among Charlotte's Latina/o musicians? How closely are they following the rules and to what end? Third, how significant are *feeling* and related notions of authentic performances of genre to how musicians and audience members conceive of their music? Finally, what does it mean to have Latin music genres performed in Charlotte, where none originated? This chapter positions genre as a socially constructed "cultural set" that, as the anthropologist Eric Wolf stated, must be understood in relation to ideology. For this analysis, I draw on the sociologist Pierre Bourdieu's theorization of taste and distinction to help explain how Charlotte musicians distinguish genres and their associated class and national affiliations.

I use ethnographic material and musicians' songs to attempt to answer these questions about genre in Charlotte's Latin music scene. The music and performances, I believe, do the best job of explaining links between genre and nationality, class, and ethnicity, the creative process and genre rules, the idea of *feeling* and its relation to authenticity, and the local geography of genre in Charlotte. When relevant, I will include web links or sources in endnotes where the reader can listen and view the music referenced.

Nationality, Class, and Ethnicity

The *regional mexicano* group Banda TecnoCaliente has performed in Charlotte since 2000. It writes and performs songs that often deal with issues of romance and intimate relationships, set to a steady backbeat of oom-pah *polca* rhythm that is typical of *norteño* music. Because of the band's lineup—it uses up to seven keyboards, a bass player and percussionist, along with shared vocals (but no other instruments)—its sound is highly synthesized, with keyboards replacing the brass section, accordion, and other instruments often used in *regional mexicano* groups. The band's name is a play on Tierra Caliente, the region of Mexico that includes Guerrero, where several members of the band are from, including the bandleader, Alejandro, and his three brothers. However, the band's contemporary, synthesized sound bears little resemblance to the traditional violin and harp music of Tierra Caliente; instead it follows the style of *norteño* that originated in the border provinces, but has become popular across Mexico and particularly among Mexican immigrants to the United States. Using TecnoCaliente as an example, we can see that *regional mexicano* as a genre relies on an appeal to modernity and technological innovation, while still constantly referencing the idea of "tradition" and the identity of immigrants who come not just from a country but a province/region within Mexico.

For example, TecnoCaliente has made several appearances on Spanish-language television shows, such as Telemundo's *Titulares y Más*.[2] On the shows, members discuss their band's cartoonish logo, an anthropomorphic flame named Pirulo, which represents the band's home region of Tierra Caliente. This type of small talk, whether on television, in radio interviews, or onstage by the bandleader between songs, serves an important purpose in framing TecnoCaliente's image and relationship with fans. It helps establish bona fides, as Mexican immigrants from a particular region, Tierra Caliente. The small talk also frames the band members as heterosexual men (writing songs for a particular unnamed woman) and family members (a group of brothers). It also is an opportunity for branding; the band markets itself with matching, brightly colored outfits with the band's name on back and even a touch of novelty with the appearance of Pirulo.[3]

Another song and video by Banda TecnoCaliente, "Así Te Amo" (2009), is a cover of a *bachata* by Elvis Martínez and a *merengue* by Banda XXI. This example shows how *regional mexicano* lends itself to interpreting material from other genres in a way that is distinctly tied to a Mexican, working-class, and immigrant identity. It also shows the influence of the band's Dominican manager/promoter, Gonzalo Pérez. While keeping the melody and lyrics, TecnoCaliente changes the rhythm and orchestration to give it a Mexican sound, adding a *polca* beat marked by synthesized tuba, bass, snare, and cymbals. The singing style draws on *norteño* phrasing and the posturing of Mexican ballad singers like Luis Miguel. The video portrays two star-crossed lovers who are kept separate by the woman's parents, who dislike the working-class origins of her boyfriend. Various scenes were shot around Charlotte, including in Plaza Fiesta Carolinas, an indoor shopping mall that re-creates a version of a Mexican town marketplace and *zócalo*.[4]

The fact that Banda TecnoCaliente can take a song from another genre and make it work as *regional mexicano* speaks to the versatility of the genre, the ability of artists trained in its rules to incorporate outside material, and some aspects that Latin American genres hold in common. In this case, *bachata* and *norteño* are genres that both draw on a working-class values system (Peña 1985; Pacini Hernández 1995), regular (yet distinct) dance steps, and themes of love and despair. This borrowing of song material is fairly common in Latin American genres, from

Leydy Bonilla and Bachata Flow

Café Tacuba's rock version (1996) of Leo Dan's "Como Te Extraño" to Los Tigres del Norte's "América" (1988) with a melody and bass line that riff on "Twist and Shout" (which is derived from the Mexican folk song "La Bamba"). Yet what makes each version distinct is the way that the genre's performers make it their own. TecnoCaliente takes "Así Te Amo" and adds rhythmic and stylistic elements to its performance, but it also situates the song through its video in an imaginary of working-class Mexican identity and immigrant striving for a better life in the United States.

Songs can sound like different things to different audiences. As part of a strategy to appeal to a wider audience, in the summer of 2010, Banda TecnoCaliente released a single with Leydy Bonilla, "A Dormir Juntitos" (2010).[5] During performances around Charlotte, Leydy Bonilla would call TecnoCaliente onstage to perform the song, or vice versa. At the Club Dominicano's annual end-of-summer picnic, Leydy Bonilla took the stage, singing a few songs with her band, Bachata Flow. Then, later in the day, she retook the stage with Banda TecnoCaliente to sing together. While many in the audience had been dancing to *merengue* and *bachata* throughout the day, when TecnoCaliente was onstage, the grass dance space in front of the stage was empty except for a lone couple dancing. Midway through the song, Leydy commented on the rhythm of the song: "¡Eso es medio como merengue ahí!" (This is almost like a *merengue* here!)[6]

Genre Rules and Boundaries

So what exactly do the rules of genre do, and where are the boundaries of genre situated? While I have already outlined some of the performance characteristics and social relations that help define the genres of *regional mexicano*, *música tropical*, and Latin rock, by now we should be aware of the fluidity of popular music genres (Walser 1993; White 2008). What may develop our understanding better is a consideration of these genres as a method, a tool, or a project that musicians and audiences engage in to interpret particular streams of popular culture. In this sense, genre becomes a process, not just a static body of work. The rules and boundaries of the genre become evident through the method, rather than the material per se. It doesn't matter, then, that TecnoCaliente is covering a *merengue* classic, if its interpretation imbues a *mexicano* method into the performance. As Bourdieu (1984) states, genre becomes a form of social distinction that marks affiliation among and difference between groups of people based on axes of class, race, ethnicity, national origin, legal status, gender, and sexuality. But the analysis can be taken a step further; genre can also be "something that does the work of a particular social relation or cultural encounter" (White 2008, 177; Fabian 1998). In the case of Latin music in Charlotte, this "work" might include voicing the immigrant experience of audience members by representing their stories of romance and love in song, such as La Rúa's "El Chanchito" or Banda TecnoCaliente's "Así Te Amo." In Charlotte, cultural encounters and social relations take place on an uneven playing field that disfavors certain groups: recent immigrants, those without legal status, monolingual Spanish speakers (and speakers of indigenous languages), immigrant women, the impoverished, and those without access to an automobile. Genres become ways to comment on these social relations and cultural encounters, to mediate a person's position by appropriating material as one's own, and to negotiate new forms of belonging and understanding the world. The following two examples illustrate how Charlotte's Latino musical communities are plying the method of genre.

At the 2010 Fanta Festival, I was working as the stage manager, helping bands set up onstage, calling bandleaders to give directions and make sure they showed up on time, and signaling to bands when it was time to stop their set. Midafternoon, a band I had never heard perform before (though I had had limited conversations with band members) took the stage. The members of Los Mentirosos were dressed in all white—white sneakers, white shorts, white designer T-shirts, and white visors—and as they took the stage, the sound guy played a long prerecorded introduction (typical for many *regional mexicano* bands) announcing the band. They launched into their set of *banda* music and I busied myself with pressing matters backstage. About midway through their set, I found myself humming along to one of their songs with a driving, up-tempo melody led by the band's trumpet player and keyboard's synthesized horns. The singer sang a few lines and then launched into the chorus: "Si no supiste amar, ahora te puedes marchar" (If you couldn't figure out how to love, then you can leave). I knew this song, this melody, but yet I did not; I had never heard this band before, nor did I recognize the words. Then it hit me: Los Mentirosos was covering a version of Dusty Springfield's (1963) pop song "I Only Want to Be with You." Later that night, I did some research on the iterations of this song. Luis Miguel, the Latin ballad singer, recorded a Spanish version, "Ahora Te Puedes Marchar" (1987) on which Los Mentirosos based its *regional mexicano* interpretation.[7]

What exactly do Los Mentirosos' cover of "I Only Want to Be with You/Ahora Te Puedes Marchar" and other covers and riffs on popular music mean? Are they representative of the overarching (and overreaching) global hegemony of American popular music and cultural taste making? What does it do for Los Mentirosos, which draws on urban, African American styles of dress, dance, and stage performance, yet makes music in a Mexican, regional style? While some might dismiss the band's use of an old pop song as derivative and uncreative, is its cover more or less legitimate than, say, Hootie and the Blowfish's cover (1995) of the song that also includes references to Bob Dylan's "Tangled Up in Blue" (1975)? Perhaps the idea of *bricolage* (Derrida 1980; Lévi-Strauss 1968) best describes the way Los Mentirosos cribs from American and Latin American popular culture, drawing on popular music history to address the identity of a transnational musical community. This type of genre mixing is part of a process of testing style and appropriating symbols that rather than just copying, creates meaning within the musical community, much as Hebdige (1979) explained for punk music in Britain.

For a second example, I turn to a band, Ultimanota, that I witnessed perform numerous times, during which I carefully noted audiences' reactions to and interactions with the band. On its website, the band gives a description of its sound and approach to genre:

> Ultimanota fuses tropical rhythms with bossa nova and rock undertones. This versatile five piece band can adapt to your event's needs; from providing ambient music at a dinner banquet, such as boleros and Cuban son, to getting a crowd on its feet dancing to salsa, cumbia and merengue. We can also do cocktail hours, weddings, private and corporate events, etc. Our repertoire includes songs from Buena Vista Social Club to Santana and from Old School Salsa to Michael Jackson with a tropical twist.[8]

Ultimanota's website also provides several sample songs: a *salsa* cover of U2's "I Still Haven't Found What I'm Looking For" (1987); a *bolero* cover of Carlos Eleta Almarán's "Historia de un Amor" (1956); another *salsa* cover of Héctor Lavoe's "El Cantante" (1978); an acoustic cover of Jack Johnson's "Upside Down" (2006); and a second *bolero* cover of Bebo

Valdés and El Cigala's version of the Cuban classic "Lágrimas Negras" (2003). The website also provides two YouTube videos from live performances, a list of upcoming shows, and contact information.

Ultimanota's website reveals its flexible approach to genre, which it reiterates in live performances. Tony Arreaza, the bandleader, first mentioned the group to me as a "project" that plays "cheesy cocktail music" at restaurants and parties around town. I knew that Arreaza had been part of several other bands in Charlotte (La Rúa, EvaFina, and Los de Paula), and he seemed to want to lower my expectations about Ultimanota. In the next few weeks, as I saw the group perform and met the other band members, they also stressed the casual nature of the band—as a way to get together and play on the weekends, to earn a little cash on the side. However, the trajectory of Ultimanota from 2009 to 2011 contradicts the band members' humble and self-deprecating assessment of their music making. Over a two-year period, they built audiences or regular customers at several restaurants, became known for playing at weddings, birthdays, and other private parties, and even edged their way into playing at festivals and opening for other bands. Ultimanota's relative success, particularly in an economic situation when other bands struggled to find shows, needs further analysis. What is "cheesy cocktail music" and why do audiences eat it up? What are the limitations and benefits to being a cover band?

Ultimanota's self-deprecation may be a posture put on when members describe their music to fellow musicians and music critics, but in fact their music does at times border on the saccharine as they cover "top forty" pop songs and romantic ballads in an intimate restaurant setting. As a "project," playing cover songs differs from the music making of Bakalao Stars, Dorian Gris, or Leydy Bonilla, who, although they occasionally play covers, spend most of their time working on their own material. Playing covers allows Ultimanota to spend fewer hours rehearsing and more time performing; performances become another rehearsal, where material is fleshed out and tightened onstage. This strategy of composition-*in*-performance (Finnegan 2007) allows for flexibility within the structure of the chords and lyrics of a song selection to bend genre boundaries according to the band's aesthetic. If a song's interpretation works for the band (i.e., not too tricky to perform with little rehearsal) and the audience likes it, then the band integrates the cover into its repertoire. For private parties, clients sometimes request that the band learn a favorite song, or that it alter its playlist—to play upbeat *salsa* at a wedding reception, for example. Over time, audiences have come to learn and appreciate Ultimanota's repertoire, requesting particular songs between sets, singing along, or dancing enthusiastically to an up-tempo number. Like the band's musicians, the audience is often made up of people approaching middle age, some with young children, middle-class or with some discretionary income to dine out at the restaurants the band plays in. The ethno-racial makeup of the audience depends largely on the location, with Latinos frequenting the suburban Cuban restaurant A Piece of Havana and more whites attending shows at an Intown steakhouse. However, it must be stressed that Latino or white, English- or Spanish-speaking, audiences are often very familiar with the songs, and audience members often would come up afterwards to remark to band members about how much they loved "that song" and the band's version of it. Coming from similar class backgrounds and with an awareness of global pop music, audiences expected the band to formulate a set that would appeal to their tastes and provide a pleasant evening at the restaurant with familiar sounds. Essentially, Ultimanota acts as a curator, compiling a canon of (Latin) American pop songs—selections that bridge the divide between Latin American and U.S. popular musics.

The canon included songs by Latin American artists juxtaposed with songs by American and British artists. Thus, Ultimanota might play Maroon 5's "Sunday Morning" (2003) back-to-back with Juan Luis Guerra's "Burbujas de Amor" (1990), or Andrés Calamaro's "Mil Horas" (1983) before Santana's "Evil Ways" (1969); or maybe start out a set with Café Tacuba's "Como Te Extraño" (1996) before launching into a cover of David Gray's "Babylon" (1999). Ultimanota gave each song a twist, whether it was adding congas to the percussion part, voicing the trumpet as a sax part, adding a blues tinge to the guitar solos, or through Fred Figueroa, the lead singer, and his personal vocal style.

Perhaps the best example of this reformulation of popular styles is in the band's cover of Michael Jackson's "Billie Jean" (1982)—which it covered often in the winter and spring of 2010.[9] Reworking the backbeat with an Afro-Cuban clave pattern rhythm, the cover became a dance song that was instantly recognizable yet subtly different from the original. "Billie Jean" became a way to engage the audience, using an American pop song that band members grew up listening to in Venezuela, Mexico, and El Salvador, that expressed some of the common musical roots and genre expressions of (Latin) American popular culture. Moreover, with the addition of Arreaza's bluesy guitar and Figueroa's vocals, the song took on new meaning as they stressed the heartbreak and betrayal of the song's lyrics, departing from the original's upbeat and casual tone. Because it was being sung in a different era, the song took on a different meaning for audience members; it expressed a bit of nostalgia for the music of their youth in the 1980s while containing novel elements that made it an interesting listen and a good dance number. For audience members approaching middle age, married and with kids, there was a certain melancholy in listening to a song about a young woman who claims to be someone's lover and to have borne his child.

Ultimanota's appropriation of popular music—American and Latin American styles, Spanish- and English-language songs—found initial success as it played in a casual setting for an audience that saw the band's performance as part of the ambience of a restaurant or private party. In this setting, there is a sort of mystification of the experience the band members present, a sublimation of the hard work and sweat that go into their performances as they present an image of relaxation and ease. This image corresponds to the "chill" atmosphere of a restaurant; their "cheesy cocktail music" fits into the experience desired by diners out on a date or a family dinner. The meager pay and long playing hours lower expectations for a band that started as a way for an older generation to get out of the house and play on the weekends with minimal rehearsal. Yet, during 2010–2011, Ultimanota evolved into a more versatile group with renewed focus. It added band members, at times using another percussionist (adding timbales to the existing congas) to play more *salsa*-infused dance numbers. It also ventured outside restaurants and private parties, playing at Latin music festivals and opening for other bands at concerts.

While the band's mix of styles and exploration of genre remained constant, this new shift raised important issues. Tensions arose between band members over increased demands on time for rehearsals and more frequent performances that took musicians away from family. As a cover band, Ultimanota cannot easily record an album to release as a CD or to send to venues for performance bookings. The band draws from recent popular music copyrighted by artists and labels with deep pockets and hefty royalty fees for recorded versions of their material. The expense of paying an artist for use of his or her song, the hassle of getting permission, and the threat of a lawsuit all restrict Ultimanota's willingness to record an album (not to mention the limited financial gains of albums in a world of MP3 downloads). Instead, the band has pursued an under-the-radar strategy of presenting its music through MP3 samples and YouTube videos on its website that do not mention the artist's name and are not transferrable through downloading. In this way, it avoids releasing the covers for public consumption as a commodity and having to pay royalties, while encouraging people to come hear the band live.

Feeling and Authenticity

Bourdieu (1984), in his analysis of style and genre, laid out a theory of distinction that focuses on the class-based aspects of aesthetic taste. For Bourdieu, taste is an "expression of a privileged position in social space whose distinctive value is objectively established in its relationship to expressions generated from different conditions." Thus, "tastes (i.e., manifested preferences) are the practical affirmation of an inevitable difference. It is no accident that, when they have to be justified, they are asserted purely negatively, by the refusal of other tastes" (Bourdieu 1984, 56).

During research in Charlotte, I heard numerous comments and witnessed situations where musicians made aesthetic judgments about taste. Middle-class and striving musicians, often members of the Intown musical community, distinguished their musical style through aesthetic judgments of music they viewed as irreconcilably different, incomprehensible, or lacking in particular musical elements they perceive as necessary. These judgments primarily focused on *regional mexicano*, but at times included other genres rooted in working-class and nonwhite racial identities such as *reggaetón*, *bachata*, and American rap. In a move to mark distinction and define taste, musicians denigrated or dismissed these styles in comparison to their own music making. However, and somewhat contradictorily, they sometimes celebrated and drew on related stylistic legacies from the African American and Afro-Caribbean traditions, in particular the blues and reggae, to help define their music.

In addition to highlighting the class differences between Mexican (and Central American) immigrants and other Latino immigrants from the Caribbean and South America, this aesthetic move reveals an often hidden narrative of racial and ethnic identity formation among Latino immigrants. The following section will analyze this phenomenon through a folk concept that many musicians deployed—the idea of *feeling*—and through debates about the use of English-language lyrics in Latin music.

Tony Arreaza, the lead guitarist for Ultimanota, often plays short guitar solos during performances that have a bluesy sound. His referencing of the African American blues is no coincidence; in conversations about music, Arreaza often stressed to me his deep appreciation of blues songs and artists like Buddy Guy and B. B. King. Listening to a song or watching a video (of any musical genre) in his office, Arreaza would call my attention to a particularly striking point in the music and remark that this artist has *feeling*. Arreaza's focus was not on the technically proficient part of the music—the orchestration, the singer's vocal range, or the dubbing and mixing that go into a good studio recording—but rather on an emotive quality of performance that brought the song out of the doldrums of being ordinary. If we were to transcribe the idea of *feeling* musically, it might be the use of minor seventh and diminished chords in a rock harmony, or the polyrhythm between the clave and timbales during the break in a *salsa* number, or the "soulful" timbre of an R&B singer's voice the third time around when she changes up the vocal attack on a chorus. But *feeling* also refers to the interaction between band and audience, the buzz in the room during an intense live performance. Sometimes this comes through in studio recordings, but often live recordings on YouTube (even with poor sound quality) reveal this quality of a band's performance abilities. Even more so, whether or not a band had *feeling* was debated among fellow musicians who had attended a group's show; being in the audience was the ultimate position from which to judge and often document (through photos and short videos taken on cell phones) the extent of a band's ability to evoke *feeling*.

The concept of *feeling* within the Latin music scene goes back at least to Arreaza's days with La Rúa, one of the pioneer *rock en español* groups in Charlotte. In an article (de los Cobos 2009a) commemorating the band's reunion in 2009, Arreaza reminisced about a series of concerts the band did with other local Latin rock groups: "Fueron eventos pequeños, pero a *full feeling*" (They were small events, but with *full feeling*). In planning festivals and concerts for the Latin American Coalition and Carlotan Rock, Arreaza has to decide which acts to bring to perform from outside Charlotte. If the band has never toured through Charlotte, he has to rely on demo recordings and online videos to understand its sound. *Feeling* plays a major part in this decision-making process; Arreaza knows that a band that lacks *feeling* will probably not move a crowd to dance and sing. Because of his years of experience, thoroughness, and skill at picking bands, Arreaza's assessment of a band's *feeling* is often correct, and the band gives a successful show with much appreciation from audience members. However, this theory of band selection is not fail-safe, and some bands do not live up to expectations. For example, at one Festival Latinoamericano, an electronica/pop group that Arreaza selected did not hold the audience's attention, and people filtered out to view folkloric dances at the other stage or went to buy food. Other band selections possess *feeling*, just not in a way that manifests in a festival performance. At the 2011 Festival Latinoamericano, the Miami band Xperimento played a mix of *merengue*, *cumbia*, and reggae on the festival main stage to an attentive but not particularly enthusiastic audience. However, Xperimento also played the after-party at the Neighborhood Theatre. Using more or less the same set list, but in a more intimate and club-like setting, the band performed to a cheering, dancing, and riveted (smaller) audience that had been warmed up by the local group Bakalao Stars.

This commitment to defining and refining the notion of *feeling* contrasts with the distaste and incomprehension that many members of the Intown community (Arreaza included) felt for *regional mexicano* music. Many Latin rock musicians could not understand the appeal of *regional mexicano*; they cringed at the nasal vocal tones, reliance on electronic keyboards, saccharine lyrics, and cowboy fashion aesthetic that for them typified the genre category. If there is one proof of inability to appreciate a genre, it is the comment that all the songs "sound the same," a phrase I often heard non-Mexican Latinos use to describe *regional mexicano*. While there was often a begrudging respect that *regional mexicano* music served an enthusiastic audience that in Charlotte's Latin scene was numerically largest and that it was important to have concerts and festivals that catered to Mexican immigrants, many Latin rock musicians dismissed the music in negative and often stereotypical terms.

Following from Bourdieu (1984), I want to stress that this expression of distinction between Latin rock (which includes a deep appreciation for Mexican rock) and *regional mexicano* follows lines of difference that are drawn between Mexican immigrants and South American and Caribbean immigrants to Charlotte. Difference is etched through geographic segregation and socioeconomic class position, and aggravated by factors of legal status, length of time in the United States, access to social capital, and physical appearance. The perceived difference of Mexican immigrants, then, is not limited to anti-immigrant politics that label them "illegal immigrants" and apply other overarching stereotypes to them. Being "Mexican" is also a racialized difference that takes on a negative connotation relating to the marginalized status of Mexican (and associated Central American) immigrants both within the Latino community and among black and white Charlotte residents. But this does not mean that Latinos who express distaste for *regional mexicano* align themselves politically with anti-immigrant positions on policing and rights; many of these same musicians expressed solidarity with fellow (Mexican) immigrants and support comprehensive immigration reform.

However, some Latino immigrants from the Caribbean, in particular Dominicans, present a different viewpoint in regard to taste and *regional mexicano* music. Many darker-skinned Dominicans, like Gonzalo Pérez, the promoter of TecnoCaliente, expressed empathy and enjoyed close social ties with Mexican immigrants, perhaps because they themselves had experienced incidents of racism and discrimination. As musical styles, *regional mexicano* and Dominican *bachata* and *merengue* share commonalities: all are primarily dance music, emerging out of nationalist musical projects that constantly reference rural life, steeped in romantic imagery and archetypical gender roles, and have been transformed by the electronic technology of keyboards, digital playback, and auto-tune. These common trajectories facilitate Leydy Bonilla's commentary that her duet with TecnoCaliente is "almost like a *merengue*." The relationship between Dominican and Mexican immigrants to Charlotte is complicated and intertwined. The Dominican-owned supermarket chain Compare Foods found success by recognizing that increased Latino immigration to the U.S. South (the majority Mexican immigrants) meant an emerging market of consumers who were not being served by regional grocery chains. Compare Foods began offering

Mexican staples—tortillas, cuts of meat, chiles, nopal, snacks—as well as food products from across Latin America that previously might be found only in a smaller Mexican-run *mercadito* or corner store. This type of ethnic entrepreneurship stems from the fact that most Dominican residents of Charlotte are not direct migrants, but transplants who first lived in the New York metropolitan area, gaining business acumen, English-language skills, and legal status and drawing on the resources of a well-established immigrant enclave before deciding to move south. While Dominican immigrants often start out living in Charlotte with limited resources, because of this social capital they often move up the economic ladder with greater ease than undocumented and newly arrived immigrants from Mexico and Central America. For example, Gonzalo Pérez remembers moving to Charlotte on a whim after visiting friends who lived there. He began working in Compare Foods to make money, but quickly moved into the music industry, where he became the manager of several Latin bands. In comparison, another musician I befriended in Charlotte, an undocumented immigrant from Central America, worked off and on at Compare Foods for several months, but could not keep up with the irregular shifts that interrupted his musical gigs. Eventually, he found another day job working as a painter and drywall installer. Dominican immigrants in Charlotte's Eastside own or run small businesses—auto repair shops, insurance agencies, and grocery stores—that position them in a somewhat exploitative relationship with Mexican immigrants, who are their main customer base, but also put them in close contact on a daily basis. This contact, perhaps even more than the technical similarity between genres, accounts for the feeling of mutual affiliation between the two groups.

A second issue regarding taste among Latino musical communities in Charlotte revolves around language—specifically, the use of English in song lyrics. Leydy Bonilla often includes *bachata* and *merengue* songs sung in English on her albums. This is an effort on Bonilla's part to appeal to non-Latino audiences and to second-generation Latinos who, having grown up in the United States, speak more English than Spanish. As the opening account of Bonilla's cover of Lady Gaga's "Bad Romance" reveals, the usage of some English-language singing in Latin music can be successful, if we judge by the audience's enthusiastic reaction. However, in other cases it falls short or does not fit into the musical community's idea of how a genre should sound. For example, singing in Spanish and even having a certain vocal attack while onstage is, for many musicians and audience members, a prerequisite for a good *salsa* song. Other genres, such as Latin rock, are more open to English-language and bilingual lyrics.

The debate about English-language use in Latin music in Charlotte is as much about generation as it is about genre. While musicians and audience members who are first-generation immigrants almost exclusively use Spanish during performances, both while singing and while interacting with audiences, musicians who are of a second generation of Latinos or who wish to count this group as a major part of their audience (Leydy Bonilla) often use English-language lyrics, or a mix of English and Spanish in between songs as they patter with audience members. Musicians and community members predicted an "inevitable" shift occurring between an older generation of musicians (relatively—many are only in their twenties and thirties) and younger musicians coming on the scene. Some were enthusiastic about this shift, while others worried about the decline of established genre categories to an onslaught of English-language dominant music.

For Latin rock musicians, the generational transition evokes mixed feelings of hope and melancholy; they are supportive of younger musicians, but face the realization that the trajectory of *rock en español* may be drawing to a close. A conversation with Bakalao Stars underlined these perceptions:

> CHRISTIAN ANZOLA: When it comes to the actual scene . . . I see it like a wave, now it's probably dying out [Bakalao's time], but there's a new generation, younger kids, maybe in two years there's going to be that new generation of Hispanic kids that grew up here . . .
>
> SB: Do you see any bands that are coming up?
>
> DANIEL ALVARADO: Avión Sans Pilot? . . . they're young kids, but they're good.
>
> JAVIER ANZOLA: Yeah, but they sing in English!
>
> SB: Yeah?
>
> JAVIER: *That's a huge thing!* It's different, you're Latino, but you're playing in English, it's not *rock en español*, it's just a completely different angle.
>
> CHRISTIAN: One of the things that I see most is Latin people play[ing] more like English bands, because . . . sixteen-year old kids . . .

JAVIER: grow up here . . .

CHRISTIAN: Most of them grow up here, unless they just move here and then it's hard to [get involved in music], but hopefully it keeps going.[10]

Avión Sans Pilot is a Charlotte band made up of teenage musicians who play heavy metal and goth rock, singing in English. In 2009–2010, it played a few shows, including one where it opened for Bakalao Stars at the Evening Muse, but also went through a period of dissolution before reuniting in early 2011. While Bakalao Stars' members appreciate the new "wave" of young(er) musicians coming up, they also reveal their opinion about how the music is different because it is sung in English. Javier, the older of the Anzola brothers, stresses that Avión Sans Pilot's music is not *rock en español*, while Christian, the younger brother, is more understanding, even recommending to Latin musicians to play music "like English bands" to appeal to a younger audience of American-born Latinos. What becomes clear is how flexible *rock en español* is in terms of including the stylistic diversity of Bakalao Stars' use of ska, reggae, and *cumbia*, but also how this breaks down in the face of linguistic and generational shifts to younger musicians singing in English and performing "like English bands." There is distance (and difference) both symbolically rooted in language usage but also real geographic distance as a second generation with American education and social capital seeks to move out of residential and performance enclaves into mainstream society.

Local Geography

Many Latin bands engage with the city's local geography in their songs and performances, especially through music videos that are posted online on YouTube, and this strategy helps connect them to their audiences. As mentioned earlier, La Rúa shot one of the first Latin rock videos in Charlotte by gathering friends and family together on a local streetscape as a backdrop to its performance of "El Chanchito." Bakalao Stars managed to get permission to shoot a music video in TimeWarner Arena, Charlotte's pro basketball stadium, for its song "Kokoa Brown" (2007). Banda TecnoCaliente and Leydy Bonilla filmed portions of their video "A Dormir Juntitos" at a public plaza overlooking the city center;

the plaza is part of a luxury condominium development with upscale restaurants and shops that replaced one of Charlotte's first shopping malls, built in the 1950s. These videos as texts reveal the desires of bands to position their musical community as belonging to Charlotte, striving for a glamorous lifestyle and access to performance spaces. Other artists' videos show little connection to Charlotte or its geography. DS The Evolution has released several new videos that take place in tropical locales—Santo Domingo and Miami. Leydy Bonilla's single "Pienso en Ti" (2011) features a dramatic story of love and betrayal but does not feature recognizable Charlotte landmarks, as she did in some of her earlier videos; instead, it is shot as if the drama takes place in a secret, "secure" location out of a spy movie. These videos shot outside the city position Charlotte musicians in relation to international and cosmopolitan visions of Latino cultural representation.

But these videos are mere representations of larger processes of class and racial formation that lead groups within the larger Latino population to position themselves as similar to or distinct from others. As we have seen, this results in musicians and their audiences forming musical communities separated by neighborhood, access to certain performance spaces, and geographic mobility. Despite the framework that I have presented (based on commentary from members of all three music districts) that classifies the Eastside, Intown, and Uptown areas into distinct purviews, there were artistic developments that complicated this categorization during my time in Charlotte. None proved more intriguing than the music of the Brazilian immigrant community in Charlotte.

Brazilian immigrants to Charlotte have largely settled in Pineville, a former small town southeast of the city that has been swallowed up by the expansion of Charlotte's suburbs. In Pineville, Brazilians own small corner stores and bakeries selling Brazilian food, soccer jerseys, magazines, and, of course, a selection of Brazilian popular music CDs. Reinaldo Brahn, perhaps the best-known Brazilian musician in Charlotte, plays weekly at a nearby seafood restaurant. This humble ethnic enclave contrasts with the other center of Brazilian social life in Charlotte, Chima—a Brazilian *churrascaria* restaurant on a prominent Uptown corner. Chima is one of the most expensive restaurants in the city, frequented by bankers and visiting businessmen for power lunches and expense-account client dinners for all-you-can-eat steak extravaganzas.

Once a month, Chima's upstairs cocktail lounge hosts Reinaldo Brahn and several members of his group, SoulBrazil, for a Friday night Brazilian party. For the first hour or two, Brahn plays solo guitar, singing *bossa nova* classics for the sparse audience of upper-middle-class businessmen grabbing a pre-dinner drink or fashionable couples out on a date. Later, groups of Brazilian men and women filter in, dressed casually but with flair, and grab tables near the music. Brahn is joined by his bandmates—a drummer and a percussionist playing a Brazilian tambourine—and they launch into *samba* covers. People get up to dance, and some of the tables are moved to the side. On occasion, a group might be celebrating someone's birthday and a cake is brought out with everyone singing "Happy Birthday" in Portuguese. Or some dancers from the local dance troupe Movimentos de Samba might emerge from a back room clad in carnival costumes—high heels, tiny miniskirts, bikini tops, and feathered headdresses—to lead the crowd in a dance.

During late 2009 and early 2010, Brazilian music also played a prominent role in a changing outlook within the Latin American Coalition and its cultural programs. In previous years, the Coalition had organized *tertulias*: sit-down events celebrating the culture of a particular Latin American country with folkloric dances, singers, and poetry readings. Due to funding cuts and staff downsizing, the *tertulias* were cancelled, and the nonprofit looked for a new model of cultural celebration that could bring in more revenue. Among the ideas that were being floated around in late 2009 was a Brazilian-themed event; Tony Arreaza, being an enthusiastic fan of *bossa nova* music, jumped on the idea and quickly found a few potential performers. The choice of Brazil as a focus was beneficial for other reasons as well. A Brazilian event could help publicize the Coalition's services and programs to a new demographic that knew little about the organization. Politically, by reaching out to the Brazilian community, the Coalition would show its inclusiveness and an expansion of what it meant to be "Latino" by including Luso-Brazilian culture in the fold.

The Latin American Coalition began organizing an event, entitled "A Night in Rio," that took place on a Thursday during the week of Brazilian Carnaval, at the Neighborhood Theatre in the Intown NoDa neighborhood. In contrast to the *tertulias*, this event was set up as a concert and dance party; although there would be interludes for cultural exhibitions, like a *capoeira* demonstration, most of the night would be dedicated to performances by musical and dance groups that would keep the audience on their feet. Revenues would be generated though participation by sponsors and vendors—a Brazilian corner market and a bakery sold food, Chima donated gift certificates—and through ticket sales for a "professional," well-produced event. Arreaza drew on his experience promoting events through the Spanish-language press and expanded this promotion to a local Portuguese-language newspaper. The imagery and timeliness of Brazilian Carnaval facilitated the promotion of the event to a wider non-Latino audience of white and black Charlotte residents. Press releases given to newspapers and posters placed around town featured photos of the dancers and linked Brazilian Carnaval to *samba*, partying, and experiencing what it might be like to spend a "night in Rio" without leaving Charlotte. In other words, unlike the *tertulias*, which to many in both the Coalition and the Latino community represented a sort of museum-ification of Latino culture, "A Night in Rio" promised authenticity and the vibrancy of contemporary Brazilian expressive culture that could bring in a wider audience.

The actual event achieved these goals, particularly by revealing the diversity and inclusiveness of Brazilian culture in Charlotte to non-Brazilians. Reinaldo Brahn's band, SoulBrazil, played two sets, with the opening set featuring Latin jazz, Brazilian popular music (MPB), and American R&B, and the closing set showcasing upbeat *samba* and *batucada*. Paulo and Ezio, another musical group, sang Brazilian country music to an audience of enthusiastic Brazilians and perplexed non-Brazilians who had never heard this genre of music before. Movimentos de Samba, the main Brazilian dance group, was led by Iya Silva, a dancer with family ties to Jamaica and Brazil. Many people expressed amazement to Arreaza afterwards—that these were local artists and that there was this unknown world of Brazilian music and dance in Charlotte.[11] The event raised money for the Latin American Coalition and became a brand, to be repeated annually and moved to a Saturday night, a more prominent night in the venue's schedule.

Conclusion

In this chapter I have analyzed the meaning of genre—as a set of rules and identifiable traits and as an expression of a community of taste

(Bourdieu 1984; White 2008)—in popular musical forms among Latino musicians in Charlotte. Genre comes to mean more than just a category of music; it also describes a method of performance, an ideology of culture, a representational product, and a philosophy of music making. At this point I would like to revisit the question from the end of chapter 3: What can genre tell us about the broader Latino experience in the U.S. South? First, in the context of labor vulnerability and the geographically segregated spaces of Charlotte's Latin music scene, genre reveals affiliations of nationality, class, language, and ethnicity in ways that foster belonging and feelings of community, but also separation and distinction from other musical communities. Second, Latino immigrants find agency through some elements of music making that are readily observable in genre (rhythmic patterns, instrumentation, song naming, language usage, dress, and so forth), while other elements are more subjective—say, the *feeling* that a good performance has. Notions of authenticity and legitimacy differ from within and between musical communities and reveal the unequal power relations between Mexican, Caribbean, and South American, documented and undocumented, dark-skinned and white Latinos. Third, the fact that among Latino musicians there is sometimes a wholesale dismissal of a genre—for example, a Latin rocker's incomprehension of *regional mexicano*—while in other instances, musicians are attempting to collaborate across genre points once again to the incompleteness of the project of formulating *latinidad* in Charlotte. Looking at genre reveals inconsistencies in Latino identity formation, particularly in ideology. Ultimanota is attempting to construct a new pan-American canon of popular music, yet its lead guitarist has an aversion to *regional mexicano*. Mexican musicians try to appeal to Dominican and Central American listeners, while still referencing the nationalist tropes that make their music distinctly Mexican. Leydy Bonilla states that her collaboration with Banda TecnoCaliente is "almost like a *merengue*," yet it does not inspire the same impassioned dancing that her other *merengues* do during live performances. And just like these genre inconsistencies, neither has the greater Latino population sorted itself out.

Perhaps this incompleteness is a positive development. One of the most important findings of this research has been that Latin genres in Charlotte follow new trajectories and form different permutations than in well-researched centers of Latin musical production like New York and Los Angeles. Although Latina/o musicians retain strong links to these musical centers and remain imbricated in musical conversations taking place there, they have created new spaces in Charlotte for explorations of what genre means. While globalization might lead one to believe that place no longer matters in music because of electronically downloaded music, Internet videos, and the demise of the dominance of major record labels as tastemakers, Charlotte's Latin music scene disrupts this conclusion. Latin genres in Charlotte grow out of a sense of place, of living on the Eastside and going to a club on Sunday night to dance to *regional mexicano*, of hanging out in NoDa and watching Bakalao Stars play a show at the Evening Muse, of dressing to the nines and going Uptown to dance *salsa* at Cosmo's Café, or taking the family to A Piece of Havana and requesting your favorite song from Ultimanota. When Tony Arreaza points to a guitar solo that has *feeling*, he is connecting Latin music to southern music—*southern* blues, rock and roll, rhythm and blues—that made the circuit through Latin America mixing with local forms to create the *rock en español* that he brought back to the U.S. South. Latin genres in Charlotte express a dialogue with the city, carving out spaces of performance and community, testing and negotiating genre boundaries, and determining what Latin music means in the U.S. South, or what it means to have southern Latin music.

7

Race and the Expanding Borderlands Condition

Francisco's Story

Occasionally, while I was hanging out with musicians between sets at the bar, talk would turn to how they immigrated to the United States. One particularly memorable narrative of passage came from Francisco, a pianist/keyboard player from Honduras who is a member of a local rock band.[1] As a teenager, Francisco left home for the United States. He first had to travel through Mexico, which in itself was a perilous journey. He spent several days riding buses and praying not to be caught by Mexican police searching for Central American migrants. To cross into the United States, his family had arranged passage with a *coyote*, or human smuggler. The *coyote* placed him in the luggage hold of a long-distance bus going to Charlotte, and Francisco remained hidden behind passengers' bags throughout the many hours' journey to the city. Once in Charlotte, he bunked with distant relatives and found odd jobs doing mostly manual labor. He began to form a sense of community with new friends he made playing music, eventually joining a band.

However, as an undocumented immigrant with brown skin and *mestizo* facial features, limited English, and little money, Francisco fears being caught up in a police checkpoint and being deported. Although he often travels to work sites during the day, he hesitates to drive at night and often asks a bandmate to pick him up or drive him home after a gig. Depending on the night, the musicians who drive him home might be documented or undocumented, but they speak better English and know alternate routes to avoid common police checkpoints, giving him some solace. He worries that one wrong turn or slipped phrase in broken English could spell the end of his time in Charlotte and thousands of dollars in smuggler's fees if he wanted to return to the United States. Francisco's precarious situation illustrates the race- (and class-) based discriminatory practices that undergird immigration policing in the U.S. South. In current anti-immigrant discourse, "illegal" and "Mexican" have become almost synonymous, with both taking on negative connotations through portrayals of working-class, brown-skinned immigrants as a threat to national integrity. Francisco embodies what it means to be "Mexican" in Charlotte (even though he is *hondureño*) because his immigration status, phenotype, and class place him in perpetual danger of arrest and deportation. However, as a musician, he uses personal connections to help avoid contact with police. Some immigrants are not so lucky. In this way, musicians show that they are somewhat more enabled members of the Latino population, using their experience and knowledge of nightlife to find their way home safely. By looking out for undocumented band members and friends, musicians also understand the fear and uncertainty that constitutes being "Mexican" in Charlotte, and they bring this empathy to their portrayals of *latinidad* in their music and performance. They also take time to think deeply about possible remedies to the situation of Latino immigrants to the city and the changing racial dynamics of the U.S. South.

A Race Problem

How does it feel to be a problem?
—W.E.B. Du Bois (1903)

The issue facing Latino immigrants in the U.S. South in the twenty-first century is not exactly the color line analyzed by W. E. B. Du Bois a century ago. Yet like African Americans at the turn of the last century (and, one could argue, still today), Latino immigrants also face the social and psychological burden of understanding their position as a racial problem. Latina/o immigrants, in particular undocumented individuals, but by association other Latinos, are cast as criminal, or what the anthropologist Jonathan Inda calls "problem elements in the social body" that constitute a major portion of the "hoards of anti-citizens" targeted by neoliberal policing regimes (Inda 2006). This is part of a larger essentialization of immigrants as the "other," savage or culturally backward (Silverstein 2005). Debates about immigration, particularly through dominant anti-immigrant discourses, take on a racialized and gendered tone that essentializes Latino immigration (by a pejorative usage of "Mexican"), correlates undocumented status with illegality (illegal means illegal), equates labor migration with invasion by foreign troops or malevolent pathogens, and stereotypes Latinas as hyperfertile and conspiring to subvert the U.S. Constitution (by giving birth to anchor babies). Moreover, this racialization takes on a sensory aspect as "Mexicans" are stereotypically seen as "dirty" and having a "smell" associated with their labor position (Holmes 2013). Paired with an expanding immigrant policing regime, this discourse makes up what Gilberto Rosas calls the "borderlands condition" that inscribes "exceptionality" (drawing on Agamben's idea of "state of exception" [2003]) on immigrant bodies through everyday violence and surveillance (Rosas 2006).

Scholars of the U.S.-Mexico border have long highlighted the region's exceptionality as a place of both lawlessness and expanding militarized policing, while also noting how regimes of racial, gender, and class exploitation help shape the political subjectivity of borderlands residents (Paredes 1958; McWilliams 1968; Montejano 1987; Peña 1985; Anzaldúa 1987; Limón 1994; Gaspar de Alba and Guzmán 2010). Informed by this scholarship, this chapter highlights how this legal exceptionalism has carried over to the treatment of Latino immigrants in other regions of the United States through the thickening of the borderlands condition (Rosas 2006) with the expansion of local immigration policing efforts. I argue that, in effect, the border has moved north, as local and state governments police immigrant communities using programs such as the 287(g) program, Secure Communities, and state laws passed in Arizona, Utah, Georgia, South Carolina, and Alabama. North Carolina has been at the forefront of implementing the 287(g) program, and the state government has expanded restrictions by prohibiting access by undocumented immigrants to driver's licenses and higher education. Under the Obama administration, deportations of undocumented immigrants have ratcheted up to around 300,000 per year, including large numbers of parents with children who are U.S. citizens.[2]

These policy changes mark new forms of social and structural racism, expressed in the racialization of Latina/o immigrants and the exceptionality of immigration enforcement seemingly exempt from civil rights oversight. The passage of anti-immigrant legislation in many southern states and the everyday policing of immigrant bodies through check-points, denial of public university admission, and refusal of access to social services for undocumented immigrants have led to a new southern landscape of Juan Crow (Lovato 2008). The U.S. South has responded to globalization by erecting a system of oppression for a new immigrant working class by marginalizing them through racial labeling, policing, social exclusion, and the delegitimation of their labor. Latina/o activists organizing to protest these conditions have mobilized mass marches and prominent actions, but face counterprotests, an entrenched class of policy makers who gain politically from targeting immigrant communities, and the failure of the federal government to construct a viable alternative to local devolution of immigration policy.[3] The immigration reform movement has been unable, nonetheless, to alter the increasing number of deportations, to fully rectify the status of the DREAM generation of undocumented students, or to exert pressure to alleviate the poor working conditions and wage theft suffered by immigrant laborers.

To understand the current racialization of Latino immigrants in the region, we must examine their plight in the context of the long history of racial segregation and violence in the U.S. South, along with the legacy of racism in Latin America from Spanish and Portuguese colonial race projects to the impact of U.S. imperialism. I briefly outline the U.S. history, and then turn to Latin America.

Despite portrayals of its monolithic and all-encompassing nature (in movies and popular novels), Jim Crow segregation varied in its implementation, legal apparatus, economic structures, and social dynamics from place to place in the U.S. South. Thus, the emergence of racially motivated terror squads and the construction of a revanchist legal and legislative system that marked the "Redemption" period of southern history occurred at varying speeds and degrees, starting with the drawdown of federal Reconstruction troops in the 1870s and intensifying with the codification of racial segregation in federal law with *Plessy v. Ferguson* in 1896 and in related state laws enforcing racial segregation enacted around the same time (Woodward 1971). Despite attempts to construct a "scientific" hierarchy of races with clearly defined and marked boundaries (greatly aided by anthropologists of the era), the ambiguity of a mixed-race individual's identity and the capricious definitions of whiteness state to state were at the heart of the *Plessy* case (Baker 1998; Dominguez 1993). The segregated labor regime of piedmont North Carolina differed greatly from those in the cotton plantations of the Mississippi Delta, the prison farms of Louisiana or East Texas, or the turpentine forests of Florida, though all resulted in inequitable and repressive regimes (Hurston 1990; Davis, Gardner, and Gardner 1988; Hall et al. 1987; Wade 2012). Segregation also developed not in opposition to modernity, but as part and parcel of a "New South" that wanted, like Henry Grady, to attract northern capital for segregated industry, or like Booker T. Washington, to attract northern philanthropy for segregated education.

The Civil Rights movement found its greatest success by revealing the shaky foundations of the segregation monolith and its relation to modernity: boycotting businesses to pressure business elites to acquiesce; questioning scientific racism as the basis for "separate but equal"; juxtaposing nonviolence with violent repression in an age of mass media (especially television) coverage; and continually pressing a reluctant federal government to intervene in the face of international embarrassment during the Cold War (Baker 1998; Branch 1989; Caro 2002). The varied nature of segregation was also evident in the uneven manner in which civil rights gains progressed, with relative ease in Charlotte and Atlanta, and with great resistance in Selma and Birmingham. The expansion of organizing efforts to housing segregation in northern cities made it obvious that racism was a national issue, and not just endemic to the U.S. South.

Unfortunately, in hindsight, the Civil Rights movement appears to have provided only a brief respite from the racial revanchism that southern whites have reasserted in recent decades. White flight from cities, expansion of private and charter schools, defunding of public transit, and hollowing out of affirmative action policies have all led to a more subtle but just as effective form of segregation (Smith 2010; Greenhaw 1982). Which is not to say progress has been stopped; African Americans have made real political, social, and economic gains in many places in the region. But what is troubling is the emergence through anti-immigrant laws and politics of a racialized other in "Mexican" and "illegal" immigrants that parallels the punitive spirit of Jim Crow laws that relegated blacks to second-class status.

The history of race thinking and racism in Latin America is as variegated, if not more so, than that of the United States. Because of the diversity of experiences, I will just discuss a few relevant examples here. The development of a Mexican national identity after the Mexican Revolution was built upon a philosophical intervention that promoted the cultural benefits of *mestizaje*, or the racial mixing of Spanish and indigenous roots to form the ideal Mexican national subject (Vasconcelos 1997). Although *mestizaje* challenged the racist philosophy of eugenics prevalent in the scientific community at the time by celebrating an interracial relationship (between Cortés and la Malinche) as the foundation of Mexican identity, it also relegated indigenous and Afro-Mexican communities to the margins of the nation-state (Hernández-Cuevas 2004). Only fairly recently, with examples like the Zapatista uprising in 1994 and the 2005 "Memín Pinguín" controversy over black print cartoon characters, have issues of indigenous and Afro-Mexican identity become prominent in national debates about Mexican culture (Hayden 2002; Krauze 2005; Global Voices 2005). This led to the Mexican government recognizing the need for land reform for indigenous communities and the role Afro-Mexicans played as the "third root" of Mexican identity. However, many indigenous and Afro-Mexican communities remain marginalized from mainstream Mexican culture and continue to face problems related to the breakup of communal lands and small holdings in the wake of economic liberalization under the North American Free Trade Agreement (NAFTA) (Hernández-Cuevas 2004; Vinson and Vaughn 2004; Lewis 2000).

The Dominican Republic undertook a national project of racial identification and gradation that had a similar effect of glossing over African heritage on the island. Under the dictator Rafael Trujillo, European and "Indian" identities were stressed in opposition to black and particularly Haitian identities (Sagás 2000). In 1937 Trujillo directed the massacre of an estimated twenty to thirty thousand Haitians working in the Dominican Republic and dark-skinned Dominican residents of areas near the Haitian border. Under a national identification card policy, mixed-race Dominicans were encouraged to stress their status as gradations of *indio* ("Indian"), such as *indio clarito, indio canelo,* or *indio quemao,* over terms that might reveal Afro-Caribbean identity. This had the effect of denigrating Afro-Dominican citizens and marginalizing their culture while highlighting a Eurocentric elite culture and an idealized indigenous past. Although Trujillo is long dead, the legacy of his national project lingers in subtle forms of racism and race thinking throughout the island and its diaspora in the United States (Howard 2001; Candelario 2007; Gregory 2006; Adams 2006).

Many of the Spanish-speaking nations of South America also have historically privileged European heritage and a Latin American concept of whiteness over indigenous and African heritage. However, unlike the stark Jim Crow system of the United States, Latin American societies perpetuated a racism that was based more on subtle gradations of perceived skin pigmentation, often accompanied by class distinction with the whitening of wealthier elites regardless of skin color, but also restricted access to certain industries and positions based on racial mores. However, social movements made up of indigenous and Afro-descendant groups have periodically made claims for greater inclusion, rights, and/or autonomy throughout the region's history, with particular success in the past few decades. The emergence of a transnational indigenous people's movement, along with organizing among Afro-descendant groups, has led to the enshrinement of specific rights and protections in the constitutions and policy frameworks of countries such as Ecuador, Bolivia, Venezuela, and Colombia (Tilley 2002; Hale 2002; Edelman 1999).

Brazil's "racial democracy" presents a related but somewhat divergent case in the region. The Portuguese colony was the largest importer of African slaves in the world; it also was the last slave-importing society in the Americas to outlaw slavery (1888). Brazil was also home to some of the most successful and long-lasting maroon colonies of escaped slaves. Brazil embarked on a twentieth-century racial project that encouraged mass immigration from Europe to whiten the population. However, an acknowledgment of widespread mixed-raced marriages led to the formation of an idea of national "racial democracy" that disavowed the overt racism of the United States or South Africa and attempted to clearly demarcate racial boundaries (even as the country eventually suffered under military dictatorship). But, as several scholars have pointed out (Telles 2004; Goldstein 2003; Twine 1997), Brazil's "racial democracy" also led to denials that racism was a problem in the country and the development of economic, educational, and political structures that favored richer, lighter-skinned citizens at the expense of the poor, Afro-descendant, and indigenous (all nonexclusive categories). By the end of military rule in the late 1980s, Afro-descendant and indigenous groups had begun a push for greater autonomy and rights that, while similar to efforts elsewhere in the region, evolved in response to specific laws meant to acknowledge the maroon *quilombo* and indigenous contribution to Brazil's "racial democracy" (French 2009).

Race in Charlotte

It is in the context of the history of racism and race thinking in the United States and Latin America that I now outline in more ethnographic detail the experience of Latina/o immigrants to Charlotte. I highlight three themes that came to the forefront during my time in the city: (1) how southern *latinidad*, particularly in music, informs how Latina/o immigrants see themselves as racial subjects—from claims of "Mexican" identity to notions of whiteness and blackness within the Latino community; (2) the detrimental effects of racial profiling in immigration policing and the geography of racism in Charlotte; and (3) how Latino residents see Charlotte, in the context of the U.S. South, as a haven from racism and a site for creating antiracist and nonracist community in the face of anti-immigrant oppression.

Southern *latinidad* informs how Latina/o immigrants see themselves as racial subjects because it is often tied into relationships that highlight perceived racial difference and experiences that crystallize a sense of marginalization from or incompatibility with mainstream American society. These relationships and experiences include connections and disconnections with other Latinos (where ethnic and cultural difference are stressed or elided) and with whites, African Americans, and Asian Americans (where racial difference is stressed more often but spaces occasionally open for interracial cooperation). Although by focusing on musicians I gathered data on only a small portion of the Latina/o immigrant population, because of their diversity they represent the racial experiences of Latinos in Charlotte. I was able to document their experiences as musicians performing in venues across town, but also through their various day jobs. Because I observed musicians playing several genres from different national backgrounds, I saw multiple sides of the Latino experience with race. Many Latinos I spoke with expressed befuddlement about their place within U.S. racial categories and often saw their identity connected more to nationality. Through interactions with the U.S. Census Bureau and other agencies asking demographic data questions, Latina/o immigrants were aware of how ill-fitting these racial categories were to their experience growing up in Latin America. Second-generation youth and immigrants brought here at a young age had the distinct experience of being accustomed to rigid racial categories, but finding themselves labeled "other." This meant that even though they felt "American," they did not belong to traditional southern racial classifications that hinged on being white or black.

I have outlined above how an expanding "borderlands condition" (Rosas 2006) in the form of immigration policing and anti-immigrant social policies has led to the framing of Latinos as a "problem." Perhaps the most insidious result of this shift has been the development of "Mexican" as a racial term. I define "Mexican" as a racial term because in anti-immigrant rhetoric and, indeed, in current popular linguistic usage it is deployed in ways that supersede a mere reference to nationality or national origin (Zavella 2011; De Genova 2005). Instead, "Mexican" has become a marker for brownness, "illegal" immigration status, indigenous facial features, working-class culture, perceived rurality, foreignness, and accented English. "Mexican" is used to describe the mass of immigrants, without actual concern for country of origin, so that many immigrants from El Salvador, Guatemala, Honduras, Nicaragua, Costa Rica, Ecuador, Peru, and elsewhere find themselves described thus, much to their chagrin. In 2008, high school students in Patchogue (Long Island), New York, who perpetuated a hate crime by stabbing to death an Ecuadorian immigrant, Marcelo Lucero, engaged in "Mexican hopping"—a sport of assaulting Latino men—and called their victim and his friend "Mexican" and "illegal" while beating them, even through the victims stated to their attackers that they were not Mexican.[4]

But the racialization of "Mexicans" extends beyond the actions of racist individuals into legal and political institutions that target immigrants. As several reports by the Southern Poverty Law Center have highlighted, the legal framework of immigration policing complements social animus toward Latinos and leads to a climate in which Latino immigrants in the U.S. South face widespread hostility, discrimination, and exploitation (Southern Poverty Law Center 2009, 2012). In the Charlotte case, the 287(g) program provides the most prominent example of this conjunction of social and legal targeting of immigrants through a racial lens—with dire results for families separated by the provision's enforcement.

The 1996 Immigration Act contained a provision, section 287(g), that gave local law enforcement agencies authority to enforce immigration law. This part of the legislation was not implemented for several years as the federal government focused on a buildup of border security and deportations of immigrants with prior criminal convictions. However, by the early 2000s, several local county and municipal governments began to clamor for the federal government to allow them to participate in immigration enforcement. The 287(g) program, as it became known, gave local law enforcement a period of training (usually a week or so) in immigration law and then gave them authority to carry out stops where a person without proper documentation could be turned over to federal immigration authorities. The former sheriff of Mecklenburg County (where Charlotte is located), Jim Pendergraph, was one of the most vocal advocates of the program and succeeded in signing the first agreement with the federal government to implement the 287(g) program in Mecklenburg County in February 2006. As of February 2012, the 287(g) program in Charlotte had resulted in the deportation of 11,480 undocumented immigrants, with the vast majority being Mexican (7,238) and Central American (3,573) (Prieto 2012).[5] In Charlotte and other places in North Carolina, 287(g) was presented as a strategy to fight crime; authorities stressed that only certain individuals would be targeted— violent criminals, gang members, and drunk drivers—while hardworking, law-abiding immigrants would have nothing to fear (Nguyen and Gill 2010). The implementation of 287(g) was paired with state legislation that cracked down on "illegal" immigration by restricting services, such as the ability to get a driver's license, for undocumented residents. Checkpoints were set up, in theory at random, by police at major intersections where drivers had to present identification. Police pulled drivers over for minor traffic violations, such as illegal turns or expired tags, and if they did not have a license, then they could be arrested and eventually deported. In practice, many people who were detained and eventually deported were nonviolent offenders or had no criminal record whatsoever.[6] The language of fighting crime bled into the idea that all undocumented immigrants were "illegal" and thus criminal.

During 2009–2010, the Spanish-language newspapers were filled with reports of families separated by enforcement of the 287(g) program. Many immigrant families in Charlotte have members with varying legal status. The father may be undocumented, the mother a legal resident, and the children U.S. citizens. News stories reported wives and partners who did not hear from their husbands for several days, only to find out that they had been detained and deported. In one case, a Charlotte resident, Roberto Medina Martínez, was arrested under the 287(g) program for driving without a license.[7] After being transferred to Stewart Detention Center, an immigration detention facility in Georgia run by Corrections Corporation of America, he fell ill, was denied medical care, and died. Medina left behind a family with young children, and his death sparked protests by immigration reform activists. Many community members I spoke with worried about driving on major thoroughfares or about family members and friends who drove without valid licenses. Among Latinos in Charlotte, it was a widely accepted fact that police mainly set up checkpoints in Latino and black, working-class neighborhoods and neglected wealthier and whiter areas such as South Park.

This mistrust of the police was exacerbated by a series of incidents that came to light in the spring of 2010. An African American officer of the Charlotte-Mecklenburg police was arrested after several Latino immigrant women complained that he had sexually harassed and assaulted them during traffic stops.[8] According to the women, the officer threatened to take them into custody or turn them over to immigration if they did not consent to his advances to have sex with them. The women were undocumented and feared that their accusations could lead to deportation. The local Spanish-language radio station and several prominent attorneys were instrumental in ensuring their safety during the investigation.

In the weeks after the arrest of the police officer, the Charlotte-Mecklenburg Police Department hosted a series of town hall meetings in immigrant neighborhoods around the city.[9] These meetings were an attempt to assure community members that steps were being taken to ensure that police misconduct would not be tolerated and to improve relations between immigrant communities and the police department. Attending an evening meeting at a church on Central Avenue, I sat in an audience of Latino and Asian immigrants as the police commissioner addressed the room. He introduced himself and then a row of about twenty officers standing behind him. Then the audience was split into two groups: English- and Spanish-speaking residents. I joined the Spanish-speaking group, where several bilingual officers were taking questions. No one brought up the accused officer, but several people asked about the 287(g) program. A few community members were concerned that the police department engaged in racial profiling of Latino residents, pulling neighbors and friends over and arresting them for drunk driving or having an expired license. While adamant that no racial profiling occurred, one officer flippantly responded that Latinos made profiling more likely by modifying their trucks with airbrushed Mexican flags and the names of their home provinces in Mexico. A Latina journalist who I ran into at the event remarked that the meeting reflected an ongoing public relations strategy that the department had engaged in for years and that nothing had really changed in terms of the antagonistic relationship between the Latino community and police.[10]

In addition to providing legal assistance to many families facing separation because of immigration policing, staff at the Latin American Coalition decided that more needed to be done to support these families and advocate on their behalf. The result was "Familias Unidas," a series of biweekly meetings where families, concerned community members, and activists from several local nonprofits meet to discuss issues related to ongoing cases.[11] The group provides a space where individuals facing deportation can tell their stories and receive emotional support from others facing similar situations. As "Familias Unidas" got off the ground, the heart-wrenching stories shared during sessions became part of online campaigns led by the Coalition and Action NC to gather petition signatures against their deportations. The group also organized rallies that gathered community support and focused attention (particularly press coverage) on individuals' cases and the fact that their deportation would leave children and spouses alone in the United States. In one prominent case, Isaide Serrano, a Mexican immigrant with six children, who was detained during a traffic stop in 2010 after living for twenty-one years in the United States with no criminal record, was required by a judge to attend her immigration hearing even though it was scheduled for five hours after she gave birth in a Charlotte hospital.[12] She ended up being granted a stay as the judge cancelled her deportation order.

Another result of "Familias Unidas" was the production of a full-length documentary film, *From the Back of the Line* (Shearer, Levinson, and Bellmas 2013), which highlights the stories of several of the families participating in the group. As Armando Bellmas, one of the producers of the film and communications director at the Coalition, relayed, the individuals featured in the film are "normal people like me, but going through this 'thing.'"[13] After several sessions he attended, Armando found himself more invested in the families' lives; he began to see them not just as clients, but as friends. He helped make the film so that their stories, and those of hundreds of other families whose situation isn't publicized, get told. After premiering in May 2013, the movie has been shown at several regional film festivals. But what has become evident to the filmmakers is the need to update the film as deportation cases drag on and shifts in immigration policy—such as pending federal immigration reform—occur.

Taken together, the cases highlighted by Charlotte's Spanish-language newspapers, "Familias Unidas," and *From the Back of the Line* reveal the extent to which immigration policing has taken on a racial pallor and punitive tone. It seems no coincidence that many of the individuals caught up in deportation proceedings because of traffic stops are brown-skinned Mexicans and Central Americans (I met several lighter-skinned Mexicans who did not face such police scrutiny). Moreover, the political marginalization and social denigration of "Mexicans" have created a climate where a black police officer feels he can take sexual advantage of immigrant women with impunity. Was this just one bad apple, or does it point to a larger uneasiness in black-brown relations in Charlotte?

Although the immigration reform movement has fostered ties with national groups like the NAACP, local collaborations between Latino and African American activists are feeble. The Latin American Coalition has partnered with a few black churches to host immigration reform rallies, but a broader coalition appears stunted. Many immigrant activists speak of the Civil Rights movement with reverence; they are inspired by nonviolent tactics like sit-ins and have co-opted strategies to organize protest and marches from the earlier movement. On Facebook and other social networking sites, activists share Civil Rights movement–era texts like Martin Luther King Jr.'s "Letter from a Birmingham Jail" (1963) as a way to instill pride and confidence in activists who get arrested during sit-ins in Washington, DC. Despite the parallels between the tactics of civil disobedience, student leaders point out that immigration reform is not the "civil rights" issue of our time because they acknowledge that the Civil Rights movement is ongoing—particularly with recent reversals to the Voting Rights Act, prominent cases of structural violence targeting black youth (such as New York City's stop-and-frisk policy), and a disproportionately incarcerated population. In addition, many immigration activists point to other sources of inspiration, such as the women's rights and gay rights movements, or the Chicano student movement and labor struggles of the United Farm Workers. Yet the message of solidarity for immigration reform seems unconvincing to many African Americans in Charlotte. Despite the support of some community leaders, few African Americans participate as rank-and-file marchers in immigration reform rallies. And despite outward appearances, many Afro-Latinos in Charlotte feel little solidarity with black residents, instead focusing their community-making efforts in collaboration with fellow Latinos, particularly Mexicans. However, solidarity does appear to be growing between Latino activists and Vietnamese and Laotian immigrants. Members of the Asian immigrant community recently founded the Southeast Asian Coalition to help advocate for individuals facing deportation and police profiling similar to those in the Latino population. As a small nonprofit, it shares office space and logistical support with the Latin American Coalition and has collaborated in organizing marches to advocate for reform.

So what does being "Mexican" in Charlotte mean? I place the term in quotation marks because of the ambiguity and shifting meaning of the term as it is deployed by whites, blacks, and Latinos. (Actual) Mexican immigrants in Charlotte approach their Mexican identity with pride but apprehension. They proudly display Mexican flags and retain linguistic and cultural ties to Mexico, while asserting a diasporic identity through Mexican institutions and businesses in Charlotte. But they are well aware of the negative perceptions of "Mexicans" in the United States and worry about how to become "American" in a place where their labor is welcome but their culture and language are not. Two contrasting examples highlight this ambiguity. At the Fanta Festival, *regional mexicano* bands play to enthusiastic audiences who display their Mexican identity proudly through flags, cowboy hats with Mexican state names etched in the hatbands, and call-and-response *gritos* between the band and audience. At immigration reform marches, however, great care is taken to de-stress Mexican (and other Latin American national) identity: marchers are asked to display only U.S. flags and to wear uniform outfits (such as white T-shirts). March organizers stress the "American" qualities of Latino immigrants: DREAM students who were brought here as children and didn't know that being undocumented would disqualify them from college, families with U.S. citizen children who face separation because of deportation proceedings, hard workers looking for a path to citizenship. Though starkly different, these two examples show the delicate balancing act that many Mexican (and Latina/o) immigrants live daily—a duality of being Mexican and becoming American, part of both worlds.

I have observed yet another layer of complexity in this duality. Some non-Mexican Latino immigrants feel a strong solidarity with Mexicans and look to some aspects of Mexican identity as a way to explain their precarious situation as working-class immigrants, in effect becoming "Mexican"—at least through performance or friendship. Since being "Mexican" has taken on a negative connotation in Charlotte, these individuals differ markedly from the many Latinos who move to disassociate themselves from cultural markers of *mexicanidad*, such as several Charlotte musicians' distaste for *regional mexicano*. The most prominent example of solidarity with Mexicans is the rock band Dorian Gris (see chapter 3). The Ecuadorian musicians in Dorian Gris, through friendships, musical performances, and their experiences laboring in service sector occupations, have developed a deep association with urban Mexican working-class culture and feel a powerful responsibility to properly convey this sense to their (primarily Mexican) audience. The concept of *el sueño gris*, which I have borrowed from Dorian Gris's incomplete dream of becoming a successful band, conveys the haltered ambitions of a generation of Latino immigrants to Charlotte who have encountered limitations to their financial and social integration into the U.S. mainstream. That Latina/o immigrants are becoming "Mexican," with its associated negative connotations, shows a further evolution of the "graying" dream: with pathways to citizenship clogged and immigrants criminalized, some Latinos look to "Mexican" identity as an oppositional frame to mainstream American and whitening Latino identities.

The importance of being "Mexican" in Charlotte is part of a context where musicians hold discussions and engage in musical collaborations that position them in relation to emerging racial constructions as part of southern *latinidad*. Carlos Crespo, the lead guitarist of Dorian Gris, struggles with the cognitive dissonance of his multiple racial and ethnic affiliations. While he identifies strongly with his Mexican friends and fans, as a light-skinned Ecuadorian of middle-class background, Crespo also participates in debates about whiteness and *latinidad*. Crespo struggles to define his identity in a U.S. urban context where race and class are paramount. His phenotype and middle-class upbringing in Ecuador facilitate friendships with "white" Latinos who frequent coffee shops, listen to indie rock, and attend art gallery openings. Yet Crespo also performs shows in Eastside venues with Dorian Gris, hangs out at his friends' homes in working-class apartment complexes, and tries to make ends meet as a poorly paid worker. Although many immigrants pointed out the incompatibility of Latin American and U.S. concepts of race, stressing their hybrid *latinidad* over a particular racial category, Crespo attempts to resolve the contradictions of a lived reality of race as a Latino immigrant in Charlotte through his questioning of whiteness and affiliation with *mexicanidad*.

Bakalao Stars' 2010 album, *Soundcocho*, provides an example of black-brown collaboration through its recording of "Gitana" with the local reggae singer Ras Congo, a Jamaican immigrant to Charlotte. Christian Anzola, the band's drummer, had played previously with Ras Congo in the band Roots Essentials. In an interview with Bakalao Stars and Ras Congo backstage before the album release party, I asked them what it was like to record a song together.[14] A song by the Argentine band Los Fabulosos Cadillacs was on the stereo, and Ras Congo started by declaring the common threads between Jamaican reggae and Los Fabulosos' music. Then he explained how even though Bakalao Stars' members were from a different culture, they had the "same heart." When he started to rehearse for the album and subsequent live performances, Ras Congo noticed how the band put "spirit in [making music]," how they weren't just showing off, but putting "soul in it" and forming a bond through music. For their part, Bakalao Stars members noted how collaborating with Ras Congo brought their music to a different level, not only through his intensive knowledge of reggae and ska music, but also by spreading "good vibes" with his enthusiastic presence. The intent of the album was to show how "Caribbeans" (by which they mean both Spanish- and English-speaking islanders) and Latinos share musical "feeling" and "flavor." While the collaboration with Ras Congo acknowledged and maintained the band's connection to Afro-Caribbean "roots" music, the album's artwork presented a pan-Latino image of the brightly decorated buses common in many Latin American countries flanked by audio speakers and pictures of the band members. According to the band, the album's music was meant to reflect this pan-Latino theme through its mixture of genres and rhythms. Thus, *Soundcocho* was a way to stay true to the band's Afro-Caribbean roots through its collaborations, while also exploring themes related to being Latino in Charlotte by juxtaposing Latin American musical styles.

The problem of race in the larger Charlotte music scene is central and vexing. As we have seen, even within the Latin music scene stark geographic segregation keeps musicians and fans in the dark about developments in parallel genres (chapter 3). The divisions between the Latin music scene and other scenes catering to whites and African Americans is oftentimes just as sharp; there is a general ignorance about what is going on in a different musical community—or even on a different night at the same club. As an outside observer, I travelled between these different worlds with relative ease, but it appears that most residents of Charlotte fail to traverse these social boundaries. One limitation, in the opinion of musicians and promoters of all races, seems to be the underdeveloped music scene in general, particularly in relation to Charlotte's size as a metropolitan area. A recent article in the *Charlotte Observer* (Reed 2013) mirrored what I often heard stated by Latino musicians: that Charlotte was not a primary destination for touring bands, and the lack of consistent concerts hurts local musicians too. Another limitation seems to be a dearth of radio stations playing local music, unlike smaller cities like Chapel Hill, Asheville, or Athens, Georgia, which have prominent college radio stations. But ignorance of what is out there, especially when segmented media of Spanish- and English-language radio and newspapers only cover limited genres of music, makes the music scene appear more parochial than it really is. Certain journalists, promoters, and organizations have made efforts to change this—*Creative Loafing Charlotte*'s coverage of Latin music under the editorship of Mark Kemp or the Latin American Coalition's marketing campaign for "A Night in Rio"—but overall it seems this type of music exchange has stalled.

Although Charlotte's Latino population has an antagonistic relationship with local police, highlighted by high-profile incidents such as those above, many musicians stressed the relative tranquility of Charlotte. In their experience, fewer examples of racism and discriminatory behavior toward Latinos occurred in Charlotte than in other places, particularly rural areas in nearby states. Some of this perceived lack of racism could be attributed to personal factors that differentiate musicians from the general Latino community—higher rates of legal status, bilingualism, access (to clubs, backstage areas), higher income levels, and increased visibility—leading to fewer individual experiences of racist behavior. Also, musicians may tend to downplay portrayals of local racism because they want to put a positive spin on their involvement in the music scene in Charlotte. The grass is sometimes greener at home; everyday forms of racism may not be as recognizable or mentionable as more blatant examples of overt racist behavior that some musicians reported having experienced elsewhere. This perception of Charlotte as a relative haven from racism and discrimination aimed at Latinos contributes to a sense of civic pride and belonging that some musicians express for the city and for Latino community institutions like the Latin American Coalition. For example, during an interview conducted in Spanish, the local music promoter Gonzalo Pérez launched into an intriguing monologue when asked about his experience with racism in the U.S. South:

> In Charlotte, there really isn't that much racism . . . there are one, two or three [cases of racism], but look, places we have gone to: Virginia, Ohio. Wow, I could tell you some stories about that! . . .
>
> I'm going to tell you one experience, my own experience. We went to Tennessee, came to a McDonald's, and I stepped off, well, I have black features—and when the guys got off the bus, the people who were there started mocking us and in the McDonald's, the area where we sat emptied out, everybody changed their seat. We didn't eat, we left and got out of there, and five minutes later the police stopped us, [asking,] "What were you doing in that McDonald's, where did you come from, and where are you going?" And they searched the bus inside and out, they searched everything top to bottom. That was an act of racism.

Yes, I eventually told the police officer let us go because I began to have strong words with him. I said, "I'm going to make a claim of racial discrimination, because you are doing something unjust." And that was the only reason he let us go.[15]

In recounting the experiences he has had traveling with Banda TecnoCaliente around the U.S. South and Midwest, Pérez contrasts Charlotte as a relative haven from racism compared to Virginia or Ohio, where he perceives racist behavior to be much more prevalent. Pérez's account has an air of bravado: as someone who speaks passable English, is secure in his legal status, and is in charge of the band, he confronted the police officer and threatened to make a complaint. He becomes an advocate for the Mexican band members, drawing on a body of experience traveling with previous bands to resolve the situation and get the band on the road again. As a touring band, TecnoCaliente sees such experiences with racism as part of the risk of traveling. They endure and even resist such hardships—actions that help them deepen their understanding of the experience of mobile and migratory immigrant laborers who make up their main audience.

Continuing with his commentary, Pérez goes into greater detail about how he envisions Latino immigrants as belonging to the city of Charlotte:

But here, at least in Charlotte really [racism] has mostly stopped, which is why it's peaceful. The American that can give you a hand gives you one. Like the Mexicans say, the *gabacho* gets along well with us.

I'm one of those who advises the Mexicans to work for [the benefit of] the state: "Don't send all your money to Mexico, it's a mistake, keep some of it here."

Mexicans earn one hundred dollars, and send ninety to Mexico. [Instead,] invest in your city, [a city] that gives you schools, gives you help, your children have good hospitals, they have everything, so invest here. Mexicans are really good [people], good laborers . . . if one invests here, they [the city] will give them more support, the institutions are going to back them with more force, and say, "Look, she is illegal, but she bought a house, he is paying taxes to the government, he is illegal but his children are professionals, he has a car and pays taxes." Understand? If we did all that, if we didn't blow it in wanting to only take from the city, and not invest, the city would go to pieces.

We have to take money and reinvest it in the city. I, the Dominican that I am, sold all my properties in my country and I am concentrating here. I take here and I spend here. I'm not able to just take and not spend. What would be left of the city? It's like if you work and work and they don't pay you [*laughs*], you will die. This happens with a city, the city has to be cared for—you have to fight for this city because the people owe it. It's not as if everybody is not giving, there are many who help, here people, the Mexican knows that if your child is born here, you have help with your [WIC] coupons, your Medicaid, the house here where we are at [Latin American Coalition] helps people a lot, with [learning] English, if one needs a lawyer they will look for one for you, because they invest in you here, we are going to work for [the benefit of] the city. That's the only thing that I don't approve of in our community, and not only, I say, it's more Mexicans than others. They are the majority [of Latinos] here.[16]

Pérez's commentary becomes an analysis of the relationship between the Latino immigrant community and the nation-state. In a somewhat stereotypical and chauvinistic manner, he advises Mexicans to be strategic about using their money, by investing in Charlotte and their local community rather than sending remittances back to Mexico. If "illegal" immigrants stake a claim to belonging in the city and invest as community members in its well-being (financially and socially) through legitimate, above-board activities like paying taxes, owning property, and having children who are "professionals" (i.e., well-educated, English-speaking, with middle-class jobs in the formal economy), then the institutions of the state (and civil society organizations like the Latin American Coalition) will be more likely to acknowledge that immigrants have a stake and say in the city's future.[17]

What is intriguing about Pérez's argument is the way it positions Mexicans and the Latino immigrant community as political actors who have important decisions to make that will determine their future. Opposing both advocates of harsher immigration laws and immigrants who themselves desire a transnational existence, Pérez advances a *realpolitik* that acknowledges what is already fact—that most Latino immigrants to Charlotte are unlikely to return to their native countries and have

strong ties to community in the city.[18] Despite recent legislation targeting undocumented immigrants, mass deportations are improbable for
economic and political reasons. Although immigration has slowed and
some migrants have returned to their sending countries during the recent economic recession (Papademetriou, Sumption, and Terrazas 2011;
Passel and Cohn 2011), most immigrants already in the United States
have decided to stay, for steadier work, because they have children who
are U.S. citizens, or because the border crossing is too perilous and expensive. These trends have contributed to place-based community formation, even among immigrants who were formerly very mobile, such
as migrant workers who decide to move to cities such as Charlotte for
more regular work.

The state as it exists along multiple scales (city, county, state, and federal) plays a major part in this politics around immigration. Although
much of the publicity focuses on actions that are anti-immigrant, such
as recent legislation passed in Arizona, Utah, and Georgia that targets
undocumented immigration, in reality, the state should be seen as en-
compassing multiple interests that at time pursue complementary and
contradictory paths. Much of the vitriol and anti-immigrant legislative efforts have centered on the rights of immigrants to participate in
government-funded, -regulated, or -mandated activities that signal participation in society, such as driver's licenses, public education, benefits
to the poor, and above-board employment. Yet while police and regula-
tory agencies may curb undocumented immigrants' rights to these activities, other government agencies, such as health, human services, or
education, may include undocumented immigrants in activities, either
through the participation of family members who are legal residents or
U.S. citizens (particularly, U.S.-born children) or participating directly
despite their undocumented status because of federal antidiscrimination mandates (such as for public primary education). The work of the
state to include undocumented immigrants acknowledges their de facto
membership in the community, city, and state, even if legally their role
is circumscribed.

In another light, Pérez's argument provides a critique of neoliberalism
and its negative effects on cities. This corresponds to the pervasiveness
of market ideology in current political thinking, and the ways people
fashion political speech on the local scale (see Holland et al. 2007). The

disinvestment in urban infrastructure and social services that first came to a head in the 1970s in New York City's fiscal crisis (O'Connor 1973; Harvey 1973, 1989; Gordon 1978; Susser 1982) is described succinctly: "What would be left of the city?," in relation to what could happen in Charlotte. However, rather than see this collapse as a result of governmental austerity and structural adjustment, Pérez sees it as a consequence of individuals shirking their civic duty to reinvest in their local government (through paying taxes), neighborhoods, and civic institutions. Immigrants are responsible for their own well-being and that of the city. Interestingly, recent studies of several U.S. cities lends support for the idea that immigration (spurring ethnic entrepreneurship and immigrant consumption) and concurrent population growth has been a major (if not *the* major) source of economic growth, particularly in places with declining or aging native-born populations (Fayde 2007; Michigan Future 2003; Fiscal Policy Institute 2009). As Pérez's argument develops, he turns to a decidedly anti-neoliberal stance on the role of the state: government agencies have provided social benefits to the immigrant community, therefore immigrants should pay taxes and fight for a government that erects more of a social safety net and expands rights and access for all.

Conclusion

Over fifty years after Martin Luther King Jr.'s "I Have a Dream" speech at the March on Washington, the United States still faces problems of racial inequality and injustice. Despite the gains of the Civil Rights movement, places like Charlotte face a retrenchment of racial segregation in housing and schools and the emergence of new forms of racism against immigrants and other minorities. The racial project of the contemporary South is one of "racism without race" (Mullings 2005; Doane and Bonilla-Silva 2003) that couches discriminatory practices and bigotry in the language of law and order—targeting immigrants because of their "illegality" and perceived-to-be inassimilable culture. The vehemence of anti-immigrant activism and the apparatus of immigration enforcement efforts create a revanchist atmosphere where families are separated, neighborhoods are on lockdown, and people fear traveling across town or out of state. This "borderlands condition" that exempts Latino immigrants (and in other places African and Middle Eastern immigrants) from fair treatment and a right to livelihood— part of an "exceptional" state that has long existed on the U.S.-Mexico border (Rosas 2006; Inda 2006)—has now spread to cities and small towns across the United States that face an immigration "problem." That immigration is a problem—causing overcrowded public schools, traffic fatalities, low-wage job competition, or a loss of "American" values— speaks to the pervasiveness of this racial project. However, like the onset of Jim Crow segregation, this developing system is incomplete and uneven, and thus can be challenged and even defeated. Will the problem of the twenty-first century be the problem of a brown color line?

For Latino immigrants to Charlotte, dealing with race has meant pursuing two parallel and intertwined strategies. First, they have created a sense of southern *latinidad* that, while developing as part of an ethnic identity, exists in concert with an awareness of race and racism in both Latin America and the U.S. South. Searching for a pan-Latino identity can be seen as a response to the general denigration of Latino immigrants, a way to form community as immigrants in a new place, or an extension of already nascent connections between outward-looking people from their home countries. But for many immigrants, being Latino in Charlotte also means being southern, and by expressing this identity they stake a claim to belonging to the region and the nation. Second, because of the specific targeting of "Mexicans" in anti-immigrant rhetoric and policy, Latinos in Charlotte assess race through the prism of how they position themselves in relation to being "Mexican." As we have seen, being "Mexican" does not always mean one is a Mexican national, but rather that one identifies with the racial, social, and economic marginalization that now accompanies the term.

Music plays a vital role in southern *latinidad*, both because of the representational qualities of genre that distill identity into performance and aesthetics and because of the power music has to help audiences form a sense of solidarity and community. Because of their experiences touring outside Charlotte, many musicians see the city as a haven from other, more racist areas of the U.S. South. Music also can be a pathway to interracial collaboration, as the case of Bakalao Stars partnering with Ras Congo demonstrates. Music is part of a larger dream they share with their audience of interracial harmony and opportunity for aspiring immigrants like themselves. However, as I argue in this chapter and else-where in this book, the dream has been graying because of the harshness of immigration policing, economic stagnation, and social segregation in the city.

Political organizing, such as the campaigns led by the Latin American Coalition, has arisen in response to the anti-immigrant climate and racialization of "Mexicans" in Charlotte. "Familias Unidas" deals with the aftermath of racial profiling in immigration policing by counseling families on legal questions and providing emotional support. DREAM activists confront authorities head-on through marches and sit-ins at politicians' offices. Both types of campaigns provide avenues for identity formation, but also have to deal with the question of race. Through political organizing there is much potential—to galvanize a generation of young activists to pursue a lifetime of advocacy and public service, to bridge organizational divides between Latino immigrant groups and other immigrant activists, to provide a balm for the anxiety and hurt of potential family separations, or to provide powerful narratives that will encourage support across racial lines for immigration reform and the social integration of immigrants into the mainstream. But as chapter 5 shows, many musicians and other Latino residents of Charlotte find overt political participation to be problematic. It remains to be seen whether musicians and political activists can find a way to overcome skepticism and hesitancy on the part of many to participate in what appears to be a lengthy struggle.

8

The Festival

Marketing Latinidad

Latino cultural festivals in Charlotte play a vital role in showcasing music, dance, and art while also giving corporations and local businesses an enthusiastic audience to market their products and services. This chapter analyzes the significance of the Latino cultural festival in relation to the production of southern *latinidad*, while also examining how festivals are essential to the process through which Charlotte's Latina/o musicians forge global connections through interactions with visiting musicians and promoters. In the first section, I provide a behind-the-scenes look at how Latino festivals are organized and the relationship between organizers and corporate sponsors. The logistics of music at festivals—that is, who decides which bands play and when and for how long they play—highlights the contingent nature of musicians' labor, but also their irreplaceable role as bearers of cultural capital. Festivals build upon the irreplaceable work musicians do forming community around music making in the local setting of the club, creating culturally "authentic" expressions that can then be inserted into a commodified festival presentation.

Enterprising musicians have used their participation in Latino cultural festivals to expand their social network to include internationally touring and often famous musicians. In the second section of the chapter, I explain how these global connections allow musicians to "jump scales" (Smith 1992) and create opportunities for their bands to tour, promote their music online through social media, or advance other creative projects such as filmmaking. However, not every musician succeeds in turning backstage friendships into something beneficial for his or her band, and there are gatekeepers that at times prevent musicians from accessing pathways to promoting their music at a larger scale.

The third section of this chapter critically examines how festivals at times produce a distorted and inaccurate picture of *latinidad*, while paying close attention to the structural and organizational limitations that influence this presentation. I argue that Latino festivals in Charlotte are sites of contestation where different groups negotiate over competing notions of what it means to be Latino, Mexican, Latin American, immigrant, and American. In addition, festivals contribute to a broader process of the commercialization and marketing of Latino identity, what might be termed, after Arlene Dávila (2012), Latin Music Inc. I situate Latino cultural festivals in the context of ongoing attempts to define (and sometimes redefine) what Latino culture is for commoditization. Musicians are well aware of this process going on around them and often provide a critical voice that questions its end result.

Latino Cultural Festivals

Latinos in Charlotte gather to attend festivals where they listen to music, watch dancers perform, enjoy food, and make the rounds at the tents of corporate sponsors. In this chapter, I examine the festival using a multifocal lens that passes through the viewpoint of artists (musicians and dancers), festival organizers, attendees, vendors, and corporate sponsors. While the outward appearance of a festival often approaches the carnivalesque, behind the scenes a regimented structure ensures that the event runs smoothly. These festivals attract thousands of attendees, including many members of the various musical communities I have outlined, and are often the result of months of planning by festival organizers and cultural brokers to recruit musicians, sign up sponsors, arrange logistics, and promote the festival through local media. Much of this analysis stems from my involvement in organizing three major festivals with the Latin American Coalition, starting with the 2009 Festival Latinoamericano, through the 2010 Cinco de Mayo Fanta Festival, and ending in the 2010 Festival Latinoamericano.[1] I also returned to Charlotte as a guest to attend several festivals in 2011–2013. The main focus of this chapter, the Festival Latinoamericano, is the culmination of a festival season that for Latinos stretches from late spring to early autumn. During some months, there are minor festivals and other outdoor events every weekend. These might include celebrations such as

Bolivian Independence Day, Parranda Venezolana, or a *jaripeo* (Mexican rodeo). For my research, I participated in the festivals' planning stages, worked as a stage manager during the events, and archived much of the festival by collecting promotional materials, photographs, video, and field notes. In addition to this work, I attended several other festivals, including Carnaval Carolina 2010 and El Grito 2010 as an observer, where I chatted with organizers, musicians, and audience members, took photos, and noted the layout, musical lineup, and general atmosphere of the events.[2]

Festival Latinoamericano

The 2010 Festival Latinoamericano begins on a Sunday morning with a torrent of preparations: trucks dropping off boxes and banners in front of sponsors' tents, sound checks, city officials arriving to inspect food vendors' equipment, volunteers directing traffic, nonprofit staff counting money boxes for beverage sales, and everyone waiting in anticipation of the rush of a long and stressful day. Backstage, I arrange couches and tables, and lay out all the food and drinks for the artists. I start calling bands to make sure they are on their way to the festival grounds and to remind them where to unload their equipment. There are two stages, one for live music and the other for dance performances, on each end of the festival grounds. In between are sponsors' tents, an aisle of food vendors, local artists and craft vendors selling their wares, and lawn for attendees to stand or set up chairs to sit and listen to music. The gates open and festival-goers start filtering into the grounds. The opening band, Rhythm +, plays a set of instrumental Latin jazz numbers to virtually no audience, as festival-goers have yet to make it around the grounds. By the time it finishes, a small group has assembled, and the *merengue* singer Leydy Bonilla croons "The Star-Spangled Banner" while a local recruiting post of the U.S. Army provides the flag corps. The next group, Bakalao Stars, plays ska and rock songs as some of its usual crowd cheers it on. Next, Orquesta GarDel, a band from Raleigh/Chapel Hill, plays classic *salsa* and *son montuno* numbers. Then SoulBrazil, a local Brazilian group, performs *bossa nova*, *samba*, and Brazilian rock.

At a smaller stage at the other end of the festival grounds, the dance stage begins to feature performances by local dance troupes. Many families come to the festival just to see their son or daughter perform as part of a *ballet folklórico*. Parents clamor for the best spots by the stage to snap photos. Troupes made up of children as young as five, teenagers, and middle-aged adults take the stage in riotously colorful costumes and perform *jarabe tapatío*, "La Bruja," and other traditional Mexican dances. Later a group of *salsa* dancers will step out for a well-choreographed ballroom-style performance.

Back at the main stage, between bands, the emcees, Sendy and Helen, take the stage and make jokes. They introduce sponsors, who send representatives onstage to talk about deals, give away free T-shirts, or announce raffle winners. Meanwhile, the stage manager, musicians, and volunteers rush to move amplifiers, tune instruments, check microphone sound levels, and get the next band ready to start its performance. If there is a delay, I give a signal to Sendy and he keeps talking, asking what countries people in the crowd are from, or telling another joke. Once everything is ready, the emcees get the crowd excited for the next band and the music starts.

Elastic Bond is the next group to take the stage; it is from Miami and plays electronic, funk, and pop styles. The crowd gives its eclectic mix of music a polite but unenthusiastic reception. The following band, also from Miami, is Locos por Juana. It plays a mix of *cumbia* and reggae in a danceable style and features a charismatic lead singer. By the last hour, when the headlining band, Plena Libre, from Puerto Rico, is due to go onstage, the crowd has reached its peak. An enthusiastic contingent of *puertorriqueños* gathers in front of the stage waving Puerto Rican flags. The band plays *bomba* and *plena*, traditional Puerto Rican African-derived rhythms that are precursors to *salsa*, but with a contemporary flair. A call-and-response pattern develops as the lead singer calls out a question, "¿Qué te pasa a ti?"(What's happening with you?), and the audience answers, "Aaaahhhhhhh!" The sun is going down and the temperature cools; the audience presses closer and dances to the encouragement of the band. The singers step to the front of the stage and get everyone in the audience jumping and shaking to the beat. The performance builds to a crescendo, ending with several encores. As the crowd disperses, some fans find their way onstage to congratulate the band, to mention their hometowns in Puerto Rico, and to take pictures with them.

Plena Libre headlines the 2010 Festival Latinoamericano

In many ways, a festival is organized chaos. For festival organizers, the trick is to manage what at times feels like an out-of-control freight train barreling down the tracks. It helps if the vision for how the event should go is well-planned and flexible enough to deal with the series of unforeseen yet inevitable circumstances that arise to derail a festival—rain, late bands, poor turnout, or failing food inspections. It takes months of groundwork to prepare for an event that is over in a matter of hours. As I have explained elsewhere (Byrd 2012), manufacturing the festival experience involves extensive planning over many months and the hard work of poorly paid staff and gracious volunteers. Here, I focus on the musical and financial aspects of this organizing process to understand what values are expressed through the festival and how the festival relates to Charlotte's Latino musical communities.

It's January and in a windowless office at the Latin American Coalition, the event manager, Tony Arreaza, and I are brainstorming about the 2010 Festival Latinoamericano.[3] The festival is ten months away, but bands are already beginning to solidify tour dates for the summer and fall. We are trying to find a headliner from out of town to fill the prime slot. For several years, the festival has featured a lineup with a mixture of two or three out-of-town bands (with one major headliner) and several local bands. The headliner helps draw in more people who pay the five-dollar entry fee, funds that go to support the nonprofit's programs. Thus it is imperative to choose someone who will appeal to a broad swath of people, both Latinos and non-Latinos. Arreaza takes pride in selecting a headliner that makes a statement about his musical taste as a musician and concert promoter. Over several days, we throw names back and forth. If we are unfamiliar with someone, we watch YouTube videos or search for the artist's website. Some of the names are promising, but too costly to bring to perform in Charlotte. Others have performed recently in town, either at a festival or at a local music venue; we don't want to repeat what has been done before. Still other bands do not appear to be touring, or are not journeying through the United States this year.

After narrowing down our list to a manageable number of artists, we make initial contact with their managers or agents, feeling out how receptive they might be to performing at the festival. This is a tenuous and somewhat frustrating process, mainly because of the financial limitations of the festival budget, but also because Charlotte is not seen as a marquee city for Latino acts. The total budget Arreaza has to pay all the bands for the festival is around fifteen thousand dollars, which is less than many major acts charge for a single performance. Some bands want a guaranteed amount to perform, but also want the festival to pay airfare, which can add thousands of dollars to the budget. We have to choose between booking one major act and having no money left over for other bands, or booking lesser-known bands and having enough to pay everyone. Also, some bands do not seem that interested in coming to Charlotte, or are surprised to learn of the festival and the fact that there is a sizeable Latino audience in the city. Arreaza employs several strategies for dealing with these hurdles. First, he pitches the festival as part of a potential southern swing of a tour, recommending that bands book gigs at clubs or festivals in nearby cities. For example, Asheville, North Carolina, holds an annual fall festival the same week as the Festival Latinoamericano; often headliners end up playing both. He presents the festival as a "professional," established (over twenty years old), and well-organized event, pointing bands to the festival website, where they can see videos of past festivals and sophisticated web design that shows that this is no fly-by-night operation.[4] He appeals to their conscience, noting the limited budget to ask for a "nonprofit rate" and linking the festival with the "good cause" of raising money for the Latin American Coalition and its community programs. Socially conscious groups—for example, the 2009 headliner Grupo Fantasma—see their participation in the festival as a way to give back to the community. Finally, Arreaza attempts to package groups together if they are represented by the same manager, agent, or record label, to get two groups to perform back to back and share expenses like equipment and travel costs.

In 2010, finding the headliner and other major acts took several months. Finally, Arreaza and I booked Plena Libre as the headliner. Slowly, the other musical pieces started to fall in place. Two acts from Miami represented by the same manager, Locos por Juana and Elastic Bond, agreed to perform. Locos por Juana had performed several years earlier at the festival and had performed at a festival in Virginia Beach alongside Arreaza's band Ultimanota, so he decided to bring it back to Charlotte. Arreaza and I came across Elastic Bond on the Internet; it had an intriguing sound, and it turned out that Arreaza knew its producer.

With the major acts selected, it now was time to choose local bands to fill in the remaining slots. Several considerations went into our decisions. First, we wanted to present a diversity of genres. Since we already had one band playing *música tropical*, we decided to select only one similar band, Orquesta GarDel, which played *salsa*. The local bands Bakalao Stars, SoulBrazil, and Rhythm + rounded out the picture. Second, the selections did not include *regional mexicano* groups because the Latin American Coalition has another festival, the Cinco de Mayo Fanta Festival, which features Mexican music. Third, we decided to exclude groups that had performed at the previous year's festival, which meant that prominent local artists such as Leydy Bonilla were not signed up. Instead, we asked her to participate by singing the U.S. national anthem.

The second phase of planning the Festival Latinoamericano involves signing up sponsors to financially support the festival and its associated nonprofit organizations. The Latin American Coalition (LAC), the Mint Museum, and the Latin American Women's Association (LAWA) are the nonprofit organizations that organize the festival; the proceeds from the five-dollar entry fee, beverage sales, and sponsorship donations are split between the organizations (after accounting for the expenses of putting on the festival). As festival organizers, Arreaza and I were in charge of enlisting sponsors. Whereas choosing music was fun, Arreaza dreaded pitching the festival to potential sponsors, which at times felt like going hat in hand to ask for alms. Occasionally we would call on the Coalition's executive director, Jess George, to lend a hand by making a call or using contacts gained through executive-level networking to win over a sponsor.

Major national corporations with a strong presence in Charlotte made up most of the sponsors of the festival. Other sponsors included local businesses, in particular Spanish-language media companies (newspapers, radio), with strong ties to the Latino immigrant community. The sponsors can sign up for several levels of sponsorship depending on how much money they are willing to donate; the donation amount determines the size of their tent space, font size of their logo on advertisements, number of times they can make announcements onstage, and proximity to the main stage (or other desirable locations). As we shall see below, the establishment of these types of sponsorships and the subsequent large corporate footprint at events have transformed Latino cultural festivals from small community events to a more commercialized and commoditized version of *latinidad*.

Jumping Scales

At the 2009 Festival Latinoamericano, the Colombian singer Jorge Villamizar was one of the featured performers. He sang an acoustic set, including several songs from his former group Bacilos. One song, "Mi Primer Millón" (2002), roused the crowd, who sang along to the performance. The chorus of the song outlines the aspirations of a struggling musician, who states, "Yo sólo quiero pegar en la radio / para ganar mi primer millón" (I only want a hit on the radio / to earn my first million). Looking back at Villamizar's performance, which was one of the first I observed in Charlotte, I can see that the song resonates as a symbol of how musicians conceive and aspire to insert themselves into global networks of musical production and socialization while attempting to retain ties to local audiences and community. "Mi Primer Millón" is a metaphor that works on several levels: it demonstrates the musical aspirations of its singer; it connects the singer to his audience (the people singing the song) who share his class aspirations; and it ties together the various locales of *latinidad* that are mentioned in its chorus (e.g., Panama, Guayaquil, Santo Domingo, and Tijuana). However, there is also a bittersweet and humorous irony to the song and its lyrics, which accompany a cheerful and upbeat melody with rhythmic elements of *cumbia* and *salsa*, because the song elides the hardship and struggle, the dashed hopes and deferred dreams that both musicians and immigrant laborers face as they pursue life in the United States. According to the song's lyrics, being released from debt and penny pinching miraculously occurs when the band says, "dejémoslo todo y vámonos para Miami" (let's leave everything and go to Miami). A rise to fame occurs as the (fictional) band arrives in Miami and promptly calls Emilio Estefan, a famous Cuban American record producer and husband of Gloria Estefan. This poetic description of social networking shows how important it is to know somebody in the music business, as a way to get a foot in the door, a recording contract, and promotion of the band.

This section analyzes the connections between local musical expressions and global and transnational networks of music. Some Charlotte musicians attempt to "jump scales" and present their music to a wider audience. While the Latin music industry neglects Charlotte in its estimation of what constitutes marketable Latin music, Charlotte musicians are proceeding with strategies to distribute their music through websites and touring and to insert themselves into global networks of music making. The question of access is political, and I argue that local musicians draw on the agency they form through making music in Charlotte's Latin music scene to challenge the industry's chauvinism and disregard of their music; the results are projects, like audio recordings and a documentary, that bypass traditional channels and rely on personal relationships with famous musicians who have visited Charlotte and admired local musical communities there.

As I have outlined in earlier chapters, Latino musicians in Charlotte face a conflicting situation: they are globally connected to transnational music networks, yet locally constrained by anti-immigrant policies, surveillance, and enforcement. Yet they are also relatively locally enabled compared to fellow immigrants because of their connections to cultural institutions and their central role in guiding Latino cultural formation.

Some musicians have taken advantage of the centrality of music in Latino cultural production in Charlotte and their position as tastemakers for a musical community to further their economic and/or social position, for example, by becoming a concert promoter or forming global social connections to expand the appeal of their music. However, just as many other musicians have faltered in connecting their creative process to professional networking that might further their musical career. The reasons for this vary, but generally many musicians point to the deteriorating economic situation (which means that fewer international bands are touring through Charlotte) and the effect of immigration policing on nightlife (with fans afraid to travel to hear bands) as limitations on their success.

What makes a hit song? This has become a more complicated question in the age of YouTube singing sensations, pop idol television shows, Internet radio, and dying record stores and bookstores. Increasing globalization means that popular music can move easily from its original local setting to new contexts as part of uneven processes of intercultural communication, leading to both exploitative appropriations and potentially counterhegemonic collaborations (Lipsitz 1994). The hegemonic influence of long-standing music production centers (Stokes 2004) should not be underestimated, as influential tastemakers and corporate structures often determine which artists gain prominence while precluding others from similar opportunities. However, as has been documented (Knopper 2009; Kot 2009), the advent of MP3 downloads on the Internet, social networking websites where bands can link directly with fans worldwide, and the rise (or reprise) of small, independent record labels have severely eroded the power of major record labels as tastemakers in the music industry. Instead of the broadly popular artists of decades past (think Elvis, the Beatles, Michael Jackson, and Madonna), popular music has splintered into microgenres, and record labels have a harder time generating hit songs than they did in the eras of Motown, disco, stadium rock, or boy bands. Yet, as I will show, the lure of these musical centers and the concurrent denigration of peripheral places like Charlotte continue. Charlotte's musicians, thus, face many challenges as they attempt to navigate the muddy and tumultous waters of fame. Many are prone to count "success" as something that only corresponds to mass record sales, something that is increasingly unlikely in a changing global music market. Instead, bands increasingly turn to live performances and royalties from music placement in commercials, television shows, and movies as primary sources of income to replace record sales. Narratives of travel, of "leaving everything and going to Miami," still create a mystique around touring for some musicians, while others create alternative visions of building "success." Yet in some ways, Charlotte's Latino musicians are well positioned to connect with well-known musicians from Latin America because of the small scale of Charlotte's Latin music scene. When famous musicians journey through Charlotte, local bands often enjoy access to them while performing as opening acts, forging relationships through backstage conversations and loans of musical instruments for performances. These bonds result in collaborations in the recording studio, access to music industry connections, and even lifelong friendships. Below I document how musicians attempt to "jump scales" through their music making, briefly outline the structural constraints of the Latin music industry, and analyze how musicians narrate the touring experience and forge connections with more famous artists.

Most, but not all, Latina/o musicians in Charlotte aspire to bring their music to a wider audience. This can mean several things, from crossing over to a non-Latino audience to touring in Latin music clubs around the U.S. South, from getting a single played on Spanish-language radio or television to getting a recording contract and invitations to music festivals in Latin America and New York. But the strategies that musicians pursue to achieve, or attempt to achieve, these goals all entail one thing: an understanding of how scales—global, local, regional, international, transnational—mediate musical expression and musicians' lives. While musicians might not use the technical terms of geographers, they are well aware of the structural constraints and connective opportunities that processes of globalization entail. Musicians follow closely the realignments and restructuring of the global music industry, developments that encapsulate broader struggles between multinational corporations and the rights of ordinary citizens, over the commons and intellectual property (Demers and Coombe 2006), and cultural chauvinism by elites toward the poor, unauthorized migrants, and the global South in general. But as I will document below, some musicians are quite resourceful and savvy in marketing their music as desirable cultural expressions.

Others involve themselves in related aspects of Latino cultural production (film, photography, concert promotion) through their connections to cultural brokers in the centers of global *latinidad*.

When I asked Gonzalo Pérez, Banda TecnoCaliente's manager and promoter, about the challenges of touring with a band, he pointed to one key factor that holds bands back from leaving their local community. Many groups, he stated, have "un miedo de inversión" (fear of investment/exchange), a reasonable hesitancy that comes from knowing the financial risks and making a rational decision not to travel. According to Pérez, bands must overcome this fear and have "faith" in their future in order to tour. Touring and other practices that help musicians jump scales (marketing, social networking, recording) require an investment of money, time, and emotional effort with little guarantee of success. In TecnoCaliente's case, this investment includes a tour bus, matching uniforms for band members, instruments and equipment, studio time to record songs, and the time that each member must dedicate to rehearsal, travel, and performances. It is this personal investment of time that is perhaps the most costly; TecnoCaliente's members have dedicated themselves fully to seeking broader success, forgoing income and free time they could have had if they chose to stay a part-time band. Other groups speak of the importance of timing. For example, the rock band La Rúa's run at fame happened when all the group's members were "young" (in their twenties), unmarried, and without careers or children; they had no fear about the financial losses they might incur by touring. The turning point in the group's trajectory came when members realized that taking that next step meant a further investment of time and money at a time when their life circumstances were changing through marriage, parenthood, and the need for job stability.

Other groups, as I have outlined earlier (chapter 4), do not hold ambitions of fame; for them a move to jump scales entails separation from the musical community that supports and inspires their musical expression. These groups (such as Bakalao Stars and Dorian Gris) engage in practices where investment is made in the musical community, rather than in outward attempts to jump scales. For example, Bakalao Stars uses a large lineup of musicians to achieve its "jam-band" sound at concerts, which is costly because members have to spend a lot of time rehearsing and pay all the musicians. At times, they held concerts frequently, within weeks of a previous show. These practices provide fodder for those who criticize Bakalao Stars as lacking ambition and not marketing its music correctly, but the band would argue (and has argued) that its local audience and the communal experience at live shows and rehearsals are more important than "making it big." For these musicians, the monetary profits they lose by staying home are offset by the local cultural capital they build within the musical community. However, this does not mean that these groups are not linked to global musical trends or do not try to connect to internationally known Latin musicians. As opening acts for touring Latin American bands, Bakalao Stars and Dorian Gris both have tried to connect their local musical community and its practices and ideas with the music of more-famous bands.

When musicians attempt to jump scales, there are gatekeepers that can help or hinder their ability to promote their music to a wider audience or create a hit song. These gatekeepers are usually what I have called the musical brokers, who have extensive connections within local, regional, and transnational musical networks. Perhaps the most important of these musical brokers are the local radio stations. Charlotte's Spanish-language radio is dominated by Norsan Multimedia, which operates two FM stations: La Raza, featuring mostly *regional mexicano* music, and Latina FM, which plays mostly *música tropical* (in addition to an AM station with talk programs). For local musicians and promoters, the radio stations represent a key entry point for promoting and marketing their music. Musicians would attempt to contact and befriend prominent DJs and the station manager, who decide to some extent what music to play on air, in order to get a new single played. Other gatekeepers include record label representatives at companies like Universal Latino and National Records. National Records releases *rock en español* and "Latin alternative" music, showcasing many of its artists at an annual event, the Latin Alternative Music Conference, in New York. Several Latin rock bands from Charlotte had traveled to the conference at one time or another to promote their band, though none had been successful in getting a slot to perform at the conference or to get signed by the label.

The influence of Norsan in Charlotte and the LAMC and National Records for the global "Latin alternative" scene points to the growing concentration of ownership of parts of the Latin music industry that are profitable. This can be seen in the consolidation of local media; for example, two Charlotte Spanish-language newspapers—*Qué Pasa* and *Mi Gente*—merged in 2011. It can also be seen in the growing influence of online sites like Amazon.com and iTunes to dictate the terms of music download pricing and promotion. This power affects musical production and consumption and helps determine who gets recognized as prominent and "successful" artists. As Ragland (2009) notes, the Latin music industry has typically ignored *regional mexicano* because of its association with working-class immigrant culture. In promotion and awards, such as the Latin Grammys, the industry has favored Latin pop, rock, and Caribbean genres that fall within what it views as the mainstream of Latin music. Whatever the genre, Latina/o musicians from Charlotte must face the fact that the city is not widely seen as a place of Latin musical production.

La Casa del Ritmo

In January 2011, I invited Juan Miguel Marín and his wife, Catalina, for dinner at my Manhattan apartment. Juan Miguel was the drummer for the Charlotte rock band La Rúa, while Catalina, a professional photographer, had taken many pictures of bands performing in Charlotte. Juan Miguel had taken a job a year earlier in New York City as a graphic designer at an advertising agency, but he quit to dedicate himself full-time to a film project documenting the lives and music of the Venezuelan band Los Amigos Invisibles. La Rúa had toured with Los Amigos Invisibles on a U.S. tour, and band members had become friends. A few days later, I received an e-mail from Juan Miguel with a link to a website, Kickstarter, where he and Catalina had started a fund-raising campaign to back the film project, entitled *La Casa del Ritmo* (The House of Rhythm). Kickstarter is an online platform that allows people to raise money for creative projects; donors pledge money through the site, and the organizers of the project must reach a goal (in this case $30,000) or the money is forfeited and donors are not charged. I pledged a small amount and was promised a DVD of the documentary and a T-shirt as a reward.

In an interview a few months later, Juan Miguel described how the idea for *La Casa del Ritmo* came about:

"La Casa del Ritmo" was a song from a Venezuelan band called Daiquiri from a few years back. Daiquiri was hot in the mid-80s; and Los Amigos Invisibles, three of them—Cheo, Catire, and Mauri—when they moved to New York they were roommates in this place in Brooklyn and they called their apartment La Casa del Ritmo . . .

I met the band on tour with La Rúa, and I became an immediate fan of their music and the hard work and the commitment with their fans and the way they treated people, so when I moved to New York I reached out to Catire, who's the bass player, more on a personal level, like, "Hey, I'm in New York, let's hang out." And we did, and after the last time we got together in May, they were going on tour to Europe, they were going to be away for like twenty days, so I wasn't going to see him anytime soon . . .

Catalina and I went to Ecuador for a friend's wedding and it was really funny, my cousin had asked me to find this bottle of rum that they sell at the Miami airport. So we had stopped at a couple duty-frees and we didn't find this rum bottle and because we had time before our flight took off, I started asking somebody in the airport if there was another duty-free that I had missed and they said, "Yeah, you should go to that other terminal."

So I got into Skytrain, the train that takes you to a different terminal, and as I get off the train on this other terminal, I bumped into Catire. He was either coming through Miami to go somewhere else and play or something. So it was very random, we just started talking. I had seen that they were gong to play the Summerstage show [last year] in 2010. I was very frustrated at my job, I was an art director in advertising, I was looking desperately to get involved into a personal project and so I started talking to him, realized that they were going to play in Summerstage and I thought, "Maybe it would be cool to document that show and how you guys get to that show because you live here in New York." That was the original idea, and during that conversation I realized they were going to celebrate twenty years together with the same lineup and . . . I immediately mentioned, "We should do something bigger." "We should tell your story, it's amazing, I mean, I'm blown away!" So that's how everything started.[5]

Although Juan Miguel describes the acquaintance he formed with Los Amigos Invisibles' band members through touring with La Rúa and the closer friendship with Catire that began after moving to New York, happenstance brought them together in the Miami airport in a situation that sparked the idea for *La Casa del Ritmo*. Before his eyes, the idea grew to include a bigger project of documenting the last twenty years of music making by Los Amigos Invisibles and celebrating their story, their connection with fans, and their friendships with each other. *La Casa del Ritmo* appeared as a natural title, because it described the band members' space in New York while also referencing the way its songs often incorporate tropical rhythms, funk and disco beats, and Venezuelan colloquialisms into a genre that could loosely be called Latin rock or Latin alternative.

Juan Miguel set up a three-person team, including Catalina and a friend, the film director Javier Andrade, to oversee the project. They interviewed band members for a week in August 2010. Because of logistical difficulties, the team was unable to record audio and video footage at the Summerstage show. Instead, Los Amigos Invisibles booked a concert in a New York concert hall in February 2011 that was recorded with multiple cameras and audio feeds. They recorded and edited a high-quality film, released in March 2012. Juan Miguel's comments about the making of the film revealed the importance of friendship to the project:

> The content, the story they shared, I don't want to say that it's impossible that they would have told somebody else, a random producer or director the same story. I feel like that was something special about the project, that everyone was comfortable enough with me, with Catalina, with Javier. It's very strange, but Julio had met Javier at one point when Javier lived here in New York and had a band called Barra Libre. I don't think they were friends but Julio knew of Javier, so even at that point when we first started, I guess there were no complete strangers to the mix, which [was] very valuable for the project.[6]

La Casa del Ritmo has also been important catalyst for Juan Miguel's personal and professional development. While organizing the successful Kickstarter campaign and filming the documentary, Juan Miguel deepened ties with friends who helped fund the project and set about creating new connections to help build a new graphic design business and music-making network in New York City. With his wife, Catalina, a professional photographer, he founded La Moutique, a "creative collective" with a studio for graphic design, photography, illustration, and film editing in Long Island City. Through connections made from the film, Catalina was able to photograph David Byrne, and her portraits were featured in a *New York Times* article and in album artwork for his release with St. Vincent. Juan Miguel was invited to participate on a panel at the 2011 Latin Alternative Music Conference to talk about *La Casa del Ritmo* and alternative sources of funding like Kickstarter. He also started performing with a new band, Legs, playing several concerts, building a fan base, and releasing an LP in August 2013. These developments demonstrate the power of global connections: through relationships started in Charlotte as part of an opening band for Los Amigos Invisibles, for Juan Miguel, and as a freelance photographer shooting at concerts, for Catalina, they were able to build a network of friends that helped them to rather quickly establish themselves professionally in New York.

Corporate *Latinidad*

In a recent book (2010), the anthropologist Hannah Gill analyzes the annual Fiesta del Pueblo in Raleigh, North Carolina, focusing on the importance of the festival as a community-building exercise, as a celebration of Latin American cultures, and as a place to dance and listen to music. Similar to the Festival Latinoamericano, the Fiesta del Pueblo is organized by a local nonprofit that provides services and advocates on behalf of the Latino community. Gill highlights the diversity of people present at this festival by providing four personal biographies of migration from individuals attending the festival. These biographies show the differences in background and life trajectory between men and women, indigenous and *mestizo*, legal and undocumented, Dominican and Mexican migrants to North Carolina, but also some of the common threads tying this diverse group together, particularly family reunification as a pull factor and a tenuous economic situation in North Carolina.

These personal stories, like many of the stories of my interlocutors in Charlotte, demonstrate the diversity of *latinidad* in immigrant communities in North Carolina. Being "Latino" has multiple and contradictory meanings, including for some the rejection of the term as a salient category.[7] While immigrants' narratives are often gripping, with tales of dangerous border crossings, class mobility, and culture shock, my purpose in this section is to juxtapose these individual formations of immigrant identity with the manner in which *latinidad* is constructed in the festival. Whereas Gill takes for granted that the surface expressions of *latinidad* at the festival—the music, dance, food, sponsor tents—are extensions of the immigrant story and one way immigrants stake a claim to public life in North Carolina, I argue that the picture is more complicated. Latino cultural festivals in the U.S. South raise important questions about *latinidad*. (How) is the festival making Latino culture in North Carolina? Who gets to decide what cultural forms will be represented in the festival, and how is Latino culture being codified? Of course, "Latino culture" is a nebulous term subject to much debate and interpretation (Delgado and Stefancic 1998; Stavans 1995; Dávila 2012; Oboler 2006). Moreover, as Arlene Dávila argues in *Latinos, Inc.*, diverse Latino identities are subject to unrelenting pressure by corporations, advertising agencies, and other interests (including, in the Charlotte case, nonprofits) to consolidate into a more homogeneous, easily marketable identity (see also Comaroff and Comaroff 2009). At the same time, various actors in the festival, whether it be corporate sponsors, nonprofit organizers, or musicians, have a stake in the festival appearing "authentic"—being a legitimate representation of *latinidad*—which often entails acknowledging Latino diversity or breaking up Latino culture into its constituent parts: national and regional identity, spicy and non-spicy food, or African and indigenous rhythms.

One way the festival constructs Latino culture is through the consumption patterns of festival-goers. While corporate sponsors and organizers often stress a pan-Latino vision, festival-goers instead mainly stress their identities as members of particular nationalities, fans of a musical genre, or proponents of a class-based aestheticism. They don Puerto Rican flag bandanas, dance Mexican *quebradita*, eat Argentine *churrasco*, or browse for homemade "Latin American" crafts. For consumers, the festival creates an imagined space apart, where the work of gathering the raw elements of expressive culture—food, music, dance, crafts, art, and games—is prefabricated into one event. The assault on the senses of masses of people, cooking food, blaring music, scorching sun, and colorful advertisements draws festival-goers into an alternate state of being that separates this space from the outside world. This carnivalesque atmosphere (Bakhtin 1984; Limón 1994) invites festival-goers to participate, to buy more, and to embody *latinidad* through their purchases and interest in products that are being marketed as "Latino." Yet many festival-goers are acutely aware of the commercialization of *latinidad*, and they act in ways that they see as counteracting this rush to consumerism—by sneaking into the festival over a fence, by gathering as many free giveaways from corporate sponsors as possible, or by bargaining with food vendors for a discount in the closing minutes of the festival. These strategies went against what organizers and sponsors envisioned for the "proper" role of festival-goers as passive consumers and showed their agency as consumers.

Festival organizers constructed Latino culture, as described above, through a process of complex considerations to select the artists, food vendors, dancers, and sponsors for a Latino festival. This construction was not automatic; in fact it developed over many years of festival organizing. The year 2010 marked the twentieth anniversary of the Festival Latinoamericano, and the festival's history presents a good example of the invention of tradition (Hobsbawm and Ranger 1983) and the gradual commercialization of the festival. From a small, casual gathering of neighborhood activists and local artists, the festival has grown to a well-choreographed event with major music groups, numerous sponsors, and thousands of attendees. The transition from an ad hoc gathering to an event produced through months of planning took place gradually and corresponded to increasing numbers of immigrants from Latin America moving to the Charlotte area during the 1990s and early 2000s. An important transition was the professionalization of the planning stages; Tony Arreaza was hired, first as a consultant to plan the festival, and then as a full-time events manager. This hiring, in effect, took everyday planning operations away from the members of the Latin American Women's Association and into the hands of a male musical broker. During my time of observation, Arreaza occasionally sparred with LAWA members who, as members of the executive festival committee, still had some say over how the festival was run. For example, during the planning for the 2010 Festival, LAWA members wanted to organize the Plaza de Artistas with a layout that involved a fountain and lights, but Arreaza argued that these additions would be costly and run over budget. In other years, they have debated musical acts and other layout issues.

Planning for the festival has followed a pattern of building upon "what we did last year" (with the notable exception of changing musical acts), so that knowingly or unknowingly, certain facets get codified through yearly practice.

Another element of the planning stage of the Festival Latinoamericano—the relationship between the nonprofit Latin American Coalition and the festival's corporate sponsors—reveals the uneven and inchoate development of corporate *latinidad* in Charlotte. As sponsors donating money to the nonprofits and receiving prominent spots on the festival grounds, major corporations are highly visible at the festival. Much has been written about the emerging "Latino" market and the growth potential for businesses in this arena. For Spanish-language television and magazines, corporations run sophisticated advertisements that rival any promotions in English-language media. Yet, during conversations with potential sponsors, Tony Arreaza, Jess George, and I often had to engage in a bit of hand-holding in terms of convincing sponsors as to the efficacy of their participation. Local representatives of national and multinational corporations seemed at times unsure about how to appeal to a "Latino" audience. In these cases, the Coalition's strategy was to portray *latinidad* and Latino consumption patterns in ways that would appeal to our perceptions of what the company's goals were. For example, Latinos who are homeowners could attract banks looking to loan money, or home improvement and electronics stores selling the accoutrements of a contemporary American home. Other company representatives needed no convincing. Some of the most successful (lucrative both for the company and the nonprofit) partnerships centered on everyday consumption items, including a regional supermarket and the beverage giant Coca-Cola. The soda company got prominent promotional space in exchange for donating sodas for the festival to sell as revenue. It also partnered with the Latin American Coalition to sponsor the Cinco de Mayo Fanta Festival, positioning a product name into the festival "brand." Organizers also urged corporate sponsors to view the festival as a way to give back to the community, to show appreciation to Latino employees and consumers, and to win goodwill in the community. This strategy had only limited success, particularly in the difficult economic climate of 2010. Banks and other corporations who had been flush with money and philanthropic benevolence two years earlier now were slicing community giving to a minimum.

This relationship between corporate capital and nonprofits around a cultural event raises interesting issues regarding the social relationships of capitalism. While corporations have embraced the productive element of low-cost immigrant labor in agribusiness, urban service employment (janitors, hotel maids, restaurants), and even high-tech labor, they appear to have not yet realized the full potential of the social consumption of Latino immigrants.[8] Those most successful at tying into this market appear to be companies that have established consumer bases in Latin America, namely, soda (and beer) companies and supermarkets carrying lines of ethnic and Latin foods. Thus, a Coca-Cola representative confided in me that Latinos are the fastest-growing consumers of soda in the region. But another question—of social reproduction—remains open-ended. Are corporations willing to view Latino immigrant labor as a disposable resource that can be renewed through continuing cycles of immigration from Latin America, or will they decide to invest resources (both marketing and philanthropic) in stabilizing and acculturating Latino immigrants to U.S. social norms and in the process creating a more clearly defined Latino market in the United States? Nonprofit organizations like the Latin American Coalition can play a major part in the stabilization of social reproduction, providing social safety net programs, job training, and English classes, and encouraging ethnic entrepreneurship. They provide a double layer of legitimacy: (1) having established ongoing relationships with community members, nonprofits can link corporations with grassroots while buffering the corporation from direct involvement in planning and implementing social programs and festivals; and (2) nonprofits provide an alternate to government social welfare programs that have been attacked in a neoliberal political climate. Partnering with a nonprofit can thus provide a corporation with an opportunity to shore up future consumers through positive branding and stabilizing community members' incomes.

However, the partnership between corporations and nonprofits raises important questions for an organization like the Latin American Coalition, which was founded as a grassroots community organization and retains the role of community advocate for Charlotte's Latinos. Does the festival reinforce deleterious relationships, say, between hack immigration lawyers and desperate migrants seeking papers, or soda companies and immigrant children struggling with obesity and diabetes? This issue was driven home to me in the planning stages for the 2010 Cinco de Mayo Fanta Festival. As Tony Arreaza and I signed up sponsors for the event, an internal debate started within the Latin American Coalition senior staff concerning whether we should allow immigration law firms to participate as sponsors. Adriana Taylor, the Immigrants Rights Program director, expressed her concern about several lawyers who had promised clients unrealistic results, in particular, that they could get them a green card or permanent residency in the United States, which they could not and did not deliver, taking clients' money in the process. These clients had then ended up at the Coalition, where Taylor was forced to tell them that they had little chance of getting legal status. She argued that accepting these firms' sponsorship was tantamount to the nonprofit endorsing the bad business practices of these firms. Others argued that sponsorship money was money nonetheless; how could we determine which law firms were suspect and which were not, and that many of these lawyers were prominent members of the Latino community and rejecting them could affect the organization's relationship with other Latino business leaders. Eventually we agreed on a compromise: we would engage with the firms and make them pay a special sponsorship rate that would go toward a "legal services fund" that would help fund the Coalition's legal services department.

At the 2011 Cinco de Mayo Fanta Festival, Adriana Taylor and I entered into another conversation about the social implications of corporate sponsorship as we sat and watched festival attendees walk past the Coalition tent. A large number of the families attending had one or several members who appeared visibly overweight or even obese. Across the grounds, the "Coca-Cola Fun Zone" featured booths with video games, basketball hoops, a soccer shooting competition, a NASCAR race car, a mechanical bull, and other kid-friendly activities. While the beverage company was encouraging physical activity and participation in sports, it was also branding its name (and partnerships with soccer, basketball, and NASCAR) in the minds and practices of Latino children. Soda consumption is rampant throughout Latin America; thus it is no wonder that Latino immigrants continue to be regular consumers of soft drinks in the United States.[9] What Taylor and I noticed was a striking gender difference, between relatively trim, fit-looking men in their twenties and thirties, and their wives and children, who were noticeably more overweight. While some of this weight difference could be attributable to the physical aftereffects of pregnancy, Taylor relayed her impression that women felt pressure to stay at home because of their legal status, while men worked in physically taxing jobs that kept them fit. Another contributing factor to this gender weight disparity might be participation in sports; on weekends when walking through neighborhood parks, I often noticed men playing soccer, while women looked after young children as they sat watching the matches. Recent studies show statewide obesity rates of around 26 percent and overweight and obesity rates of 64 percent for Latino adults in North Carolina (Trust for America's Health 2011; North Carolina State Center for Health Statistics 2010). According to a study by the North Carolina State Center for Health Statistics (2010, 5), "Hispanics were more likely than whites not to get the recommended level of physical activity or not to engage in any leisure time activity. Hispanics were also less likely to consume the recommended amount of fruits and vegetables each day. A slightly higher percentage of Hispanic adults were overweight or obese, compared to white adults."

Corporate *latinidad* at a festival

The Latin American Coalition and other nonprofits that engage in similar campaigns to raise funds for operational and programmatic expenses must walk a fine line to coax corporate donations while not abandoning their mission to serve the Latino community. While they dubbed this relationship a "partnership," that name hides many of the conflicting interests and uneven power relationships between corporations and nonprofits. Corporate sponsorships for festivals do not take shape overnight; a lot of social capital is needed to bring them to fruition. Executive directors must network at parties and events; nonprofit staff must present a package and, as stated above, convince corporate representatives of the efficacy of their participation. While for a corporation, pulling out of a sponsorship might just be part of cutting a budget or a department's reorganization, for a nonprofit like the Coalition, a loss of just ten thousand dollars can mean the cutting of an entire service program or the elimination of a part-time staffer.

Conclusion

Latino residents in Charlotte use festivals as an important means to negotiate *latinidad*. Festival-going is a cultural practice common in Latin America, with national independence day celebrations, saints' days, rodeos, or outdoor music concerts, but certain behaviors are learned (or reinforced) by immigrants as they acculturate to American and Latino lifestyles in the United States. Radio listeners are encouraged to attend festivals by radio DJs hyping the event and giving on-air updates from a mobile transmission vehicle (usually a brightly painted Hummer SUV) at the event. Members of a certain community, whether by national origin or musical affiliation to a band performing there, attend, especially if they have gone in years past. Friends and family attend together, particularly if a child is performing in a *ballet folklórico* onstage. And passersby wander in when they hear music or notice a crowd. There are community leaders who play a prominent role in organizing the event and who are recognized and saluted by the emcees onstage. At festivals, attendees are encouraged to consume: corporate sponsors give away free samples of their products; food and craft vendors form a phalanx of enticing stalls that festival-goers pass through on their way to listen to music; banners, inflatable signs, and company representatives advertise brands to the audience. Festival-goers dress in outfits that openly mark their identity as belonging to a nation, state, ethnicity, or class. For example, many Puerto Ricans dressed with bandanas or T-shirts with the Puerto Rican flag prominently displayed. Mexican immigrant men dressed in cowboy boots, button-down shirts, and wide-brimmed hats that sometimes had the name of the province they hailed from sewn on the hat band. These differences showed the diversity of the audience, but also connections as Latinos from different backgrounds danced to the same music or engaged in similar consumption practices. The festival represents a holdover of practices from Latin America but also proof of an ongoing process of acculturation.

Charlotte's Latino musicians engage with the festival as a way to "jump scales" that connects them to global networks of music making. They see performing at local festivals as part of a larger strategy that includes touring and promoting their music. Often, the process of "jumping scales" is mediated by local power brokers in the Latin music scene, as radio station managers, promoters, and concert organizers decide which bands get maximum exposure to the world beyond Charlotte's musical communities by acting as gatekeepers. But occasionally, musicians are able to establish their own connections, whether backstage at a festival or by chance encounters that lead to opportunities for collaboration with international artists of greater renown.

These transnational connections with famous musicians warrant further discussion. What does it mean when the periphery connects with the center, bypassing the many levels in between? Through easy access to backstage areas during festivals, demand for opening acts, and the small social circle of musicians, Charlotte musicians may come into contact more often with famous musicians than in industry centers where these musicians are sequestered in guarded social settings. Thus, Charlotte's Latina/o musicians are somewhat locally enabled. David Coplan (2008) describes a parallel situation in South Africa, where during the 1970s and 1980s, black South African musicians were able to forge personal and professional collaborative relationships with visiting European and U.S. musicians. Musicians and musical forms that were relegated to second-class status under apartheid were repackaged and repurposed, finding enthusiastic audiences through the brokerage of Western musicians active in the global anti-apartheid movement—for example, Paul Simon's *Graceland* (1986).[10] Musicians are able to move from the local context into transnational networks through the access, cultural capital, and relationships they harvest at festivals. These are the "cosmopolitan" actors that Appadurai (1996) describes emerging out of global "ethnoscapes" and "mediascapes," but mediated by the gatekeeping of local power brokers and the temporal and structural limitations of global networks (at least for the non-elite).

Becoming "cosmopolitan" for local actors is a process with uneven results; for Charlotte's Latino musicians, some prove better than others at "jumping scales," whether because of skill at forming collaborative relationships, ability to maintain connections over time, or being at the right place at the right time. The uneven success of touring musicians cannot be attributed to genre. Each genre (*regional mexicano, música tropical*, Latin rock) connects to its own, somewhat separate global network within the music industry, networks that very clearly have centers of production and taste making and peripheries that exist in an inferior, somewhat neglected, dialogic relationship with the center. Charlotte as a place of Latin music production and consumption must continually vie for the attention of the Latin music industry, competing with other cities for tour dates and exposure. The pride with which Charlotte musicians speak of their brushes with fame while touring elsewhere and playing shows in Charlotte, not to mention the friendships that they have forged, demonstrate some benefit to "jumping scales" that makes touring worthwhile, even if few of them have yet to earn their *primer millón*.

From its giant corporate banners to its promotion of various forms of consumption, the Latino cultural festival is a prime example of how *latinidad* is being increasingly commoditized and connected to corporate brands, even at a local level. But it is also clear that this corporate form of *latinidad* does not go uncontested and that Latino cultural festivals are sites where Latinos negotiate the rituals of consumption and public portrayals of their culture. Some audience members eagerly participate as active consumers of the products peddled at festivals. But they also stress the importance of companies providing a culturally relevant message to their background and thus not treating all Latinos as the same market; they want messages that speak to them as Dominicans, Mexicans, or Colombians, as working-class or middle-class consumers, or as cosmopolitan individuals who may defy stereotypes about the typical Latino consumer (see Dávila 2012). Other festival-goers ignore the giveaways and go straight to the parts of the festival they enjoy most: the main stage, the food vendors, or the craft vendors. They see the corporate presence as an unavoidable (they still see giant banners and hear onstage plugs by corporate representatives) but tolerable part of the event. But seeing and hearing corporate messages are not the same thing as listening and paying attention to these messages. Although corporate sponsors pay extra to get time onstage where they can burnish their community image, few are successful at actually gaining the full attention of audience members, who are often using the time in between musical acts to talk with friends, take pictures with artists beside the stage, or find the nearest restroom.

At times, organizers also contest the corporatization of *latinidad* through their participation in festivals. Although the organizers of the Festival Latinoamericano, for example, are beholden to their corporate sponsors as a way to raise money for the Latin American Coalition, they can choose not to work with sponsors they see as engaging in unethical behavior or promoting harmful business practices. Festival organizers also shape the ways corporations display their branding on the festival grounds—say, by not allowing a soda company to place inflatable bottles too close to the stage, or by facing a radio station's mobile unit away from the main stage so its blasting music does not compete with music from the main stage. But perhaps the most important way that organizers assert their agency is through the selection of musicians and other performers. Tony Arreaza of the Festival Latinoamericano pointedly chooses bands that reflect the diversity of *latinidad* in Charlotte, and curates a festival that not only is marketable, but also upholds what he sees as a high standard of musicianship. He resists selecting what is easiest or even what other people (LAWA members, corporate sponsors) recommend, instead trusting his own aesthetic judgment to make final decisions about the lineup.

As we have seen, the festival is a site where *latinidad* is constructed through festival organizing practices, the performances and interactions between audiences and musicians, and a process of commoditization of ethnic identity. Yet festival-goers negotiate—and at times contest—the creation of a corporate *latinidad* that would facilitate the marketing of mass consumption goods to a diverse group by homogenizing their tastes into bounded categories. Musicians also negotiate the festival, turning a job into a tool for jumping scales. They see the festival as a site of contestation where various gatekeepers restrict communication between prominent global and struggling local musicians. In the next chapter, I show how musicians develop a sense of ethics that is tied to their professional training and experiences interacting with fellow musicians; I also analyze how this ethical compass guides their visions of what it means to be successful.

9

Musicians' Ethics and Aesthetics

Whereas the previous chapter showed how the festival is a site of contestation over the meaning of *latinidad*, this chapter demonstrates how the festival (and other prominent performances) facilitates communication between Latina/o musicians across genre boundaries and between musical communities. During and after their participation in these events, musicians engage in heated intellectual debates about the proper way to organize festivals and treat performers, constructing social rules that guide their sense of ethics and their judgments about the success of an event. These ethical sensibilities stem from musicians' training, whether in a music school or informal setting, and their relationships with fellow musicians and audience members that shape professional behavior. By situating musicians' labor in the nexus of cultural production and consumption practices associated with festivals, the analysis shows how working musicians face many of the same political and economic limitations that dull to gray the immigrant dream.

If festivals are a way to mark the calendar into intervals (Leach 1966), they also create a sense of community through ritual behavior, in this case tied to musical expression (Finnegan 2007). The festival is a different kind of public space from the regular performance spaces of most bands and their musical community. Playing in a club, bar, or restaurant involves a different scale of performance; at the festival the crowds are bigger, the "regulars" mix with new, potential fans (often families with children) who must be won over by the strength of the performance as bands compete with the other forms of entertainment present: kiddie rides, food trucks, folkloric dancers, and sponsor booths. The festival is also one of the few spaces where Latina/o musicians from different musical communities come together and share their music with any regularity. Moreover, festivals are where Latino musicians present their work to the largest audiences. Often, this performance beyond the friendly confines of the musical community entails recalibrating or refining aesthetic choices for musicians as they encounter a wider audience and contact musicians from outside Charlotte. Festivals also crystallize ideas about morality, as musicians interact with organizers who have different priorities concerning what should happen onstage. Much of this negotiation takes place behind the scenes, before the festival even starts, among festival organizers and prominent musical brokers who decide which musical acts and dancers will perform (and how they will be treated), what types of food will be offered, and which corporate sponsors will be positioned favorably to plug their products. Other negotiations take place backstage during the festival as schedules are squeezed or rearranged, for example, when a band gets lost and arrives late for its set, or when an assembled crowd enthusiastically responds during a band's performance.

By examining the festival, I link together musicians' training and their intellectual endeavors with their ideas of morality and ethics. Just as performances within their musical community contribute to intellectual debates such as those represented by the "collective circle," so too do musicians draw on their experiences in festivals, most often to formulate aesthetic norms and debate what is ethical. Musicians' ideas of aesthetics connect to an evolving consciousness about how the structure of corporate *latinidad* limits their expressive range and ability to subvert genre boundaries. Also, musicians increasingly are calling for a more ethical system of interaction, even if just on a personal level, among musicians and between musicians and organizers, although this push has not yet transformed the way festivals are organized.

Carnaval Carolina

Another annual Latino cultural festival in Charlotte, the Carnaval Carolina, operates on a more profit-driven model than the Festival Latinoamericano presented in chapter 8. When I attended in 2010 (its thirteenth year), Carnaval Carolina took place at the Metrolina Expo, a large fairground with warehouses and an open, blacktop-paved staging area. This festival claims to be the region's largest Latin festival, and features numerous *regional mexicano* groups, both local and from Mexico and the U.S. Southwest, playing on two stages, food and craft vendors, corporate sponsors, carnival rides, and a BMX bike stunt demonstration course. Alex Ruiz, the festival's organizer, is a local radio personality and singer of *regional mexicano* music. He promotes several other events throughout the year, including concerts and a beauty pageant, La Chica Carolina. Newspapers often profile Ruiz as Charlotte's biggest Latino celebrity, and at these events he somehow manages to entice minor celebrities from Spanish-language television to make an appearance and take photos with him onstage.

However, Ruiz also has a negative reputation among many musicians. One musician relayed a story of a past Carnaval Carolina where Ruiz had neglected to reserve port-a-johns, so that fifty thousand attendees ended up going in the bushes. Other musicians questioned his musical talent, remarking that his relative (and limited) success as a singer was only due to his radio show (where he could self-promote his latest single to a wide audience). A concert promoter complained that Ruiz had hired him to organize a concert and as they discussed the specifics of the event, Ruiz asked him what sound company and what promotional contacts he was going to use. A few weeks later, after Ruiz would not return his calls, the promoter realized that Ruiz had stolen his professional contacts and never really wanted to hire him to organize the concert. Other musicians warned me that Ruiz often promised blockbuster concerts with numerous, well-known bands playing back to back, but when the show started, only one or two groups would show up.

Hoping these tales would be proven wrong, I entered Carnaval Carolina with some trepidation on a muggy June day. People milled about the spacious festival grounds, many searching for a bit of shade from the punishing sun and roasting pavement. Three stages were set up: two main stages were right next to each other—the idea being that while one band was performing, another could be setting up next door—while the third (smaller) stage was some distance away across the grounds. The two main stages had catwalks that ran out into the crowd, with stanchions and intimidating security personnel keeping open a gap between the crowd and the stage. The multiple stages created a problem for the enterprising ethnographer (and other music lovers with short attention spans) trying to hear as many bands as possible. After a few hours, the main stage got so crowded that I had to squeeze my way through the crowd to get a good view of both the stage and audience around me, but then I would have to find my way back out again to reach the opposite stage.

The smaller third stage presented local bands, including some that I knew, and provided a more intimate interaction between audience and band, so for several sets I concentrated my attention there. In the crowd by the sound board, I found Gonzalo Pérez, whose bands, Banda TecnoCaliente and DS The Evolution, were performing; he was excited to present *banda* and *música latina urbana* to the mostly Mexican crowd. But the third stage had a problem: it faced the main stages with their larger speakers, so its music routinely got drowned out. I found this frustrating, and eventually abandoned ship to join the burgeoning crowd at the main stages.

A traditional *banda* was performing on the right-hand stage, with acoustic instruments and several vocalists. When they finished, DJs from a local radio station, who were emcees at the event, came onstage and started telling jokes. They sprayed a water hose into the crowd to help relieve the intense heat. People used other strategies to stay cool: umbrellas to block the sun, fans, and munching on watermelon given away by a supermarket chain. Then it was time for the next group to perform, Rey Norteño from Raleigh, North Carolina. I wrote in my blog about its set:

> The musicians were not pleased when, two songs into their set, the radio DJs rudely cut them off and started talking to the audience. I could tell from my spot next to the stage that the lead singer was pissed, and the band kept playing, until the organizer cut their mikes. As someone [who was backstage] told me after the event, the first song was spent trying to get the sound right, and just when musicians were getting into a groove in the second song, they were cut off.

So after two songs, Rey Norteño left the stage. In its place, radio DJs switched gears and introduced several government officials who read proclamations (in halting Spanish) and then a television celebrity, La Chilindrina, who told corny jokes for almost thirty minutes. By the end of this extended interlude, the audience, and especially the young men in the area near me, started calling loudly for "Music!" La Chilindrina was followed by another celebrity, Carmen Salinas, a *telenovela* star and singer. Salinas's appearance created an interesting dynamic in the crowd. Many were starstruck and rushed forward to take photographs of her.

But blocked by a throng of onstage media photographers, the crowd grew frustrated and expressed their discontent by throwing empty plastic bottles and directing obscenities at the media. Salinas finally noticed and defused the situation by getting the photographers to step back. She then spoke very forcefully to the politicians, who had just made cheery but empty proclamations about the festival, and lectured them not to pass a law similar to Arizona's harsh immigration policy in North Carolina and moreover, to get rid of the 287(g) program.

At a festival purported to feature back-to-back music, over an hour of the evening was dedicated to celebrity appearances. From there, the musical sets went downhill. Alex Ruiz performed a set where he prefaced his first song by saying he was hoarse from announcing so many celebrities and would sing only a couple of numbers. He proceeded, with a raspy voice, to sing a full set. He was accompanied onstage by his band and three bikini-clad dancers who gyrated and pranced around the catwalk. During another band's performance, high winds ripped the ropes holding a sponsor's advertising banner and it fell behind the stage.

In the days following Carnaval Carolina, I caught up with several musicians who had performed at the festival. As with every concert, there were little backstage dramas that, in this case, I was not privy to. Several musicians complained that the festival had not provided backstage refreshments for the performers; they had to go out into the festival and purchase water after their set in ninety-five-degree heat. Gonzalo Pérez volunteered to drive back home and pick up a set of conga drums after the headlining band showed up expecting congas to be provided and they were not. Other musicians complained about the meager pay; Ruiz gave them no pay or only offered a small honorarium in exchange for promising a large crowd that did not materialize at the third stage. Some artists were given VIP passes, yet the VIP area turned out to be a warehouse behind the stage with no air conditioning and no privacy to change into street clothes.

Musicians' Training and Ethics

Juxtaposing the Festival Latinoamericano, Carnaval Carolina, and other festivals and concerts highlights a central ethical concern for many working musicians: their treatment on the job site. Festivals highlight how musicians occupy a tenuous position, as leaders of their musical communities, but also as contingent labor. The festival brings this contradiction to the surface: the status of musicians is put on display and they are expected to "bring in" a certain amount of their musical community as festival-goers and to translate their repertoire to a festival audience in order to make a successful event. But backstage (and sometimes onstage), they receive variable treatment, sometimes being feted as VIPs, other times suffering disregard and disrespect. Festival organizers construct a festival with many moving parts, including the musicians' labor costs, which they try to reduce to a minimum, either because of the constraints of nonprofit funding streams or to maximize profit. Festivals allow musicians to build social capital through their exposure to larger audiences, through connections they make with visiting musicians, and through the interactions with fellow local musicians backstage. In essence, the festival becomes a major point of training and socialization where musicians develop their professional personae and negotiate relationships with each other.

When I spoke with musicians, the conversation often turned to what constitutes the proper conditions and respect for their artistry during a performance and backstage. I observed instances of what I thought constituted fair or unfair treatment of musicians by concert organizers and would ask musicians what they thought about certain situations. These conversations were an important method that musicians used to compile an unwritten list of standards and notions of respect that, rather than being passed down from elite values, was constructed from the intellectual work that musicians undertake as part of their musical communities. Musicians' assessments of stage situations resulted from the culture of their musical community and their dialogic relationship with their audience members. Many musicians tempered their performances to reflect interactions they had with working-class immigrants during concerts, in their neighborhoods, or at their day jobs; these experiences also influenced the positions musicians took in relation to festival organizers, whom they viewed as belonging to a different class, or at least traveling in elite circles.

Musicians appreciated honesty, and were quick to acknowledge that concert promoters often work on shoestring budgets and that they, as performers, are not big-name acts attracting a large audience. But musicians were also damning in their criticism of concert organizers who just could not seem to "get it right," whether in terms of the quality of sound equipment or providing a few snacks backstage before the show. After a bad experience, some musicians would vow never to work with a certain promoter again; others did not have that luxury and continued to take any gig they could get, even if they were quick to protest onstage, like Rey Norteño did, if they felt they were being cheated.

Musicians' conversations about their treatment become a body of ideas that they use as a moral compass and a way to construct norms of professional behavior. Because of their structural position as contingent laborers, Latina/o musicians have limited formal power in negotiating their working conditions. Their strong social ties to networks of other musicians and their ability to bring out a group of fans are their main negotiating chips. Musicians agree to perform with a handshake deal, or by contracting out one performance at a time. These informal labor agreements make musicians very suspicious of and vulnerable to shifting conditions—say, a promoter backing out of a show, not providing equipment, or skimping on food—that might signal a reduction in their monetary or other compensation for performing. However, Charlotte's Latino musicians do not have a musicians' union where they could complain about working conditions or seek recourse for lost pay; North Carolina is a right-to-work state where unionization is weak and there are very few full-time musicians in the community.

Instead, musicians coalesce into informal networks of friends and collaborators who share information about working conditions and potential gigs. These networks serve as the forum where musicians debate personal behavior and the relative success or failure of concerts and festivals. For example, after almost every major Latin music concert in Charlotte, musicians and other prominent cultural brokers would stop by Tony Arreaza's office at the Latin American Coalition (or call on the phone) to discuss the audience turnout, the level of excitement, and the musical competence of the performance, and, if conditions were imperfect, to complain about their treatment. These sessions act as a sort of training where musicians develop professional standards. Stories about promoters and venues would take on a life of their own, sometimes accurate, sometimes reflecting the biases of the narrator, as they were retold from person to person. Whether gripe session or comedy hour, these conversations helped build solidarity among musicians. Often, musicians were friendly with other musicians in their musical community—for example, Intown musicians who practiced in the same space—but through festivals these bonds would extend between musical communities as musicians chatted backstage or shared musical equipment. Feelings of mutual respect sprang from realizations of musicians' similar positions and problems. Much of this solidarity occurred behind the scenes, even as bands strove to assert the uniqueness of their sound and differentiate themselves from other, competing groups—for example, TecnoCaliente's professionalism or Bakalao Stars' jamming sound and energy.

Where does musicians' sense of ethics come from? In interviews and conversations, many musicians pointed to early training in Latin America as being a major factor in their professionalization and sense of fair treatment. Avenues for achieving musical proficiency reflect class structures in Latin America. Immigrants of middle-class background spoke of receiving training in special music academies or through private lessons, and forming garage bands with classmates as teenagers, while immigrants from working-class backgrounds remembered more informal training such as learning from relatives, in church, or apprenticeships with older musicians. For example, the saxophone player Oscar Huerta recalled the intense training he received attending a music school in Monterrey as a teenager, including learning various regional Mexican styles. Although now he plays a more jazz-infused style, this training prepared him to play with numerous bands playing different styles of music. Helder Serralde, trained at a conservatory in Mexico City, ended up starting a *salsa* band in Charlotte, Orquesta Mayor, which he continues to manage with a professional hand. In an interview in Spanish with Serralde, he recalled the genesis of the group:

> HELDER SERRALDE: When I arrived in Charlotte, North Carolina, I realized that there wasn't an *orquesta de salsa*,[1] on top of that a musical *orquesta* that could play here, so because I'm a professional musician, having studied at the Escuela Libre de Música de Mexico [Mexican Free School of Music], I started to look for musicians and organized them and what came out of it was an *orquesta*, what it is now, the end result, no? So Orquesta Mayor started working . . .
>
> SB: There wasn't another *orquesta* here, at that time?

Orquesta Mayor backstage before a concert

HECTOR: If there was, then it did not have the same, the same—I don't know—"musicalization."[2] There were no more than five, six musicians, or at most seven [in a group]. We are twelve, eleven—it's a real *orquesta*![3]

Another aspect of the professionalization of musicians in Latin America involves their experiences as performers in music venues there, often at a young age. Social class tempers this early experience. Carlos Crespo (of Dorian Gris) and his friends jammed on expensive equipment in his middle-class Ecuadorian family's home and went on escapades to hear punk rockers in Guayaquil clubs. On the other hand, the Brazilian musician Reinaldo Brahn started playing his guitar in bars in his hometown as a teenager. Brahn described his formative years:

SB: When did you start learning music, and learning how to play guitar?

REINALDO BRAHN: When I started guitar, I was thirteen.

SB: And did you take lessons, go to school?

REINALDO: No I didn't. . . . actually it was very fun[ny], because I quit school, 'cause I couldn't learn anymore in the school.

SB: And would you just play at home, or . . . would you go out? When did you start playing with other musicians, in a band?

REINALDO: Actually it was at this bar. I played . . . worked in there and they had this open mike, but the musicians [playing] in there had breaks, and in the breaks sometimes they would put somebody to play, so that was the opportunity.

SB: During the breaks?

REINALDO: Yeah, during the breaks, I played for my first time, and then, this bar hired me for just playing the breaks, because the breaks were huge, because the guys—it's insane, you have to play like four hours, five hours, so then the guys played for two hours, and then he got a break for forty minutes, so that's a terrible business for the bar.

SB: Yeah, they want to keep the music going . . .

REINALDO: So what they do, they hire me, they fired me in my position I was in, and hire me for covering just the breaks. That was awesome too, because I was making more money then . . . when I was seventeen, around seventeen, I was already playing in bars professionally.[4]

Brahn's class background, as a son of a working-class family in a city in central Brazil, influenced how he became involved in playing music. When Brahn made the decision to start seriously playing guitar at thirteen, he dropped out of school and dedicated himself full-time to the musical profession. His parents supported his decision; already working in a bar as a busboy, he could now make more money filling in during the regular musicians' set breaks. The money he made went toward making him self-sufficient and supporting his family. Brahn saw his choice to drop out of school as an opportunity to work hard to perfect his craft. He continued playing in bars and small clubs for fifteen years, moving up the music world from his hometown to a regional city, Uberlândia, to touring around São Paulo. Eventually he met an American woman visiting Brazil, they fell in love and got married, and Brahn decided to move with her to Charlotte. After years of performing almost nightly, Brahn took a four-month hiatus before starting to perform Brazilian music in Charlotte.

Brahn's musical training and expertise are extensive. During interviews and conversations, we spent hours discussing Brazilian music, but also jazz, blues, rock, and other genres. Other Latin musicians in Charlotte often comment on his skill as a guitarist. I witnessed his prowess during performances with his band, SoulBrazil, which involved covers of Brazilian classics, but with extended jazz-like improvisation, and on several occasions when other Latin groups, such as Ultimanota, would invite Brahn to join them onstage for a song.

However, some musicians received much of their socialization as musicians after they arrived in Charlotte. They moved to Charlotte as teenagers along with their families, growing up playing Latin music in an American setting. These musicians' experience reveals a constant tension between embracing American norms and retaining the professional characteristics of Latin American musicians, many of whom are their peers. For example, members of Bakalao Stars lack much of the apprenticeship professionalization of Latin American musicians, but they compensate by stressing the familial aspect of their band and the seriousness of attendance at their Thursday jam/practice sessions. Other young musicians have been taken under the wing of more experienced performers who train them in ethical, upstanding behavior. For instance, Gonzalo Pérez, who sees the two young men of DS The Evolution as not just musicians to promote but also his wards, stresses their moral character, especially as they embarked on a spring 2011 tour. While they may shake their hips and sing suggestive lyrics to women in the crowd, Pérez is quick to check any behavior he sees as unprofessional (drug or alcohol use) and to stress the difference between their style of *música latina urbana* and the negative reputation he associates with *reggaetón*.

The Tour

For many musicians, the experience of traveling with a band is one of the most important moments in their professional development. On tour, they gain knowledge of the music scenes in different places, meet musicians from other bands, and learn how to present their music in varied formats. When musicians tour, they are extending a tradition that goes back to the mid-twentieth century, when Mexican musicians toured the southwestern United States on the Taco Circuit (Ragland

2009), and African American musicians traveled on the Chitlin' Circuit (Lauterbach 2011). Touring also connects to the working-class Mexican and Caribbean concept of traveling for work (Ragland 2009; Freeman 2000; Smith 2005). The tour can consist of a short weekend trip to a nearby city—say, Atlanta or Virginia Beach—or a more extended jaunt of several weeks across the country or even overseas. The shorter trips were more common during the time I spent in Charlotte, and these tours around the region built upon an emerging network of Latin music clubs and festivals in southern cities and towns. The support of local radio stations, particularly for *regional mexicano* groups, to promote shows is essential to bands touring through Virginia, North Carolina, South Carolina, and Georgia because they provide bands with an already cultivated fan base and potential radio airplay. But the most important asset on tour is a network of locally connected fellow musicians and concert organizers who can ease the process of traveling. Charlotte musicians often acted as these local guides when touring musicians arrived in Charlotte, lending bands equipment, giving directions over the phone when someone got lost on the freeway, pointing the way to a cheap, all-night diner, and helping promote a show by drawing on their musical community. In return, when Charlotte-based musicians traveled, fellow musicians elsewhere would lend their local expertise.

During interviews and conversations with musicians, narratives of the tour emerged that stressed both the upside and difficulties of traveling with a band. The tour is both hard work and the good life. Musicians recounted driving long distances, eating bad food, getting cheated out of paychecks by unsavory club owners, and sleeping in crowded hotel rooms. But they also remembered bonding with fellow band members, partying backstage, finding enthusiastic new audiences, and being part of "something big," whether it was a major festival or opening for a famous artist. A major part of this experience involves overcoming a fear of losing money by assuming an attitude of positive thinking. In practice, this strategy becomes affect, an optimism that weighs the losses of touring (a night or two lost on the road, money spent) against the potential gains of fame and selling a musical product.

The touring affect, as an emotive positionality, becomes a way for musicians to justify, and perhaps obscure, the degraded material conditions in which their creative work takes place. While the labor regime of the local club or festival is exploitative, it is also a familiar interaction; by leaving Charlotte, musicians enter into a less familiar and more uncertain world where the risks and rewards are greater. As lesser-known bands, they are rarely extended the courtesies (really part of the pay package) of hotel, transportation, or meals paid for by the concert promoter that more famous groups sometimes receive. Instead, they are expected to book a hotel or drive through the night to get back home, while often receiving the same low pay as in Charlotte. In this context, musicians stressed the need to "think positive" and spoke of the "faith," "dedication," and "persistence" that accompany a total investment (both physically and emotionally) in the future of the band.

Camaraderie established through joking, sharing food and drink, and impassioned debates about music, sports, and women becomes a path to heteronormative intimacy that helps male musicians endure long drives and cramped quarters. For example, when I accompanied Ultimanota on a weekend journey to Virginia Beach to play the Hardee's Latin Fest, five of us squeezed into an SUV loaded with musical equipment and luggage. On the ride north, we killed time by listening to music, telling jokes, and passing around snacks. Looking for a cheap place to eat, we found an all-you-can-eat buffet and filled up on barbecue and fried food. Arriving the night before their performance, we listened to bands playing at the festival and wandered the boardwalk. Finding a liquor store and supermarket, we bought a bottle of scotch and food for the next day and headed back to the hotel. At the hotel, we visited another band in their room and had a few drinks. The next day, the band hung out by the hotel pool in the morning, before heading over to the festival site to perform. After the performance, as we finished off the scotch in a backstage bathroom and the bandleader, Tony Arreaza, counted out each member's share of the pay, I took photographs as we joked about the scatological and sexual significance of getting paid in cash in a bathroom on the Virginia Beach boardwalk. This high point of camaraderie lasted just a few hours. On the drive back to Charlotte, weariness set in and an argument started between two band members about scheduling future gigs.

For some bands, touring also provides an opportunity to forge ties with musicians from other bands, sometimes connecting with members of more famous groups as they tour together. Band promoters attempt to utilize their connections within the music industry to help their bands during a tour. For example, Gonzalo Pérez organized a collaboration between the Charlotte band DS The Evolution and Kinito Méndez, a *merengue* singer for whom he had previously worked as a manager. DS and Kinito recorded a song together and performed live together several times. Through these types of connections, musicians better the chances of success by linking their efforts to more established and experienced artists. These bonds form between individuals who share the same nationality (Méndez and Pérez are both Dominican), share stylistic and aesthetic philosophies, or belong to the same generation. Even if the initial touring collaboration does not pan out, local musicians often continue cultivating personal friendships with fellow artists when they come through Charlotte to play at festivals or music venues. Local musicians might be asked to be the opening act at a concert for a well-known touring group, or they might reconnect by sneaking into the theater early to listen to a sound check, or chatting backstage after a show.

So what makes touring worth the difficulty and risk for musicians? There are always musicians who find fame through touring, perhaps signing a record contract or having a hit single. But during my time in Charlotte, no local band of Latina/o musicians had met with this kind of success. Some musicians described wanderlust, a need to travel and play music in other cities. They described the excitement they felt when performing in the same festival lineup with famous bands, or playing in a music venue with historic importance. For example, La Rúa members recalled fondly the experience of performing at the Cat's Cradle in Carrboro and the Orange Peel in Asheville, both North Carolina clubs that hosted important rock and rhythm and blues bands in decades past. For some musicians, touring acts as an escape from everyday life. The members of Ultimanota treated their trip to Virginia Beach as a miniature vacation, a time to relax with fellow band members, take a break from the world of children, and play and listen to music all weekend.

Touring can also be an opportunity to explore new aesthetic possibilities by testing new material or reinterpreting old songs in an atmosphere that does not have the same established connections with the musical community that exists in Charlotte. Even if this effort fails, it can help bands find more confidence in the direction of their musical creativity. For example, the new material that Ultimanota began to play around the time of its trip to Virginia Beach (in rehearsing for this festival and a few other concerts) eventually resulted in a change in instrumentation (adding timbales) and the addition of a new member of the group.

"Success"

What is "success"? Despite what self-help books advocate and musicians might wish, positive thinking does not lead directly to success (Ehrenreich 2010). Nor does cultivating the trappings of a "creative class" (Florida 2003) necessarily lead to an environment more favorable to musicians. As the political analyst Thomas Frank explains in a recent critique of Florida's ideas, notions like the "Bohemian index" obscure the class differences between economic winners and losers in the postindustrial landscape (Frank 2011). For Latinos, the prospects are dim for economic success: for example, from 2005 to 2009 median household net worth among Hispanics fell from $18,359 to $6,325, mainly as a result of the housing crisis (Kochar, Fry, and Taylor 2011). While the household net worth for whites also fell during this period, what is significant is that the "wealth gap" increased significantly between whites and other groups (Latinos and African Americans), representing a bifurcated path that corresponds to the predatory lending practices of banks and mortgage companies that targeted black, Latino, and poor white communities for adjustable-rate mortgages and biased lending practices. Charlotte was an epicenter for these sorts of monetary dealings, and the cultural milieu benefitted from the heady days of a booming real estate market. But Latino musicians were largely excluded from direct access to "creative class" formation; instead, they exist on the margins of Charlotte's slice of bohemia. They understand the hard work and persistence, the social capital and connections that must be developed in order to achieve success, which does not appear out of thin air.

Musicians rely upon webs of knowledge to achieve "success," cultivating friendships by building acquaintances into relationships of mutual benefit where musicians share information and connections. Through friendships, musicians can share their deep knowledge of the style and distinctive properties of musical genre, even with musicians who do not belong to that particular musical community, in return for favors that benefit them later on. For example, Tony Arreaza's ability to organize a "successful" Cinco de Mayo Fanta Festival is a testament to his network of friends rather than his limited knowledge of *regional mexicano* music. During the planning stages of the Fanta Festival, Arreaza relies on the judgment of other musicians and cultural brokers to help discern the best artists. He calls in favors from earlier events, and promises the limited fringe benefits that are available to him as a nonprofit events manager—VIP passes, stage time, T-shirts, backstage access—to entice unpaid labor out of friends who volunteer and are key to running the festival behind the scenes. This volunteer help might be as simple as lending a drum kit for the festival bands to use, or as taxing as distributing ice to beverage stands on a hot, dusty day. Musicians often visit Arreaza in his office, dropping off their latest demo recording or trying to get booked in the next event. Rather than treating them as supplicants, he takes the time to discuss professional matters—how they are promoting their band, if they have a booking agent, where they recorded their music—in order to see whether he can give them any advice and whether they can collaborate in the future. Even if these sessions do not result in an immediate hiring for the event on hand, often more fruitful results occur months later, when Arreaza connects the band with a promoter from another city who has called him looking for a good *regional mexicano* band.

Many musicians I spoke with in Charlotte equated "success" with fame and chart-topping status, listing best-selling artists as the most successful in their genre. However, there were caveats to this idea of "success," the most vital being that musicians should always maintain connections with their audience. Charlotte musicians praised famous artists who cultivated an intimacy with audiences and treated fellow musicians with respect. They were also quick to criticize artists whom they perceived as aloof and out of touch. Although behavior varied between genres, there were particular activities that musicians and audience members saw as key in maintaining this connection. First, musicians should connect with audience members during performances through their performance style and casual conversations between songs. Also musicians often would give away a few copies of their latest album during a show, creating excitement as fans rushed to the side of the stage where a band member or promoter was passing out CDs. Second, there should be opportunities for audience-musician interaction before and after shows. For example, at *regional mexicano* festivals and concerts, it is customary for fans to take photos with musicians from bands they like, posing in the areas beside or behind the stage. At times, bands would spend up to thirty minutes after a show taking pictures with fans. Some bands would also set up tables where they sold CDs and T-shirts to fans. Third, famous musicians were expected to play the hits, songs that made them famous or that they are known for covering. Promoting a new album or playing a few numbers that are in development is fine, but audiences want to hear the standards. Musicians, heavily attuned to musician-audience interaction, also were sensitive to how approachable and friendly visiting artists were during interactions backstage.

Conclusion

Performance at festivals results in an evolving aesthetics tied to musicians' interactions with other bands and the crystallization of a sense of ethics based on prior professional training and musicians' treatment by festival organizers. Festivals, even more than concerts in clubs or bars, bring to a head the conflicting class loyalties of Latinos, and the festival itself becomes a stage where diverse notions of *latinidad* are negotiated and debated. Local musicians, even if they hail from different musical communities, experience similar treatment by organizers at a festival. As they recollect after performances, they rely on shared experiences to begin a process of reckoning—how things went, who slighted whom, what could have been done better. During this process, they bring a strong identification with their fans' class and ethnic positionality as marginalized groups in Charlotte, and many see parallels to the ways they are treated as working musicians. For the musicians, festivals become not just an opportunity to perform in front of their musical community, but also a chance to share their music with members of other musical communities and network with fellow musicians.

At the festival, organizers and musicians play by different sets of rules. The dominance of corporate *latinidad* channels certain preconceived and "acceptable" notions of being Latino to the forefront, often at the expense of other, less marketable folk traditions or even cutting-edge creative endeavors. Organizers must perform roles that adhere to the constraints of corporate *latinidad*: limited budgets, cult of celebrity, product placements, and limited political activism. They must follow these rules even if, like Tony Arreaza, they show some concern for the low pay of local musicians. Musicians have their own set of standards, which, under the yoke of corporate *latinidad*, often leads to conflicts and dissatisfaction. At times, musicians engage in small acts of resistance. Some vote with their feet, by refusing to work with unscrupulous organizers. Others, like Rey Norteño, express their discontent while onstage. Still others engage in backstage antics. For example, at one festival, to make up for their low pay, members of a local rock band stashed numerous cans of beer in their backpacks from the coolers that had been provided as refreshments for the headliners.

During conversations with musicians, the richness and depth of their intellectual engagement with the meaning of festivals were most apparent when they talked about music. Many spoke of juggling the novelty of playing music for a new audience with the familiarity of performing for their musical community, both in attendance at a festival. Musicians take seriously the challenge of presenting their talent and ideas on a larger stage. The Brazilian musician Reinaldo Brahn explained how he makes an effort to replace songs in his repertoire annually. That way, if he plays a festival two years in a row, the audience does not hear the same set as the year before. While he keeps a few Brazilian standards, like "Garota de Ipanema" and "Mas Que Nada," he always comes up with a variety of new songs to cover. The Dominican promoter Gonzalo Pérez urges his artists to give an energetic show and to not venture too far away from road-tested crowd pleasers. For example, DS The Evolution performs "lo que la calle quiere" (what the street wants) to stay true to its urban, Afro-Caribbean roots.

Although there is a growing awareness of the exploitative conditions of festival labor among Latina/o musicians and of the limitations of its brand of corporate *latinidad*, this consciousness has not led to any sort of widespread action to remedy the situation. Perhaps because of the informal nature of the business (where organizers sign up bands with a handshake and a promise, or a minimalistic contract with few guarantees), musicians appear to have few options for rectifying their mistreatment. Unionization seems a pipe dream in a right-to-work state with a barely functioning state bureaucracy to hear labor rights' cases, not to mention the fear that undocumented musicians have of interacting with state agencies. Instead, many musicians advocate a more personalized approach of developing good working relationships with festival organizers and trying to gain more pay through a sense of mutual obligation, the potential for future collaboration, or a professional demeanor. But this also does not change the drive by corporate sponsors, nonprofit boards, and festival organizers to ceaselessly reduce costs, nor does it lessen the structural limitations imposed by corporate *latinidad* that curtail many local musicians from achieving what they see as success—whether that be a record deal or a sense of unadulterated local musical community. The potential for a political transformation is there, but as of yet it remains incomplete.

Conclusion

This book began by outlining the policies and political developments that have led to a climate of fear and hate and intensive policing aimed at immigrants in the United States, particularly in southern states such as North Carolina. It concludes by returning to this context and examining what is at stake in the struggle over immigration policy and how musicians and their audiences position themselves in this struggle. In the face of intensive policing that disrupts people's lives and wrenches families apart, attempts to form community and stake a claim to belonging to the city become all the more important. As we have seen, making music constitutes a form of individual and collective agency and political action. This research has ramifications for conceptualizations of the city as a center of music making, for what it means to be southern, and for the future of Latino music in the U.S. South. We can best comprehend them by traveling through various scales, from the global to the local, and from the national to the community, in order to understand the implications of this book's findings for Latino immigrant residents of Charlotte.

Global

If Charlotte is a "globalizing city" (Graves and Smith 2010) (as it most certainly appears to be), then Charlotte's Latino immigrants are its most vital link to a transnational cosmopolitanism and emerging regional demographic and cultural transformation. As Charlotte's largest (but not only) immigrant community, Latinas/os provide a steady supply of low-wage labor that supports the machinations of global capital cycling through Uptown Charlotte's bank towers. Immigrants' wages in turn create a market for entrepreneurship that is revitalizing the city's Eastside neighborhoods with ethnic businesses. Charlotte's financial industry and corporations have put forth a socially liberal agenda for the city by supporting infrastructure projects that revitalize the center city and philanthropic efforts that support nonprofits like the Latin American Coalition. However, this is a tenuous elite project, at risk from populist libertarian politics that vilify immigrants and decry progressive taxation, and threatened by the very monetary risks through which the finance industry makes its profits.

Charlotte's Latina/o musicians approach the global scale through their transnational networks of friends, family, and acquaintances. These networks mean that Latina/o musicians in a relatively small city in a region not renowned for its Latino culture nonetheless are able to attract "world-class" touring artists to perform at festivals and to draw on their own pool of talented musicians to put on well-regarded show-cases of Latino culture, such as the Coalition's "Azúcar" and "A Night in Rio" series. These global connections also mean that musicians can at times "jump scales" by touring or by drawing on friendships to pursue new projects, like the film *La Casa del Ritmo*. But these global connec-tions also create a "dangerous crossroads" (Lipsitz 1994) where musical brokers may perpetuate inequalities in cross-cultural communication and musicians may find themselves distorting their musical aesthetic to fit a marketable style. While they face social marginalization in Char-lotte, local musicians find themselves relatively enabled through these global networks to take part in a cosmopolitan world that has yet to fully establish itself in the city. Latina/o musicians' position reveals the contradictions that many Latino residents of Charlotte face: they may belong to the world, but many feel they don't belong to North Carolina. They represent a potential future city—cosmopolitan, multicultural, but also immersed in a supportive, engaging local community—that has yet to be embraced by everyone.

National

What is also at stake is a question of who belongs to the nation. The current legal and political climate places immigrants under a regime of militarization, racialization, and social segregation. As much as the U.S. historical narrative celebrates a "nation of immigrants," the current political situation reminds us that who gets accepted into the nation has always been contested terrain tied to how society constructs racial, ethnic, and class boundaries (Jacobson 1998; Takaki 2000). The lives of immigrants should not be separated from the context of the often fraught situations in their homelands, situations that remind us of the long and continuing history of U.S. imperialism in Latin America (Galeano 1997; McCullough 1978; Smith 2004; Leogrande 1998). The current "great wave" of immigrants faces a thirty-year ratcheting up of immigration enforcement that began with the militarization of the U.S.-Mexico border and American inner cities to fight the "War on Drugs" and codification of "illegality" in immigration law starting with the 1986 Immigration Reform and Control Act (IRCA) (Dunn 1996; De Genova 2002; Inda 2006). This enforcement structure has been intensified by numerous increases in funding for border enforcement, the development of the 287(g) and Secure Communities programs, and increased surveillance of immigrant communities after 9/11. In Charlotte, these policies have resulted in police checkpoints, families torn apart when fathers are deported, and residents afraid to venture out of their neighborhood at night.

The consequences of immigration policy include new forms of social and structural racism, expressed in the racialization of Latina/o immigrants. The correlation of Latina/o immigrants and what has been socially constructed as "illegal" behavior—crossing an international border to find work, operating a taco truck, driving without a license, public alcohol consumption, speaking Spanish—is increasingly codified into laws and policies that target "illegal" immigrants. Each new law further legitimizes the deportability and "illegality" of undocumented immigrants. Although federal immigration enforcement policy is often framed as nondiscriminatory, the numbers of deported individuals and concentration of ICE agents on the U.S.-Mexico border tell a different story of overwhelming force being used to send black and brown bodies back to Mexico, Central America, and the Dominican Republic.[1]

States' Rights

In recent years, the struggle over immigration has centered on the local and state level, where most new laws and policies have been implemented. As noted earlier, the border has moved inland as local police take on immigration enforcement responsibilities and state governments institute restrictive laws and policies targeting immigrant populations.

What is taking shape is a battle over immigration politics that again tests the boundaries between federal and state authority. The series of local and state laws that target immigrants were the result of activism by groups opposed to illegal immigration. These anti-immigrant groups face off against groups of Latino activists and their allies, who support comprehensive immigration reform at the federal level and oppose these state laws. Pro-immigrant activists have also promoted the idea of "sanctuary cities," where individuals would not be asked about their legal status by city officials nor turned over to federal immigration authorities, and protested the enforcement practices of the 287(g) and Secure Communities programs. Activists on both sides frame their movements as struggles over rights to the public sphere, or what can be conceptualized as the "right to the city" (Lefebvre 1996; Harvey 1973). Anti-immigrant groups deploy the idea of freedom from "illegality" and the alleged illegal behavior of unauthorized migrants—from drug dealing, drunk driving, petty crime, and violating housing codes to the simple fact of being "illegal." They also frame anti-immigrant laws as upholding the right of taxpayers and citizens to deal with government waste through denial of social services to undocumented immigrants. Immigration reform groups, on the other hand, frame their protests in the language of the Civil Rights movement and Chicano activism, stressing antidiscrimination and antiracism, but also the basic humanity of immigrants, their contributions to society, and their desire to become "American."

The author Ralph Ellison once wrote that American life since the abandonment of Reconstruction has been a reversal of Clausewitz's dictum, and thus "the continuation of the Civil War by means other than arms. In this sense the conflict has not only gone unresolved, but the line between civil war and civil peace has become so blurred as to require of the sensitive man a questioning attitude toward every aspect of the nation's self-image" (Ellison 2003, 119). While Ellison was writing about the "guerrilla politics" of the South that resulted in Jim Crow, lynching, and race riots and how these phenomena colored his appreciation of Stephen Crane's fiction, his analysis can be extended to the Civil Rights movement and the current struggle over immigration. Some of the more successful moments of the Civil Rights movement occurred when activists challenged the boundaries between federal and state authority, pressuring the U.S. government to overrule recalcitrant state and local government officials (Branch 1999; Caro 2002; Carmichael and Hamilton 1967). This resulted in court-ordered desegregation of schools (e.g., Little Rock, Charlotte, Ole Miss, University of Georgia), prosecution of violent acts, including killings of civil rights activists, and federal civil rights legislation (e.g., the Civil Rights Act, the Voting Rights Act, the Fair Housing Act), actions that helped turn the tide in the push to ensure basic civil rights for African Americans. Some of these developments were long lasting; for example, the Voting Rights Act still directs how southern states must apportion their legislative districts after each U.S. census.[2] Others, such as school desegregation, were slowly undermined by the retrenchment of "guerrilla politics," first as white southerners pulled their children out of public schools and then as they resisted a Carter administration federal tax policy requiring private and religious schools to desegregate (Johnson 2010). More recently, southern cities like Charlotte (once famed for its embrace of school desegregation) have all but abandoned school busing efforts in a turn to "neighborhood schools" that results in de facto resegregation along racial and class lines (Smith 2010).

The long-standing tension between federalism and states' rights now centers on immigration. New state laws are being challenged, in whole or in part, in federal courts, where supporters argue that they fill in the gaps of federal enforcement efforts, while opponents protest that the laws usurp federal authority on immigration enforcement granted in the U.S. Constitution and violate federal civil rights codes. Many of the state laws are eventually defanged, as courts find parts of or entire laws unconstitutional, but not before they spread a climate of fear and uncertainty in immigrant communities. Immigration reform activists in Charlotte have attempted to balance local and nationally focused efforts to roll back anti-immigrant laws and policies. But they face the limitations of this same tension: how do they balance local actions, such as protests against family separations, with broader organizational efforts to change federal policy? How do they reconcile appeals for immigrants' inclusion in the nation with demands they make for "urban citizenship" as residents of Charlotte?

The Gray Dream

The cultural effect of conflict over immigration policy has been what I call the graying of the immigrant dream. The inability of the immigration reform movement to achieve success, particularly the failure to get the U.S. Congress to pass meaningful immigration reform or the DREAM Act legalizing undocumented students, has sullied hopes that many immigrants held of becoming full-fledged members of U.S. society and dampened the enthusiasm of the mass marches of 2006. Having left their home countries, but not fully welcomed in the United States, many Latinos feel they are "neither here nor there" (Zavella 2011; Tigres del Norte 1997), instead occupying an in-between state at the margins. The economic recession of 2008 further darkened the horizon for immigrant workers, affecting industries such as construction that employed an immigrant workforce, so much so that significant numbers of immigrants returned to their home countries.

As I conducted this research, *el sueño gris* (the gray dream) became more than just a band's slogan; it came to represent how musicians and their audiences were persisting in attempting to create community despite a set of serious obstacles placed in their way. Musicians have occupied a vulnerable position, stemming from their contingent labor conditions, their training and experiences growing up in Latin America, their often insecure legal status, and their daily interactions with policing in neighborhoods and job sites. Yet, in their way(s), musicians asserted their agency by building common cause with their audience through processes of music making, practicing genre, and discussions about music. This dialectical process often involves synthesizing disparate elements—nationalities, class backgrounds, ages, and migration experiences—into creative expression. Latin music in Charlotte helps its listeners work through a process of defining how they live and see the world. The result has been the creation of group solidarity and agency in the face of oppressive anti-immigrant policies. I adapt the historian E. P. Thompson's idea of a class "in itself" (Thompson 1963) as a way to analyze how musicians and their audiences recognize their common experience—as immigrants, as musically inclined people, as speakers of a shared idiom—to form musical community.

Musical Community

This type of community does not just exist, but arises from a process of music making in a hyper-local setting that at times jumps scales to engage with global musical networks. Rather than deploy "community" as a commonsense and general term, I have attempted to outline the social interactions, ideas, and attitudes that lead musicians and fans to envision themselves as belonging to a cohesive social group. Using community as an analytical and descriptive tool does the "sociological and ideological work" (Creed 2006) of allowing us to understand how Latino immigrants have picked up the pieces of a world that has been shattered by neoliberal economic restructuring and the 2008 recession, the upheaval of transnational migration, and the tightening of a regime of anti-immigrant surveillance and enforcement.

Musical community is a sense of belonging and shared affiliation around notions of class, ethnicity, language, style, and taste expressed through music and other creative cultural expressions. The personal relationships formed among musicians and between musicians and their fans support community formation and often act as a form of fictive kinship. These personal relationships become a prism through which musicians interpret the city, at times leading to memorable linkages, such as Juan Miguel Marín's experience with La Rúa, which he describes as "kind of like our first girlfriend," or Gonzalo Pérez's exhortation that Mexican immigrants need to "invest in our city."[3] Musical community exists at the intersection of local and mass consumption, often serving as a point of mediation between locally produced, "grassroots" expressions of music and nationally and globally popular mass expressions of music. While each musical community centers on a particular band and its genre(s) of music and is situated in the segregated geography of the city, musicians often framed their music as representing Charlotte through their interpretations of the city and *latinidad*. Their experience with the city varies, in large part based on where they live and perform and how their band positions itself in terms of labor conditions, politics, genre boundaries, and moral and ethical questions. Bars, clubs, restaurants, and other music venues host performances by Latino musicians and become spaces where musicians and audiences feel comfortable engag-

ing in musical conversations. Bands begin to belong at certain clubs—
Dorian Gris at Skandalos on the Eastside, Orquesta Mayor at Cosmo's
Café downtown, Bakalao Stars at the Evening Muse, Intown, Ultimanota
at suburban A Piece of Havana—corresponding to how music making
fits the style and aesthetics of fans who live and go out in these neighborhoods. These musical communities illustrate the diversity of Charlotte's Latino population. It is impossible to talk of one Latino experience
in the city; instead, there are multiple experiences fractured along lines
of national origin, immigration status, class, genre, race, gender, and
sexuality. But to some extent, each musical community unites its members around an effort to come to terms with what it means to be Latino
in a southern U.S. city.

The City

Too often in anthropology and urban studies, music and other cultural expressions are dismissed as trivial in analyses of contemporary
urban life, or added in like spices to flavor descriptions of neighborhoods, social gatherings, or street life. I have argued instead that music
is central in the lives of many Latino residents in Charlotte, vital to
how community members present "Latino" culture to the world, and
key to understanding how Latino immigrants are adapting to, adopting, and transforming southern culture. This dynamic is best revealed
when musicians describe how they see the city of Charlotte and envision
what type of city it will become. The promoter Gonzalo Pérez situates
Charlotte as a city that has less racism and discrimination against Latino
immigrants than cities in neighboring states. He also sees a Charlotte
that needs investment from its immigrant community as a way to repay
and continue the support that city agencies and nonprofits give through
social safety net services. The drummer for La Rúa, Juan Miguel Marín,
sees Charlotte evolving and changing from "being a city that was not
diverse to a really, really diverse and dynamic city."[4] This transition
did not happen overnight, and it involved growing pains and the hard
work of people like him who acted as "mediators" and "ambassadors"
representing Latino culture and convincing native-born southerners
to be open to new experiences with other cultures. Members of Bakalao Stars stress the importance of place and how location affects what

type of crowd attends a show. Because of fears of deportation, potential fans from Charlotte's Eastside who are undocumented will not travel to see the band in clubs in NoDa, an Intown neighborhood. Conversely, when Bakalao Stars has played at Skandalos, an Eastside venue, its Intown crowd does not attend because they dislike the place and they are afraid of petty crime in what they see as a dangerous neighborhood. An Eastside band, like Dorian Gris, has experienced the same effect in the opposite direction, receiving negative feedback after playing Intown from fans who prefer that it play at Skandalos. For musicians who come up against these barriers to audience mobility, the city is a fragmented landscape that highlights difference in status, class, race, and ethnicity through its residents' ability to access neighborhoods and feel comfortable making music there.

How might we imagine the southern immigrant experience in this context? Latino immigrants in Charlotte are creating a vision of southern *latinidad* that draws from elements of southern, Latin American, and Latino culture(s), but with unique elements that reference the local neighborhoods and musical communities of the Latin music scene in Charlotte. The southern immigrant experience parallels themes in regional literature and expressive culture. Take, for example, the title of the southern writer Thomas Wolfe's novel *You Can't Go Home Again* (2011), which takes on a new meaning in relation to how immigration laws and enforcement policies restrict migrants' ability to return to the United States if they visit family in their home countries. The 1996 Immigration Act (IIRIRA) includes stiff penalties for entering the United States as an unauthorized migrant, criminalizing labor migrations across the border that have been routine since the early twentieth century. Penalties for repeat violations of the law include restrictions on a migrant's future ability to apply for citizenship, and when migrants are detained, they often face periods of imprisonment or deportation to remote outposts on the U.S.-Mexico border. Many undocumented immigrants who in the past would have returned annually to Mexico now remain for extended periods in the United States, setting down roots but unable to go home again.

Attention must also be given to the long-standing but often hidden connections between southern and Latin American cultural expressions. Several scholars have been reconstructing the history of these musical connections (Roberts 1979; Sublette 2004; Brennan 2008). The Colombian author Gabriel García Márquez credits reading Faulkner's work with inspiring him to become a writer; it is not coincidental that the magical realism of Macondo builds upon the techniques of and attention to local history that run through Faulkner's writing. Latino musicians in Charlotte are beginning to connect the dots between these two literary traditions, whether by linking musical *feeling* to the blues or writing down new stories of the southern experience, like the immigrant love story in La Rúa's "El Chanchito." As musicians debate the morality and ethics of being a performer, form connections to a neighborhood's people and landscape, or construct musical genealogies of their influences, they are engaging with themes they hold in common with many southerners. And as people of all political persuasions now argue, immigration is the flashpoint issue in the South, perhaps beginning to replace or give a new permutation to black-white racial tensions that have long dominated political calculations in the region. Latin music in Charlotte is but the first wave of Latino storytelling about life in the South; perhaps we should think of southern *latinidad* as another chapter in the regional experience. What future stories will emerge from a dialect that includes Spanish with a southern accent and southern English with a Latin American accent?

Music Making as Politics

This book has documented how making music is a process that gives agency to Latina/o immigrants in Charlotte, North Carolina, and helps to position them in the context of the "globalizing city" (Graves and Smith 2010; Smith and Furuseth 2006). The fate of current immigrant laborers, including "working musicians" who struggle with freelance and contingent work arrangements, should be understood in the context of a city and region that have long regimented labor under an uneven racial, gendered, and class order and been tied into the volatile swings of the international market (whether it was cotton prices or mortgage derivatives). The layers of the "globalizing city" are evident in the landscape of Central Avenue, a thoroughfare that begins within shouting distance of Uptown skyscrapers, passes through gentrifying Intown neighborhoods, and ends up in the Latino immigrant Eastside. Charlotte's Latin music scene engages with all three of these districts, but in ways that reveal the social segregation, class divisions, and genre boundaries of Latino musical production in the city. These divisions have roots in the histories of each musical genre in Latin America and in the life trajectories of immigrants of a particular national origin, both in their home country and in the United States.

As we have seen in Charlotte, making musical community is a fragile process; it requires hard work to make sure music venues feel like home, that they are welcoming to fellow fans of genres, and that opportunities open for connections to the Latin music industry (e.g., touring artists, radio DJs). It is also transitory; some musicians have argued that the "height" of *rock en español* in the city had already passed and that I was viewing the dregs of a moment that began in the early 2000s. However, the persistence of musicians and musical community means that, in a musical city,[5] music becomes inscribed in the landscape and ingrained in how people interact with one another. The Eastside, Intown, and Uptown musical districts are not natural geographic areas, but are socially constructed in response to social networks, patterns of performance, fears of deportation because of immigration policing, and real estate trends. The "musical city" is a process that builds (and sometimes dismembers) the brick-and-mortar places, demographics, social relationships, consumption and production patterns, and popular practices that make music possible. Thus, the Latin music scene in Charlotte would not have been possible without an influx of Latino immigrants, bars and clubs, friendships established between musicians, learned leisure habits of dancing, drinking, listening to music, and "going out," and a need to belong to a musically framed community of peers. These factors delineate an Intown club as the best place to hear Bakalao Stars, an Uptown dance hall as the best place to dance *salsa*, or an Eastside park as the best place to organize a *regional mexicano* music festival.

Bourdieu (1984) made the point that artists, a group within which we can include musicians, have a unique vision of the relationship between money and time that causes them to exchange (or forgo) money for time to spend on the creative process. We have seen how different bands position their music making on a spectrum that includes work, professionalism, play, and hobby. But no matter the outlook of the band, from Banda TecnoCaliente's touring ambitions to Bakalao

Stars' jam-band stance, every musician stressed the sacrifices he or she makes for music. The investment (of both time and money) that goes into creating a new song is not an empty gesture, but rather a role that musicians take on as creative leaders in their musical community. It is important to emphasize the labor power of musicians who work long hours and put in effort behind the scenes rehearsing, setting up, and promoting so that a performance has that magical quality of musical spectacle. Often the extent of this labor remains hidden from the ordinary audience member, particularly if the genre and setting favor audience interaction that stresses celebration and enjoyment through dancing, drinking, and banter.[6] For example, when Ultimanota performs at a restaurant, the primary goal of the band is to perform in a manner that allows customers to enjoy their meal, to groove to familiar covers of songs, and to remember the evening as a pleasant experience. When musicians take requests, or, as Dorian Gris did, change the direction of their music based on audience feedback, they are acknowledging the importance of their fans. Although some musicians recognized the idea of playing music "for music's sake," every musician I spoke with regarded his or her relationship with the audience (and fellow musicians) as *the* reason behind continuing to create music. As creative leaders who produce and "discover" objects (to use Bourdieu's terms), they feel a sense of mutual obligation and entanglement in a musical project with their audience.

We have seen how musicians engage with (or choose not to engage with) political and social issues in their music and personal lives, with relative lack of overt political activism among working musicians, mainly because they are acutely aware of their multiple vulnerabilities. While musicians were too busy or uninterested in engaging in overt political activism through protests and political parties, they did insert politics into their music making, often by acting as "grassroots intellectuals" making conscious decisions about the direction of their music in relation to audiences and through discussions about aesthetics and morality (Susser 2011b). By creating a comfortable atmosphere where musical community can express itself—the *circular colectivo* described by Jacobo Strimling (2010)—musicians position themselves as political actors who lead the intellectual charge by encouraging a certain ethnic, class, and sonic identification.

Through genre, this identification is paired with style of dress, speech, dance, and singing and marked in opposition to other genres or social classes. For example, Bachata Flow's New York fashions and R&B-infused playing style match its audience of established immigrants with affiliations to African American popular culture, but members of DS The Evolution complicate this affiliation by making clear that they are not *reggaetoneros*, but play *música latina urbana*. Bakalao Stars often performs in costumes—gorilla masks, Hawaiian shirts, and so forth— and references Rastafarianism and other Afro-Caribbean cultural traditions to stress its fun-loving and pan-Caribbean style. Some musicians stake claims of difference between their music and other genres, for example in rock musicians' incomprehension of *regional mexicano*, while other musicians attempt to find common ground between genres—for example, when Leydy Bonilla points to the similarity between a *banda* beat and the pulse of *merengue*. Latino musicians also constantly evaluate their music in relation to other genres. Tony Arreaza expresses the importance of music with *feeling*, relating Latin music to the southern blues idiom. Ultimanota has created a (Latin) American repertoire of U.S. and Latin American pop songs with shared themes. Intown musicians fret over ways to cross over to rock audiences who frequent the same clubs they play in, just on different nights. Eastside community members fear traveling outside their neighborhood at night, worrying about police checkpoints and deportation. For them, cross-town music is a foreign, inaccessible world.

Because taste is socially constructed and mediated, musicians' metadiscourse about music represents a key element of their politics: talking about music is how they negotiate and comprehend interactions of social class, racial, ethnic, and community identity. When a musician complains to a friend about the unfair treatment he received from a concert organizer, he is not just warning a fellow musician to watch out, but fleshing out a moral position about how professionals who represent a certain working-class aesthetic should treat each other. If a percussionist, like Sendy Méndez, approaches learning a new timbale lick with care and dedication, recording another drummer's performance and then slowing it down to reconstitute all its relevant pieces, that is because he recognizes the importance of having proper respect for the music's origins, particularly the African-derived percussive elements that course throughout *salsa*. And if a musician covers a popular song in an original way—Leydy Bonilla opening with Lady Gaga's "Bad Romance," Los Mentirosos remaking "Ahora Te Puedes Marchar," or Ultimanota covering "El Cantante"—it is because she recognizes the power of familiar songs, but also how southern *latinidad* is giving those songs new meaning. When audience members shout out requests during a concert or come up after a show and comment about the performance, they are asserting their right to direct the trajectory of a band as active members of the musical community.

By examining Latin music and immigration reform activism in the context of new forms of social and structural racism, we have seen the impact that this emerging racialization has had on the everyday lives and political consciousness of Latino residents. For one, southern *latinidad*, particularly in music, informs how Latina/o immigrants see themselves as racial subjects, and some musicians embrace being "Mexican" (even if they are not) in defiant response to the negative portrayals of "Mexicans" and "illegals" in mainstream English-language media. The detrimental effects of racial profiling in immigration policing have a heavy influence on the segregated and diffuse Latino musical communities, and the denigration of immigrants certainly hampers ties that might be formed with white or black musicians outside these insular communities. Yet Afro-Latina/o musicians have attempted to develop ties across nationality—say, between Dominican musicians and Mexican musicians from Tierra Caliente. Despite its problems, many Latina/o musicians see Charlotte as a haven from regional thickets of racism and even as a site for creating antiracist and nonracist community in the face of anti-immigrant oppression.

Observation of several Latino festivals gave a behind-the-scenes look at how Latino festivals are organized, how organizers market "Latino" culture, and the role of musicians in these events. At festivals and other large concerts, a symbiotic relationship has formed between Latino musical communities and multicultural, progressive corporate Charlotte. In other words, it has become convenient for the corporate business community in Charlotte in its efforts to conceive of and market the city as a multicultural and "progressive" place to attach itself through sponsorship to Latino musical communities who practice "authentic" representations of urban diversity. Musicians play an irreplaceable role in festivals as bearers of cultural capital and connectors to musical communities. They do the hard work of forming community around music making in the local setting of the club, creating culturally "authentic" expressions that can then be inserted into a commodified festival presentation.

Yet musicians' labor at festivals, especially members of local bands, is seen by organizers as just another cost and as a series of interchangeable parts. Organizers legitimize the low pay musicians receive by highlighting the chance bands get to promote their music in front of a large audience with quality sound equipment and network with famous, visiting musicians. Musicians engage in heated intellectual debates about the "proper" way to organize festivals and treat performers, constructing social rules that guide their sense of ethics and their judgments about the "success" of an event—a judgment that often differs from the assessment of festival organizers. These ethical sensibilities stem from musicians' training, whether in a music school or an informal setting, and their relationships with fellow musicians and audience members that shape what constitutes "professional" behavior. By situating musicians' labor in the nexus of cultural production and consumption practices associated with festivals, the analysis shows how "working musicians" face many of the same political and economic limitations that dull to gray the immigrant dream. Moreover, the internal divisions and structural constraints facing festival organizers illustrate how difficult it is to construct an accurate vision of *latinidad*, even on the scale of a single cultural event.

The "popular practice" (Fox 2004) of music making and expressing local musical culture that Charlotte's Latino musicians and audiences engage in differs from the fields of production and consumption produced by and mediated through the Latin music industry. Yet these two fields are not entirely separate: Charlotte musicians attempt to forge connections between local musical expressions and global and transnational networks of music making. Musicians put intellectual effort into assuming postures toward the global music industry, formatting their music, dress, and promotional materials to look and sound "professional" or through an attitude of nonchalance and disinterest in becoming "famous." Some musicians and promoters have invested a considerable amount of time and money in convincing international artists to stop in Charlotte for a tour date, and some have benefited from their access to transnational networks within their genre(s). Others have toured and traveled in an attempt to gain the attention of the Latin music industry by breaking out of the geographic and social limitations of a local scene, widening their audience and perhaps "catching a break." But in "jumping scales," musicians acknowledge that they must form the same types of relationships—with audience members, fellow musicians, and cultural brokers—outside Charlotte in order to be successful; building social capital is a slow and painstaking process, especially when it takes place over great distances. Technology, particularly mobile phones, e-mail, and websites, greatly aids these connections, but sometimes a chance encounter, like Juan Miguel Marín running into a member of Los Amigos Invisibles in the Miami airport, is what deepens these ties.

Musical City

Charlotte offers an important case study of the issues around immigration, cities, and music. Although certainly not the only metropolitan area that can lay claim to being a "musical city" (Graf 2007; Waxer 2002; Berry, Foose, and Jones 1986), Charlotte presents an interesting case of a place where much of the mainstream, non-Latino population is largely unaware of how Latino musicians are forging a music scene across the urban landscape. This phenomenon follows a trend of marginalized populations—Appalachian whites recording "hillbilly" records in the 1920s, African American singers laying down gospel tracks in the 1970s, or Latino musicians singing in Spanish today—making music that through its very existence counters the master narrative of "progressive" industrialization and business boosterism put forth by city elites for over a century.

The "musical city" emerges out of a particular moment and landscape. For example, New Orleans jazz at the turn of the twentieth century arose out of the city's location as a port, its racial gradation of neighborhoods, and its red-light district set aside for prostitution, drug use, and entertainment. All cities abound with sound; yet this does not make a city musical. Whether it is the roar of car traffic, the screech of subway trains, the music bumping from a passing car's speakers, or the Muzak piped into a retail store, these soundscapes are more often regarded as noise and noisome by city dwellers. Music makes the "musical city" not just because it sounds pleasant—that is a subjective judgment that relates to fans of a particular type of music—but because of the community that forms around music making. In Charlotte, a musical city formed around the wake of Latino immigration in the 1990s corresponding to the housing boom and following the geography of the city, where aging Eastside and inner-ring suburban neighborhoods provided inexpensive housing and business opportunities for Latino residents. The labor of "working musicians," the politics inscribed in music making, and negotiations of genre boundaries all facilitate the formation of musical community in Latino Charlotte.

The musical city, then, is a political place, defined by its geography of music making and the social relationships that are embedded in musical community. Sometimes despite their best intentions, musicians are political actors who negotiate a field where they must position themselves as part of a community and in relation to others. In the Latin music scene in Charlotte, musicians are making popular music in the midst of immense political, economic, and social change and despite the indifference of the Latin music industry. Their popular practice will leave a legacy, in musical recordings, in musical communities, and in ways of thinking about the world. In practices such as the "collective circle," they are demanding a right to the city and making spaces where music lives and thrives as a uniquely southern and Latino cultural expression.

NOTES

INTRODUCTION

1 I use the term "rhythm and blues" and "soul" to refer to respective African American musical genres from the 1950s to 1970s, whereas I use the term "R&B" to refer to the African American musical genre from the 1980s to the present, following from its music industry designation and popular terminology.

2 I use the term "grassroots intellectual" rather than "organic intellectual" to differentiate musicians, who act as leaders in their musical community, from intellectual leaders involved in organizational or formal party politics. Latina/o musicians in Charlotte have little or no involvement in the latter type of formal political activism.

3 Connecting these terms to their linguistic origins, *hermano* seems to be a common term of friendship across nationalities, while I heard *'pana* used mainly by musicians from Ecuador. *Marico* is specific to Venezuelans, and although it is derived from *maricón* (faggot), it is used like *'pana* in Venezuelan Spanish, signaling familiarity and taking on the linguistic role of placeholder in speech, much like "dude" in English. It appears that most musicians developed speech patterns connected to their nationality before emigrating, but some have picked up elements of other nationalities through participation in bands, such as the Ecuadorian members of Dorian Gris embracing Mexican slang.

4 Juan Miguel Marín, interview by Sam Byrd, New York, NY, July 18, 2011.

CHAPTER 1. CHARLOTTE, A GLOBALIZING CITY

1 Patricia Zoder, interview by Sam Byrd, Charlotte, NC, April 28, 2010.

2 The Penguin Diner is consistently rated one of the top places to eat in Charlotte and is one of the oldest restaurants in the area, dating from the 1950s. In late 2010 the Penguin Diner was bought by new owners, who instituted menu and decorative changes and are attempting to open other locations. Many local residents were appalled and some stopped eating there, instead frequenting the Diamond restaurant, another old diner down the street, which had just reopened after a hiatus.

3 ACORN was targeted by right-wing activists who posed as a pimp and prostitute seeking government-subsidized housing. This also can be seen as a right-wing versus left-wing fight over the "right to the city."

4 A marketing campaign by a rival supermarket chain, Food Lion Sabor Latino, began in 2009. Food Lion, a southern supermarket chain, created "Latin" food sections at its stores and promoted its products in the Latino community through advertisements on radio and in newspapers and through sponsorship of festivals, including the Festival Latinoamericano.

5 Some speculate that the song "So. Central Rain (I'm Sorry)," on REM's second album, *Reckoning* (1984), was written while band members were in Charlotte. Reflection Sound Studios (where the album was recorded) is located on Central Avenue.

6 In 1952 the collector Harry Smith assembled the *Anthology of American Music* (Smith 1997) from commercial records released between 1927 and 1935, to preserve these important commercial recordings. The anthology has had a far-reaching influence on folk musicians, but was also unique for its time in that it assembled songs based on theme and not on the race of the musicians. Some listeners had difficulty discerning whether certain lesser-known artists were black or white. The British music historian Tony Russell in *Blacks, Whites, and Blues* (1970) puts forth the simple but striking thesis that only with the advent of phonograph recordings did black and white music in the U.S. South begin to travel on separate paths.

CHAPTER 2. THE LATIN MUSIC SCENE IN CHARLOTTE

1 A *regional mexicano* dance style.

2 Fred Figueroa, interview by Sam Byrd, Charlotte, NC, March 13, 2010.

3 I would like to briefly translate some of these names and analyze why this naming is important in terms of genre. First, there is a tendency among rock groups to use wordplay and a mixture of English and Spanish to name their groups. Dorian Gris is a reference to Oscar Wilde's *Picture of Dorian Gray* (2008) and is a reflection of the private school, anglophile education of the band's members in Ecuador and their goth, punk, and heavy metal musical tastes. Bakalao Stars references *bacalao* (codfish), a food commonly eaten, particularly among the working class, in Spain, Portugal, Brazil, the Spanish Caribbean, and coastal Colombia and Venezuela. The "Stars" portion of Bakalao Stars refers to its self-categorization as a jam band playing a mixture of styles, such as the reggae group Easy Dub All Stars or the Afro-Cuban All Stars. Another group, Avión sans Pilot, weaves words from Spanish, French, and English into its name to describe its runaway plane death-metal sound.

Second, among *regional mexicano* groups, there are multiple naming traditions. The most famous *norteño* group extant, Los Tigres del Norte, epitomizes the classic naming equation Animal/person + *del* (of) + place/landscape. A band from the Charlotte area that follows this pattern is Los Forasteros del Norte (the Outsiders of the North, highlighting its marginal immigrant identity). Another tradition involves naming the band using the formula *Banda* (band) + name/

descriptive term. Banda TecnoCaliente fits this mold. A third tradition involves a descriptive name using animals or adjectives as nouns. Los Mentirosos (The Liars) fits this formula.

Third, *música tropical* groups tend to have names that reflect their perspective of the band's musical direction. Thus, one finds names like Furia Tropical (Tropical Fury), a local band that plays *merengue, bachata,* and *salsa.* Bachata Flow's name reflects its affinity both for playing *bachata/merengue* and for mixing in R&B and hip-hop elements to its music and dress styles. DS The Evolution is a name that reflects its changing viewpoint and presentation. The duo started out as D.S. or Dominican Squad and rapped and sang *reggaetón.* In its new guise as DS The Evolution, it continues to play *reggaetón* mixed with the occasional *bachata,* but has shed the "squad" part of the name, associated with rap groups.

Finally, some bands also give nicknames to bandmembers as part of the process of making music. The core members of Bakalao Stars all have nicknames, such as Reggaeman, Mr. Popo, and Gorilla. These nicknames correspond to the sense of playfulness and acting that Bakalao Stars engages in when it takes the stage. Leydy Bonilla (pronounced like lady), however, is not a stage name, but her birth name; in several Latin American countries like the Dominican Republic and Venezuela, this reflects a common creativity in naming children; see Simon Romero, "Venezuelan Parents Love a Famous Name," *New York Times,* January 7, 2007.

4 However, one Eastside club, Skandalos, was known for the high quality of its sound system and sound guy. In a conversation I had with a journalist who covered the Latin club scene (both live and DJ music), he declared that out of all the clubs in Charlotte, "in my opinion Skandalos has the best sound."

5 Gonzalo Pérez, interview by Sam Byrd, Charlotte, NC, September 20, 2010.

6 I have included Brazilian music within the fold of the Latin music scene in Charlotte for several reasons. First, the musical similarities are unmistakable. Brazil shares many of the African influences that shape Spanish Caribbean genres like *salsa, merengue,* and *cumbia.* Brazilian music has long engaged in a dialogue with Latin American music, both firsthand through the regional popularity of individual artists, and secondhand through the amalgamation of Brazilian and Cuban influences in Latin jazz. Musicians from other Charlotte bands, for example, Tony Arreaza from Ultimanota said that they enjoyed listening to *bossa nova* and other Brazilian genres. Second, Brazilians and Latino immigrants, although speaking different languages, share a common history of tumultuous political and social upheaval in their home countries throughout the last fifty years, with military coups, economic crises, and massive urbanization. Moreover, they share a common experience as immigrants to the United States, living in the same neighborhoods, working in the service economy, and facing uncertainty about legal status and rights. Third, while I was in Charlotte, there were concerted efforts, by musicians and organizations, to include Brazilian culture as part of Latino-themed performances and concerts. Thus, Reinaldo Brahn, the vocalist/

guitarist for SoulBrazil, was invited to perform with Ultimanota at several shows. SoulBrazil and a Brazilian dance troupe, Movimentos de Samba, were featured performers at Latin festivals, culminating in the establishment of "A Night in Rio."

7 The exception to this may be Mexican rock, specifically the working-class styles of heavy metal and punk covered by Dorian Gris, which is why I often group it with *regional mexicano* groups that play at Charlotte's Eastside clubs.

CHAPTER 3. BANDS MAKING MUSICAL COMMUNITIES

1 *Culero* is a Mesoamerican Spanish colloquialism that has varied meanings. From the word *culo* (ass, butt) and the personal suffix *-ero*, the term can mean an asshole, a mean or bad person, or ass-fucker in reference to a person's alleged homosexuality (the latter particularly used by Salvadorans and Hondurans). Usually the term is deployed as an insult, although in the case above and most musical settings it is used as friendly criticism to be yelled when a singer forgets lyrics or a DJ miscues a record. It has less gravitas than similar homosexual insinuations attached to the verb *chingar* (to fuck, penetrate) (Paz 2001; Byrd 2000).

2 *Naco* is a colloquial term that means base, lower-class, or "ghetto." The term may originate from Totonaco, the name of a group of indigenous people from the eastern coastal and mountain regions of Mexico, present-day Veracruz, Puebla, and Hidalgo (see Cabrera 1974). However, Marco Polo Hernández-Cuevas asserts that the term originates from *chinaco*, a term referring to African descendants in Mexico, and must be understood in the context of the *mestizaje* racial project that erased Afro-Mexicans from Mexican national identity (Hernández-Cuevas 2004, 2011).

3 Larry Hernández is a young *norteño* singer of *narcocorridos* and love songs. Banda Recodo is the oldest continually performing *banda sinaloense* group. Los Tucanes de Tijuana is a *norteño* group whose song "Mis Tres Animales" (1995) is arguably the most renowned *narcocorrido*.

4 According to a local Spanish-language newspaper, Latino drivers devised ingenious ways to warn other drivers about an impending police roadblock. Drivers passing a checkpoint in the opposite direction would flash headlights and use hand signals outside rolled-down windows to warn oncoming drivers to turn around. José Cusicanqui, "'Los puntos malditos': Sin papeles se las ingenian para evitar los retenes policiales," *Qué Pasa*, August 11, 2010, B1.

5 Fito Páez is an Argentine rock singer known for his political lyrics. Charly García is an Argentine singer and keyboardist who played in the bands Sui Generis and Serú Girán and wrote outspoken songs against the military dictatorship. The Argentine rock band Soda Stereo was the first to achieve success throughout Latin America. After suffering a stroke in May 2010, Soda Stereo's lead singer, Gustavo Cerati, remained in a coma until September 4, 2014, when he died from respiratory arrest. El Tri is Mexico's oldest and most famous rock band. Its lead singer, Alex Lora, is known for his piquant exchanges with audiences during performances and for writing songs about working-class Mexican life. Molotov is an alternative rock/rap band known for its vulgar and political lyrics.

6 Carlos Crespo, interview by Sam Byrd, Charlotte, NC, March 5, 2010.
7 By 2012, Tropic Culture had broken up as a band. Several band members began sitting in with other local groups.

CHAPTER 4. "THURSDAY IS BAKALAO'S DAY!"
1 Bakalao Stars (Christian Anzola, Javier Anzola, and Daniel Alvarado), interview by Sam Byrd, Charlotte, NC, July 20, 2010.
2 Bakalao Stars interview, July 20, 2010.
3 The Fania All Stars included singers and instrumentalists who performed on the Fania label, including Héctor Lavoe, Celia Cruz, Johnny Pacheco, Willie Colón, Rubén Blades, Ray Barretto, Cheo Feliciano, and other Latin stars of the 1960s and 1970s. Their recordings mixed *salsa* (which itself was a fusion of several dance styles) with other Caribbean and Latin American musical styles, as well as R&B, disco, rock, and funk.
4 Spanish-language television has a number of talk and variety shows that provide chances for lesser-known bands to promote their songs. TecnoCaliente has appeared on several shows produced in New York or Miami throughout the past few years, such as *Despierta América*. One locally produced show, *Mi Tierra TV*, is broadcast on satellite television and features local bands, interviews, and community news.
5 Since this research was completed, Gonzalo Pérez has moved from Charlotte to Houston, Texas, and now promotes an all-woman group, Las Fenix. He no longer represents any Charlotte bands.
6 Gonzalo Pérez interview, September 20, 2010.
7 Gonzalo Pérez interview, September 20, 2010.
8 Bakalao Stars interview, July 20, 2010.
9 Former singer with *rock en español* band Héroes del Silencio.
10 See http://www.carlotanrock.com/portafolioshows.php.

CHAPTER 5. THE "COLLECTIVE CIRCLE"
1 Translation: "Thanks . . . to our families and friends for supporting us in this gray dream. And hyper-special gratitude to *la raza* that comes to all our shows, without you the Dorians wouldn't exist." *La raza* (literally "the race") refers to people from Mexico of *mestizo* and/or indigenous descent.
2 Portions of this chapter appear in Byrd 2014.
3 See http://www.youtube.com/watch?v=FkH1wrLvgHk.
4 Juan Miguel Marín interview, July 18, 2011.
5 A popular English-language learning program.
6 Rosario Machicao, "Masivo pedido de reforma migratoria en Charlotte," *La Noticia*, January 13, 2010, 1; Ileana Pauly, "Miles gritaron reforma: Tres mil personas en Carolina de Norte prenden la campaña," *Qué Pasa*, January 20, 2010, B1; "Charlotte se moviliza por la reforma migratoria," *El Progreso Hispano*, January 14, 2010, 1.

7 Organizers would often stress during planning meetings and during phone calls to recruit protesters that participants should only bring the U.S. flag and not the flag(s) of their home countries so that the protesters' loyalty to the United States could not be questioned. This became an issue after the 2006 immigrant-rights marches, when some marchers carried flags from other countries. Organizers also encouraged participants to dress in neutral colors, usually a white T-shirt, so that the group would appear uniform and easily recognizable.

8 "Multitudinaria marcha nacional se unió a una voz: ¡Reforma!," *Mi Gente*, March 23, 2010, 1; "Inmigrantes demonstraron su poder," *El Progreso Hispano*, March 25, 2010, 1; Rosario Machicao, "Miles marcharon por una reforma migratoria," *La Noticia*, March 24, 2010, 1.

9 *Qué Pasa*, March 24, 2010, A1.

10 Ileana Pauly, "Rechazo a la injusticia: Grupo de teatro callejero presenta obra contra la ley Arizona," *Qué Pasa*, July 21, 2010, B1.

11 Alberto Benítez, "Nueva generación: Son jóvenes y comprometidos con vivir con las mismas oportunidades," *Qué Pasa*, February 24, 2010, B1.

12 Lee Shearer, "Voices Raised against Regents' Policy on Undocumented Students," *Online Athens/Athens Banner-Herald*, August 24, 2011; Jose Antonio Vargas, "My Life as an Undocumented Immigrant," *New York Times*, June 22, 2011, MM22.

13 "Drop the I Word" is a campaign to pressure media to stop using the word "illegal" to describe undocumented immigrants in news stories.

14 Lacey Williams, interview by Sam Byrd, Charlotte, NC, October 26, 2013.

15 Franco Ordoñez, "Charlotte Women Arrested in Immigration Protest," *Charlotte Observer*, August 1, 2013 (video).

16 Armando Bellmas, interview by Sam Byrd, Charlotte, NC, August 3, 2013.

17 See http://obracollective.wordpress.com/about/.

18 For a recap video of the march with these performances, see http://www.youtube.com/watch?v=b4i7oa9eZcg.

19 Billy Bragg. "Why Music Needs to Get Political Again," *New Significance*, August 25, 2011.

20 However, the Los Angeles band La Santa Cecilia has released a song with strong political commentary about family separations entitled "ICE—El Hielo" (2013).

21 On September 30, 2010, Ecuador's national police went on strike. In a confrontation with President Rafael Correa, the police attacked him and took him hostage. After being held inside a hospital, Correa was rescued by an elite army unit and restored to full power. The Tropic Culture concert took place on October 1, 2010.

22 For a counterexample of a political, environmentally concerned song that does offer specific condemnations and recommendations, see the Atlanta rap group Goodie Mob's "public service announcement" at the end of its song "Beautiful Skin" (1998).

23 Forgacs 2000, 425.

24   Sendy Méndez, interview by Sam Byrd, Charlotte, NC, May 7, 2010.

25   Gustavo Cerati, lead singer of the Argentine rock band Soda Stereo, and Beto
Cuevas, lead singer of the Chilean rock band La Ley.

26   Ricardo de los Cobos, "Honor a los grandes," *Mi Gente*, November 24, 2009, 31.
Translation mine.

27   *Pachuco* is a term that describes Mexican American/Chicano working-class youth
from the 1930s to the 1950s who wore zoot suits and engaged in a subculture that
mixed Mexican and American working-class style, language, and attitudes.
Maldita Vecindad members often dress in zoot suits when they perform; one of
the band's songs is entitled "Pachuco."

28   *Ska-neando* is a play on words combining "ska" with *sonando* (sounding) and
perhaps *sondeando* (sounding out) to describe Maldita Vecindad's relationship
with its audience.

29   When I attended a Maldita Vecindad concert in New York in July 2010 at Central
Park Summerstage, this exact dance formation occurred as soon as the band
started playing and went on for the entire performance, despite the efforts of the
security personnel, who had to try to prevent crowd surfers from jumping
onstage.

CHAPTER 6. SHIFTING URBAN GENRES

1   The fact that Leydy is a Hispanicization of "lady" is also part of this affiliation.
Unlike Lady Gaga, Leydy Bonilla is not a stage name.

2   See http://www.youtube.com/watch?v=_Y4NrLboDiQ.

3   Matching outfits and name branding on instruments (especially drum sets) and
clothing are common practice among *regional mexicano* groups.

4   See Marske 2008 for an analysis of Plaza Fiesta as a reimagined homeland for
Latino immigrants. In late 2013, Plaza Fiesta Carolinas closed for business.

5   Itself a cover of a song by the Dominican *merengue* singer Eddy Herrera and the
Venezuelan singer Liz.

6   See http://www.youtube.com/watch?v=pHwyyJxtTfc.

7   I wrote a blog entry outlining the song's different cover versions: http://sams-
sounds.blogspot.com/2010/05/ahora-te-puedes-marchar.html.

8   See http://ultimanotamusic.com/. Full disclosure: after Ultimanota's bandleader,
Tony Arreaza, wrote this description, I helped him edit the statement.

9   This is an intriguing connection, particularly since Michael Jackson at times
borrowed elements of Latin (and African) music, such as the coda of "Wanna Be
Startin' Somethin'" (1982), which borrows the phrase "Mama say, mama sah,
ma-ma coo-sah" from the Cameroon saxophonist Manu Dibango's "Soul
Makossa" (1972), also covered by Fania All-Stars in the 1970s (n.d.).

10   Bakalao Stars interview, July 20, 2010.

11   This matches Maxine Margolis's analysis that Brazilian immigrants are the
"invisible minority" among Latino immigrants (2009).

CHAPTER 7. RACE AND THE EXPANDING BORDERLANDS CONDITION

1 Not his real name. To protect his identity and because of his undocumented status, I have slightly altered certain details of the narrative.

2 Michael D. Shear, "Seeing Citizenship Path Near, Activists Push Obama to Slow Deportations," *New York Times*, February 22, 2013; American Immigration Council, "Falling through the Cracks: The Impact of Immigration Enforcement on Children Caught Up in the Child Welfare System," December 12, 2012.

3 As this book went to press, the U.S. Congress was still debating immigration reform legislation.

4 See Manny Fernández, "Layers of Contradiction in L.I. Hate-Crime Trial," *New York Times*, March 26, 2010.

5 By the spring of 2012, the Department of Homeland Security (DHS) decided to reduce funds for Charlotte's 287(g) program, for which the agreement was set to expire in October. DHS now favors the Secure Communities program as a tool for local enforcement of immigration law. See Prieto 2012.

6 The counterproductive results for law enforcement, such as underreporting of crimes and fear of police in immigrant communities, are just beginning to be analyzed for the 287(g) program. See Vidales, Day, and Powe 2009; Nguyen and Gill 2010; Capps et al. 2011. De Genova (2002) has written about the broader negative social implications for this association of "illegality" with immigrant communities.

7 Ileana Pauly, "Justicia con Roberto: Entierro simulado de Roberto Medina en cárcel de Stewart," *Qué Pasa*, December 2, 2009, B1.

8 "Policía acusado de asaltar sexualmente a Latina," *La Noticia*, January 6, 2010, 5; Cheris Hodges, "Community Violations: Crimes Drive a Wedge between CMPD and Hispanics," *Creative Loafing Charlotte*, February 10, 2010, 9.

9 Rosario Machicao, "Policía pide confianza a inmigrantes," *La Noticia*, March 24, 2010, 10–11.

10 Rosario Machicao, "¿Como mejorar la relación entre la policía y los latinos?," *La Noticia*, June 14, 2010, 8.

11 Whitney Smith, "Familias Unidas," Latin American Coalition blog, August 10, 2012, http://www.latinamericancoalition.org/blog/111/familias-unidas.

12 Roque Planas, "Isaide Serrano Wins Deportation Case Five Hours after Giving Birth," *Huffington Post*, November 30, 2012.

13 Armando Bellmas interview, August 3, 2013.

14 Bakalao Stars and Ras Congo, interview by Sam Byrd, Charlotte, NC, December 18, 2010.

15 Gonzalo Pérez interview, September 20, 2010.

16 Gonzalo Pérez interview, September 20, 2010.

17 In fact, city officials from the Health and Human Services Department hold office hours weekly at the Latin American Coalition, where they help families fill out paperwork for Medicaid and other public benefits. Some of the Coalition's

funding comes from grants from city agencies and prominent statewide foundations.

18 See Massey 2011 for an explanation of the decreased mobility and limited economic prospects of Mexican and Central American migrants to the United States.

CHAPTER 8. THE FESTIVAL

1 Festival Latinoamericano is also called by its English name, the Latin American Festival. To avoid confusion and to stress the importance of Spanish language usage during the event, I use its Spanish name.

2 I take caution to note my role in the events described below and assess the limitations and benefits of my position as an insider at these festivals. I have also taken care, when necessary, to hide the identities of certain individuals whose reputations or interpersonal relationships could be damaged by conversations we had in private.

3 To be clear, while I did give advice and opinions as to which artists and sponsors should be selected, Tony Arreaza and other executive staff at the Latin American Coalition made all significant decisions. My role was that of apprentice being trained by a master craftsman, which in describing Arreaza is not hyperbole.

4 See www.festivallatinoamericano.org. The website and the festival's promotional materials are designed by the Carlotan Rock co-investor and former La Rúa member Juan Miguel Marín.

5 Juan Miguel Marín interview, July 18, 2011.

6 Juan Miguel Marín interview, July 18, 2011.

7 While I have deployed "Latino" as a descriptive term of convenience (see chapter 1), it is important to highlight the ways "Latino" materializes in practice, in this case through conversations, marketing, and promotion of the Festival Latinoamericano.

8 Charlotte recently emerged as the fastest-growing Latino market in the United States, according to Nielsen (2013).

9 It is estimated that Mexicans (in Mexico) drink on average 40 percent more soft drinks per person than people in the United States. Mexico is Coca-Cola's biggest market by volume outside the United States; see *Economist*, October 19–25, 2013, 70.

10 However, Lipsitz (1994) critiques Simon for appropriating the music of South African and other nonwhite musicians without understanding the consequences of his repurposing of their music to appeal to white audiences.

CHAPTER 9. MUSICIANS' ETHICS AND AESTHETICS

1 An *orquesta* is a specific musical term in Spanish that means a full band with proper instrumentation for the musical genre—*salsa* or Tejano—being played. I have avoided translating the term as *orchestra* because of the latter's association with classical music. An *orquesta de salsa* features two or three vocalists and may

include trumpets, trombones, timbales, congas, bongos, clave, piano, bass, and other instruments.

2 Serralde used the Spanish term *musicalización*.

3 Helder Serralde, interview by Sam Byrd, Charlotte, NC, June 25, 2010.

4 Reinaldo Brahn Fermino, interview by Sam Byrd, Charlotte, NC, June 16, 2010.

CONCLUSION

1 Immigration, Customs and Enforcement (ICE) deported 396,906 individuals in fiscal year 2011, the most to date. Deportation Nation, "Round-Up: Immigration and Enforcement Systems under Fire amidst Record-Number Deportations," October 20, 2011, http://www.deportationnation.org/.

2 A recent U.S. Supreme Court decision, *Shelby County v. Holder* (2013), however, modified aspects of this law.

3 Juan Miguel Marín interview, July 18, 2011; Gonzalo Pérez interview, September 20, 2010.

4 Juan Miguel Marín interview, July 18, 2011.

5 By "musical city," I refer to how the city becomes a site for music and shapes and directs how music making occurs among its residents.

6 One counterexample was the onstage presentation of James Brown as "the hardest-working man in show business."

BIBLIOGRAPHY

Adams, Robert L. 2006. "History at the Crossroads: Vodú and the Modernization of the Dominican Borderlands." In *Globalization and Race: Transformations in the Cultural Production of Blackness*, edited by Kamari Maxine Clarke and Deborah A. Thomas. Durham: Duke University Press.

Adorno, Theodor W. 1941. "On Popular Music." *Studies in Philosophy and Social Sciences* 9: 17–48.

Agamben, Giorgio. 2003. State of Exception. Chicago: University of Chicago Press.

Allman Brothers. 1971. "Statesboro Blues." *At Fillmore East*. Capricorn B000003CMB.

Almarán, Carlos Eleta. 1956. "Historia de un Amor." From film *Historia de un Amor*. Internacional Cinematográfica.

Anderson, Benedict. 2006. *Imagined Communities: Reflections on the Origin and Spread of Nationalism*. London: Verso.

Anglin, Mary K. 2002. *Women, Power and Dissent in the Hills of Carolina*. Urbana: University of Illinois Press.

Anzaldúa, Gloria. 1987. *Borderlands/La Frontera: The New Mestiza*. San Francisco: Aunt Lute Books.

Appadurai, Arjun. 1996. *Modernity at Large: Cultural Dimensions of Globalization*. Minneapolis: University of Minnesota Press.

Austerlitz, Paul. 1997. *Merengue: Dominican Music and Dominican Identity*. Philadelphia: Temple University Press.

Bacilos. 2002. "Mi Primer Millón." *Caraluna*. Warner Music.

Bakalao Stars. 2007. *Péguele al Trifásico con Azpero Sumbein*. Kukaracha Records.

———. 2010. *Soundcocho*.

Baker, Lee. 1998. From Savage to Negro: Anthropology and the Construction of Race: 1896–1954. Berkeley: University of California Press.

———. 2002. "The Color-Blind Bind." In *Cultural Diversity in the United States: A Critical Reader*, edited by Ida Susser and Thomas Patterson, 103–19. Malden, MA: Blackwell.

Bakhtin, Mikhail. 1984. *Rabelais and His World*. Bloomington: University of Indiana Press.

Banda TecnoCaliente. 2008. "Porque Me Enamoré de Ti." Performance on *Titulares y Más*, Univision.

———. 2009. "Así Te Amo." Freddie Records.

Banda TecnoCaliente and Leydy Bonilla. 2010. "A Dormir Juntitos." Tecno Records.

Benjamin, Walter. 1999. *The Arcades Project*. Cambridge: Harvard University Press.

Berry, Jason, Jonathan Foose, and Tad Jones. 1986. *Up from the Cradle of Jazz*. Athens: University of Georgia Press.

Boellstorff, Tom. 2010. *Coming of Age in Second Life: An Anthropologist Explores the Virtual Human*. Princeton: Princeton University Press.

Bonilla, Leydy. 2011. "Pienso en Ti." Leybo Records.

Booth, Stanley. 1993. *Rythm Oil: A Journey through the Music of the American South*. New York: Vintage.

Bourdieu, Pierre. 1984. *Distinction: A Social Critique of the Judgement of Taste*. Translated by Richard Nice. Cambridge: Harvard University Press.

Branch, Taylor. 1989. *Parting the Waters: America in the King Years, 1954–1963*. New York: Simon and Schuster.

———. 1999. *Pillar of Fire: America in the King Years, 1963–1965*. New York: Simon and Schuster.

Brennan, Timothy. 2008. *Secular Devotion: Afro-Latin Music and Imperial Jazz*. London: Verso.

Byrd, Samuel. 2000. "Gender Construction in the Contemporary Narcocorrido, 1967–2000." B.A. honors thesis, Oberlin College.

———. 2009–2011. *Sam's Sounds*. Weblog. http://www.samssounds.blogspot.com/.

———. 2012. "Making Music in Latino Charlotte: Politics and Community Formation in a Globalizing City." Ph.D. diss., City University of New York Graduate Center.

———. 2014. "'The Collective Circle': Latina/o Immigrant Musicians and Politics in Charlotte, NC." *American Ethnologist* 41, no. 2 (May): 246–60.

Cabrera, Luis. 1974. *Diccionario de aztequismos*. México DF: Ediciones Oasis.

Café Tacuba. 1996. "Como Te Extraño Mi Amor." *Avalanche de Exitos*. Warner Music Latina B00000 5TLT.

Calamaro, Andrés (with Los Abuelos de la Nada). 1983. "Mil Horas." *Vasos y Besos*. Interdisc.

Caldeira, Theresa. 1999. "Fortified Enclaves: The New Urban Segregation." In *Cities and Citizenship*, edited by James Holston, 114–38. Durham: Duke University Press.

Candelario, Ginetta. 2007. *Black behind the Ears: Dominican Racial Identity from Museums to Beauty Shops*. Durham: Duke University Press.

Capps, Randy, Marc R. Rosenblum, Cristina Rodriguez, and Muzaffar Chishti. 2011. "Delegation and Divergence: A Study of 287(g) State and Local Immigration Enforcement." Migration Policy Institute, Washington, DC, January.

Carmichael, Stokely, and Charles V. Hamilton. 1967. *Black Power: The Politics of Liberation in America*. New York: Vintage.

Caro, Robert. 2002. *Master of the Senate: The Years of Lyndon Johnson*. New York: Knopf.

Carter, Jimmy. 1995. *Keeping Faith: Memoirs of a President*. Fayetteville: University of Arkansas Press.

Charters, Samuel. 2009. *A Language of Song: Journeys in the Musical World of the African Diaspora*. Durham: Duke University Press.

Cobb, James C. 1988. *Industrialization and Southern Society, 1877–1984*. Chicago: Dorsey.

Comaroff, John L., and Jean Comaroff. 2009. *Ethnicity, Inc*. Chicago: University of Chicago Press.

Conway, Cecelia. 1995. *African Banjo Echoes in Appalachia: A Study of Folk Traditions*. Knoxville: University of Tennessee Press.

Coplan, David. 2008. *In Township Tonight! South Africa's Black City Music and Theatre*. 2nd ed. Chicago: University of Chicago Press.

Crapanzano, Vincent. 2006. "The Scene: Shadowing the Real." *Anthropological Theory* 6, no. 4: 387–405.

Creed, Gerald, ed. 2006. *The Seductions of Community: Emancipations, Oppressions, Quandaries*. Santa Fe: School of American Research Press.

Crehan, Kate. 2012. *Community Art: An Anthropological Perspective*. London: Berg.

Cvetkovich, Ann. 2003. *An Archive of Feelings: Trauma, Sexuality, and Lesbian Public Culture*. Durham: Duke University Press.

Dávila, Arlene. 2012. *Latinos, Inc.: The Marketing and Making of a People*. Berkeley: University of California Press. First published 2001.

Davis, Allison, Burleigh Gardner, and Mary Gardner. 1988. *Deep South: A Social Anthropological Study of Caste and Class*. Los Angeles: Center for Afro-American Studies, University of California. First published 1941.

Davis, Mike. 2006. *City of Quartz*. London: Verso.

De Genova, Nicolas. 2002. "Migrant 'Illegality' and Deportability in Everyday Life." *Annual Review of Anthropology* 31:419–47.

———. 2005. *Working the Boundaries: Race, Space, and "Illegality" in Mexican Chicago*. Durham: Duke University Press.

De Genova, Nicholas, and Ana Ramos-Zayas, eds. 2003. *Latino Crossings: Mexicans, Puerto Ricans and the Politics of Race and Citizenship*. New York: Routledge.

De la Fuente, Alejandro. 2001. *A Nation for All: Race, Inequality, and Politics in Twentieth Century Cuba*. Chapel Hill: University of North Carolina Press.

Delgado, Richard, and Jean Stefancic, eds. 1998. *The Latina/o Condition: A Critical Reader*. New York: New York University Press.

De los Cobos, Ricardo. 2009a. "Es sólo Carlotan Rock, pero me gusta . . ." *Mi Gente* (Charlotte), August 4, 30.

———. 2009b. "Honor a los grandes." *Mi Gente*, November 24, 31.

Demers, Joanna, and Rosemary Coombe. 2006. *Steal This Music: How Intellectual Property Law Affects Musical Creativity*. Athens: University of Georgia Press.

DeParle, Jason. 2011. "The Anti-Immigration Crusader." *New York Times*, April 17.

Derrida, Jacques. 1980. *Writing and Difference*. London: Routledge.

Dibango, Manu. 1972. "Soul Makossa." *Soul Makossa*. Atlantic Records.

Doane, Ashley, and Eduardo Bonilla-Silva, eds. 2003. *White Out: The Continuing Significance of Racism*. New York: Routledge.

Domínguez, Virginia. 1993. White by Definition: Social Classification in Creole Louisiana. New Brunswick: Rutgers University Press.

Dorian Gris. 2009. *Live at the Dark Room*. Mono Gris Mobile Recordings.

Doyle, Don H. 1990. *New Men, New Cities, New South: Atlanta, Nashville, Charleston, Mobile, 1860–1910*. Chapel Hill: University of North Carolina Press.

Drake, St. Clair, and Horace Cayton. 1993. *Black Metropolis: A Study of Negro Life in a Northern City*. Chicago: University of Chicago Press. First published 1945.

Du Bois, W. E. B. 2003. *The Souls of Black Folks*. New York: Barnes and Noble Classics. First published 1903.

Dunn, Timothy. 1996. *The Militarization of the U.S.-Mexico Border, 1978–1992*. Austin: Center for Mexican American Studies.

Durkheim, Emile. 1997. *The Division of Labor in Society*. New York: Free Press. First published 1893.

Dylan, Bob. 1975. "Tangled Up in Blue." *Blood on the Tracks*. Columbia.

Edberg, Mark Cameron. 2004. *El Narcotraficante: Narcocorridos and the Construction of a Cultural Persona on the U.S.-Mexico Border*. Austin: University of Texas Press.

Edelman, Marc. 1999. *Peasants against Globalization: Rural Social Movements in Costa Rica*. Stanford: Stanford University Press.

Ehrenreich, Barbara. 2010. *Bright-Sided: How Positive Thinking Is Undermining America*. New York: Picador.

Ellison, Ralph. 2003. "Stephen Crane and the Mainstream of American Fiction (Introduction to *The Red Badge of Courage*, 1960)." In *The Collected Essays of Ralph Ellison*, edited by John F. Callahan. New York: Modern Library.

Erlmann, Veit. 1996. *Nightsong: Performance, Power and Practice in South Africa*. Chicago: University of Chicago Press.

Fabian, Johannes. 1998. *Moments of Freedom: Anthropology and Popular Culture*. Charlottesville: University Press of Virginia.

Fania All-Stars. N.d. "Soul Makossa." *Fania Salsa Classics*. Charly Records SNAD523CD.

Fayde, Reese. 2007. "Reviving South Minneapolis." *Next American City Magazine*, Winter.

Feld, Steven. 1976. "Ethnomusicology and Visual Communication." *Ethnomusicology* 20, no. 2 (May): 293–325.

———. 1990. *Sound and Sentiment: Birds Weeping, Poetics, and Song in Kaluli Expression*. Philadelphia: University of Pennsylvania Press.

Ferguson, James. 1994. *The Anti-politics Machine*. Cambridge: Cambridge University Press.

Fernández-Kelly, María Patricia. 1983. *For We Are Sold, I and My People: Women and Industry in Mexico's Frontier*. Albany: State University of New York Press.

Fink, Leon. 2002. *The Maya of Morgantown: Work and Community in the Nuevo New South*. Chapel Hill: University of North Carolina Press.

Finnegan, Ruth. 2007. *The Hidden Musicians: Music-Making in an English Town*. Middletown, CT: Wesleyan University Press. First published 1989.

Fiscal Policy Institute. 2009. "Immigrants and the Economy: Contribution of Immigrant Workers to the Country's 25 Largest Metropolitan Areas." December.

Flores, Juan. 2000. *From Bomba to Hip-Hop: Puerto Rican Culture and Latino Identity.* New York: Columbia University Press.

Florida, Richard. 2003. *The Rise of the Creative Class.* New York: Basic Books.

Floyd, Samuel A., Jr. 1995. *The Power of Black Music.* New York: Oxford University Press.

Flynt, J. Wayne. 1979. *Dixie's Forgotten People: The South's Poor Whites.* Bloomington: Indiana University Press.

Foner, Philip. 1972. *The Spanish-Cuban-American War and the Birth of American Imperialism.* Vol. 1, *1892–1895* and vol. 2, *1895–1898.* New York: Monthly Review Press.

Forgacs, David, ed. 2000. *The Antonio Gramsci Reader: Selected Writings, 1916–1935.* New York: New York University Press.

Fox, Aaron. 2004. *Real Country: Music and Language in Working-Class Culture.* Durham: Duke University Press.

Frank, Thomas. 2011. "The Bleakness Stakes." *Harper's Magazine,* November, 8–13.

Freeman, Carla. 2000. *High Tech and High Heels in the Global Economy: Women, Work, and Pink-Collar Identities in the Caribbean.* Durham: Duke University Press.

French, Jan Hoffman. 2009. *Legalizing Identities: Becoming Black or Indian in Brazil's Northeast.* Chapel Hill: University of North Carolina Press.

Fry, Richard. 2008. "Latino Settlement in the New Century." Pew Hispanic Center, Washington, DC, October 23.

Funk, Tim, Steve Harrison, and Théoden Jones. 2010. "End Is Near for Charlotte's Eastland Mall." *Charlotte Observer,* April 19.

Galeano, Eduardo. 1997. *Open Veins of Latin America: Five Centuries of the Pillage of a Continent.* New York: Monthly Review Press. First published 1971.

García, David. 2006. *Arsenio Rodríguez and the Transnational Flows of Latin Popular Music.* Philadelphia: Temple University Press.

Garreau, Joel. 1992. *Edge City: Life on the New Frontier.* New York: Anchor.

Gaspar de Alba, Alicia, with Georgina Guzmán, eds. 2010. *Making a Killing: Femicide, Free Trade, and La Frontera.* Austin: University of Texas Press.

Gates, Henry Louis, Jr. 1994. "Multiculturalism and Its Discontents." *Black Scholar* 24, no. 1 (Winter): 16–17.

George, Nelson. 1988. *The Death of Rhythm and Blues.* New York: Penguin.

Gill, Hannah. 2010. *The Latino Migration Experience in North Carolina: New Roots in the Old North State.* Chapel Hill: University of North Carolina Press.

Gilroy, Paul. 1991. "There Ain't No Black in the Union Jack": The Cultural Politics of Race and Nation. Chicago: University of Chicago Press.

Global Voices. 2005. "Cross-Border Conversation on Race." Global Voices weblog. July 9. http://globalvoicesonline.org/2005/07/08/cross-border-conversation-on-race/.

Goffman, Erving. 1959. *The Presentation of Self in Everyday Life.* New York: Doubleday Anchor.

Goldstein, Donna. 2003. *Laughter out of Place: Race, Class, Violence, and Sexuality in a Rio Shantytown.* Berkeley: University of California Press.

González, Juan. 2000. *Harvest of Empire: A History of Latinos in America.* New York: Penguin.

Goodie Mob. 1998. "Beautiful Skin." *Still Standing*. Arista, LaFace Records 73008–26047–2.

Gordon, David M. 1978. "Capitalist Development and the History of American Cities." In *Marxism and the Metropolis: New Perspectives in Urban Political Economy*, edited by William Tabb and Larry Sawers, 25–63. New York: Oxford University Press.

Gordon, Robert. 2002. Can't Be Satisfied: The Life and Times of Muddy Waters. Boston: Little, Brown.

Gorter, Durk. 2004. "Introduction: The Study of the Linguistic Landscape as a New Approach to Multilingualism." *International Journal of Multilingualism* 3, no. 1: 1–6.

Graf, Max. 2007. *Legend of a Musical City: The Story of Vienna*. New York: Philosophical Library.

Graves, William, and Heather A. Smith, eds. 2010. *Charlotte, NC: The Global Evolution of a New South City*. Athens: University of Georgia Press.

Gray, David. 1999. "Babylon." *White Ladder*. IHT.

Green, Archie. 1972. *Only a Miner: Studies in Recorded Coal-Mining Songs*. Urbana: University of Illinois Press.

Greenhaw, Wayne. 1982. *Elephants in the Cottonfields: Ronald Reagan and the New Republican South*. New York: Macmillan.

Gregory, Steven. 2006. *The Devil behind the Mirror: Globalization and Politics in the Dominican Republic*. Berkeley: University of California Press.

Griffith, David. 2006. *American Guestworkers: Jamaicans and Mexicans in the U.S. Labor Market*. University Park: Pennsylvania State University Press.

Griswold del Castillo, Richard, and Arnoldo de León. 1996. *North to Aztlán: A History of Mexican Americans in the United States*. New York: Twayne.

Grossman, James R. 1991. *Land of Hope: Chicago, Black Southerners, and the Great Migration*. Chicago: University of Chicago Press.

Guerra, Juan Luis. 1990. "Burbujas de Amor." *Bachata Rosa*. EMI Records.

Habell-Pallán, Michelle. 2005. *Loca Motion: The Travels of Chicana and Latina Popular Culture*. New York: New York University Press.

Hale, Charles. 2002. "Does Multiculturalism Menace? Governance, Cultural Rights and the Politics of Identity in Guatemala." *Journal of Latin American Studies* 34:485–524.

Hall, Jacquelyn Dowd, James Leloudis, Robert Korstad, Mary Murphy, Lu Ann Jones, and Christopher Daly. 1987. *Like a Family: The Making of a Southern Cotton Mill World*. Chapel Hill: University of North Carolina Press.

Hanchett, Thomas W. 1985. "Recording in Charlotte, 1926–1945." *History South*. Weblog. www.historysouth.org.

———. 1996. *Sorting Out the New South City: Race, Class, and Urban Development in Charlotte, 1875–1975*. Chapel Hill: University of North Carolina Press.

———. 2010. "Salad-Bowl Suburbs: A History of Charlotte's East Side and South Boulevard Immigrant Corridors." In Charlotte, NC: The Global Evolution of a New South City, edited by William Graves and Heather A. Smith, 247–62. Athens: University of Georgia Press.

Harrison, Faye V. 2008. "The Politics of Antiracism and Social Justice: The Perspective of a Human Rights Network in the U.S. South." *North American Dialogue* (Society for the Anthropology of North America) 11, no. 2: 7–17.

Harvey, David. 1973. *Social Justice and the City*. Baltimore: Johns Hopkins University Press.

———. 1989. *The Condition of Postmodernity*. Malden, MA: Blackwell.

———. 2006. *Paris: Capital of Modernity*. New York: Routledge.

Hawkins, Martin. 2007. *A Shot in the Dark: Making Records in Nashville, 1945–1955*. Nashville: Vanderbilt University Press.

Hayden, Tom, ed. 2002. *The Zapatista Reader*. New York: Nation Books.

Hebdige, Dick. 1979. *Subculture: The Meaning of Style*. London: Methuen.

Helg, Aline. 1995. *Our Rightful Share: The Afro-Cuban Struggle for Equality, 1886–1912*. Chapel Hill: University of North Carolina Press.

Helm, Levon, and Stephen Davis. 2000. *This Wheel's on Fire: Levon Helm and the Story of the Band*. Chicago: Chicago Review Press.

Hernández-Cuevas, Marco Polo. 2004. *African Mexicans and the Discourse on Modern Nation*. Lanham, MD: University Press of America.

———. 2011. "We Count: Identity, the Census, and Visibility." Paper presented at "Afro-Latin@s Now! Strategies for Visibility and Action" conference. New York, November 3–5.

Herrera-Sobek, Maria. 1990. *The Mexican Corrido: A Feminist Analysis*. Bloomington: University of Indiana Press.

———. 1993. Northward Bound: The Mexican Experience in Ballad and Song. Bloomington: University of Indiana Press.

Herskovits, Melville. 1990. *The Myth of the Negro Past*. New York: Beacon. First published 1941.

Hill, Jane. 1999. "Language, Race, and White Public Space." *American Anthropologist* 100, no. 3: 680–89.

HipHoods. 2008. "Morningside Village to Include 400 Apartments." February 13. http://www.hiphoods.com/blog/2008/02/13/morningside-village-to-include-400-apartments/.

Hirsch, Jennifer. 2003. *A Courtship after Marriage: Sexuality and Love in Mexican Transnational Families*. Berkeley: University of California Press.

Hobsbawm, Eric, and Terence Ranger. 1983. *The Invention of Tradition*. New York: Cambridge University Press.

Holland, Dorothy, Donald Nonini, Catherine Lutz, Lesley Bartlett, Marla Frederick-McGlathery, Thaddeus Guldbrandsen, and Enrique Murillo Jr. 2007. *Local Democracy under Siege: Activism, Public Interests, and Private Politics*. New York: New York University Press.

Hollinger, David A. 1993. "How Wide the Circle of the 'We'? American Intellectuals and the Problem of the Ethnos since World War II." *American Historical Review* 98, no. 2: 317–37.

Holmes, Seth. 2013. *Fresh Fruit, Broken Bodies: Migrant Farmworkers in the United States*. Berkeley: University of California Press.

Hood, John. 1996. "Charlotte: The Queen of Southern Banking." *Policy Review* 75:10–12.

Hootie and the Blowfish. 1995. "Only Wanna Be with You." *Cracked Rear View*. Atlantic.

Howard, David. 2001. *Coloring the Nation: Race and Ethnicity in the Dominican Republic*. Boulder, CO: Lynne Rienner.

Hurston, Zora Neale. 1990. *Mules and Men*. New York: HarperPerennial. First published 1935.

Inda, Jonathan Xavier. 2006. "Border Prophylaxis: Technology, Illegality, and the Government of Immigration." *Cultural Dynamics* 18, no. 2: 115–38.

Inda, Jonathan Xavier, and Renato Rosaldo, eds. 2008. *The Anthropology of Globalization: A Reader*. Malden, MA: Blackwell.

Irvine, Judith T., and Susan Gal. 2000. "Language Ideology and Linguistic Differentiation." In *Regimes of Language: Ideologies, Politics, and Identities*, edited by Paul Kroskrity, 35–83. Santa Fe: School of American Research Press.

Jackson, Michael. 1982. "Billie Jean." *Thriller*. Sony B0000025RI.

Jacobs, Jane. 1992. *The Death and Life of Great American Cities*. New York: Vintage. First published 1961.

Jacobson, Matthew Frye. 1998. *Whiteness of a Different Color: European Immigrants and the Alchemy of Race*. Cambridge: Harvard University Press.

Johnson, Jack. 2006. "Upside Down." *Sing-a-Longs and Lullabies for the Film Curious George*. Universal.

Johnson, Olati. 2010. "The Story of *Bob Jones University v. United States*: Race, Religion, and Congress' Extraordinary Acquiescence." Columbia Public Law and Legal Theory Working Papers, Columbia Law School, New York.

Jones, Jacqueline. 2008. *Saving Savannah: The City and the Civil War*. New York: Vintage.

Juris, Jeffery S. 2012. "Reflections on #Occupy Everywhere: Social Media, Public Space and Emerging Logics of Aggregation." *American Ethnologist* 39, no. 2 (May): 259–79.

Keil, Charles. 1966. *Urban Blues*. Chicago: University of Chicago Press.

Kemp, Mark. 2004. *Dixie Lullaby: A Story of Music, Race, and New Beginnings in a New South*. New York: Free Press.

King, Martin Luther, Jr. 1963. "Letter from a Birmingham Jail." Originally titled "The Negro Is Your Brother." *Atlantic Monthly* 212, no. 2 (August): 78–88.

Kingsolver, Ann. 1991. *Tobacco, Toyota, and Subaltern Development Discourses: Constructing Livelihoods and Community in Rural Kentucky*. Amherst: University of Massachusetts Press.

Knopper, Steve. 2009. *Appetite for Self-Destruction: The Spectacular Crash of the Record Industry in the Digital Age*. New York: Free Press.

Kochar, Rakesh, Richard Fry, and Paul Taylor. 2011. "Wealth Gaps Rise to Record Highs between Whites, Blacks, Hispanics." Pew Research Center, Washington, DC.

Kopple, Barbara. 1976. *Harlan County U.S.A.* Film. First Run Features.

Kot, Greg. 2009. *Ripped: How the Wired Generation Revolutionized Music.* New York: Scribner.

Krauze, Enrique. 2005. "The Pride in Memín Penguín." Op-ed. *Washington Post*, July 12.

Lady Gaga. 2009. "Bad Romance." *The Fame Monster.* Interscope/Streamline.

Lauterbach, Preston. 2011. *The Chitlin' Circuit and the Road to Rock 'n' Roll.* New York: Norton.

Lavoe, Héctor. 1978. "El Cantante." *Comedia.* Fania Records.

Leach, Edmund. 1966. "Time and False Noses." In "Two Essays Concerning the Symbolic Representation of Time." *Rethinking Anthropology.* London: Athlone.

Lefebvre, Henri. 1996. *Writings on Cities.* Oxford: Blackwell.

Lemann, Nicholas. 1991. *The Promised Land: The Great Black Migration and How It Changed America.* New York: Vintage.

Leogrande, William M. 1998. *Our Own Backyard: The United States in Central America, 1977–1992.* Chapel Hill: University of North Carolina Press.

Lévi-Strauss, Claude. 1968. *The Savage Mind.* Chicago: University of Chicago Press.

Levitin, Daniel J. 2006. *This Is Your Brain on Music: The Science of a Human Obsession.* New York: Penguin.

Lewis, Laura A. 2000. "Blacks, Black Indians, Afromexicans: The Dynamics of Race, Nation, and Identity in a Mexican 'Moreno' Community (Guerrero)." *American Ethnologist* 27, no. 4 (November): 898–926.

Limón, José. 1994. *Dancing with the Devil: Society and Cultural Poetics in Mexican-American South Texas.* Madison: University of Wisconsin Press.

Lipsitz, George. 1994. Dangerous Crossroads: Popular Music, Postmodernism and the Poetics of Place. London: Verso.

Lovato, Roberto. 2008. "Juan Crow: The Deep South's New Second-Class Citizens." *Nation*, May 21.

Low, Setha. 1996. "The Anthropology of Cities: Imagining and Theorizing the City." *Annual Review of Anthropology* 25:383–409.

Loza, Steven. 1993. *Barrio Rhythm: Mexican-American Music in Los Angeles.* Urbana: University of Illinois Press.

Lynyrd Skynyrd. 1974. "The Ballad of Curtis Loew." *Second Helping.* MCA Records.

Malone, Bill C. 1979. *Southern Music, American Music.* Lexington: University of Kentucky Press.

———. 2006. *Don't Get above Your Raisin': Country Music and the Southern Working Class.* Urbana: University of Illinois Press.

Manu Chao. 1998. *Clandestino.* Virgin Records.

Manuel, Peter, Kenneth Bilby, and Michael Largey. 2006. *Caribbean Currents: Caribbean Music from Rumba to Reggae.* Philadelphia: Temple University Press.

Marable, Manning. 2011. *Malcolm X: A Life of Reinvention.* New York: Viking.

Margolis, Maxine. 2009. *An Invisible Minority: Brazilian Immigrants in New York City.* Gainesville: University of Florida Press.

Maroon 5. 2003. "Sunday Morning." OctoScope Music.

Marske, Sarah. 2008. "Plaza Fiesta: A Re-imagined Homeland Contributing to Latino Identity and Community." Master's thesis, Communication Theses 39, Department of Communication, Georgia State University.

Marx, Karl. 1976. *Capital*. Vol. 1. New York: Penguin Classics.

Massey, Douglas, ed. 2007. *New Faces in New Places: The New Geography of American Immigration*. New York: Russell Sage.

———. 2011. "Isolated, Vulnerable and Broke." Op-ed. *New York Times*, August 4.

McCann, Bryan. 2004. *Hello, Hello Brazil: Popular Music in the Making of Modern Brazil*. Durham: Duke University Press.

McCullough, David. 1978. *The Path between the Seas: The Creation of the Panama Canal, 1870–1914*. New York: Simon and Schuster.

McWilliams, Carey. 1968. *North from Mexico: The Spanish-Speaking People of the United States*. New York: Greenwood.

Meléndez, Maudia. 2010. "¿Donde están los líderes?" *La Noticia*, February 24, 17.

Mendoza, Vicente T. 1939. *El romance español y el corrido mexicano*. México DF: Universidad Nacional Autónoma de México, Instituto de Investigaciones Estéticas.

Mentirosos, Los. 2009. "Ahora Te Puedes Marchar." *Ahora Te Puedes Marchar*.

Michigan Future, Inc. 2003. "Revitalizing Michigan's Center Cities: A Vision and Framework for Action." March.

Miguel, Luis. 1987. "Ahora Te Puedes Marchar." *Soy Como Quiero Ser*. Warner Music.

Miller, Marc S., ed. 1974. *Working Lives: The Southern Exposure History of Labor in the South*. New York: Pantheon.

Mintz, Sidney. 1974. *Worker in the Cane: A Puerto Rican Life History*. New York: Norton.

———. 1986. *Sweetness and Power: The Place of Sugar in Modern History*. New York: Penguin.

Montejano, David. 1987. *Anglos and Mexicans in the Making of Texas, 1836–1986*. Austin: University of Texas Press.

Morgen, Sandra, and Jeff Maskovsky. 2003. "The Anthropology of Welfare 'Reform': New Perspectives on U.S. Urban Poverty in the Post-Welfare Era." *Annual Review of Anthropology* 32:315–38.

Mullings, Leith. 2005. "Interrogating Racism: Toward an Antiracist Anthropology." *Annual Review of Anthropology* 34:667–93.

Mumford, Lewis. 1961. *The City in History: Its Origins, Its Transformations, and Its Prospects*. New York: Harcourt, Brace and World.

Nash, June, and María Patricia Fernández-Kelly, eds. 2001. *Women, Men, and the International Division of Labor*. Albany: State University of New York Press.

Nielsen. 2013. "Latino Populations Are Growing Fastest Where We Aren't Looking." May 1. http://www.nielsen.com/us/en/newswire/2013/latino-populations-are-growing-fastest-where-we-arent-looking.html.

Nguyen, Mai Thi, and Hannah Gill. 2010. "The 287(g) Program: The Costs and Consequences of Local Immigration Enforcement in North Carolina Communities."

Latino Migration Project, Institute for the Study of the Americas and the Center for Global Initiatives, University of North Carolina, Chapel Hill.

North Carolina State Center for Health Statistics. 2010. "North Carolina Minority Health Facts: Hispanics/Latinos." July.

Oboler, Suzanne, ed. 2006. *Latinos and Citizenship: The Dilemma of Belonging*. New York: Palgrave Macmillan.

OBRA Collective. N.d. Weblog. http://obracollective.wordpress.com/about/.

O'Connor, James. 1973. *The Fiscal Crisis of the State*. New York: St. Martin's.

Omi, Michael, and Howard Winant. 1994. *Racial Formation in the United States: From the 1960s to the 1990s*. New York: Routledge.

Ong, Aihwa. 1999. *Flexible Citizenship: The Cultural Logics of Transnationality*. Durham: Duke University Press.

Pacini Hernández, Deborah. 1995. *Bachata: A Social History of a Dominican Popular Music*. Philadelphia: Temple University Press.

Pacini Hernández, Deborah, Héctor Fernández L'Hoeste, and Eric Zolov, eds. 2004. *Rockin' Las Americas: The Global Politics of Rock in Latin/o America*. Pittsburgh: University of Pittsburgh Press.

Papademetriou, Demetrios G., Madeleine Sumption, and Aaron Terrazas. 2011. "Migration and the Great Recession: The TransAtlantic Experience." Migration Policy Institute, Washington, DC.

Paredes, Americo. 1958. *With His Pistol in His Hand: A Border Ballad and Its Hero*. Austin: University of Texas Press.

Passel, Jeremy, and D'Vera Cohn. 2011. "Unauthorized Immigrant Population: National and State Trends, 2010." Pew Hispanic Center, Washington, DC.

Paz, Octavio. 2001. *El laberinto de la soledad*. Madrid: Catedra.

PBS. 1998. "The Two Nations of Black America" (with Henry Louis Gates Jr.). *Frontline*, February 10.

Peacock, James, Harry Watson, and Carrie Matthews, eds. 2005. *The American South in a Global World*. Chapel Hill: University of North Carolina Press.

Pecknold, Diane. 2007. *The Selling Sound: The Rise of the Country Music Industry*. Durham: Duke University Press.

Peña, Manuel H. 1985. *The Texas-Mexican Conjunto: History of a Working Class Music*. Austin: University of Texas Press.

Pope, Liston. 1942. *Millhands and Preachers: A Study of Gastonia*. New Haven: Yale University Press.

Prieto, Rafael. 2012. "El 287g dejaría de funcionar en octubre." Qué Pasa/Mi Gente online, March 2.

Ragland, Cathy. 2009. *Música Norteña: Mexican Migrants Creating a Nation between Nations*. Philadelphia: Temple University Press.

Razsa, Maple, and Andrej Kurnik. 2012. "The Occupy Movement in Žižek's Hometown: Direct Democracy and a Politics of Becoming." *American Ethnologist* 39, no. 2 (May): 238–58.

Reed, Bryan. 2013. "Charlotte Struggles to Become a Live Music Landmark." *Charlotte Observer*, July 15.

Regis, Helen. 1999. "Second Lines, Minstrelsy, and the Contested Landscapes of New Orleans Afro-Creole Festivals." *Cultural Anthropology* 14, no. 4: 472–504.

REM. 1984. "So. Central Rain." *Reckoning*. I.R.S. Records.

Roberts, John Storm. 1979. *The Latin Tinge: The Impact of Latin American Music on the United States*. New York: Oxford University Press.

Rolling Stones. 1974. "It's Only Rock and Roll (But I Like It)." *It's Only Rock and Roll*. Rolling Stones Records WEA.

Rosaldo, Renato. 1994. "Cultural Citizenship in San Jose, California." *PoLAR* 17, no. 2 (November): 57–63.

Rosas, Gilberto. 2006. "The Thickening Borderlands: Diffused Exceptionality and 'Immigrant' Social Struggles during the 'War on Terror.'" *Cultural Dynamics* 18, no. 3: 335–49.

Rose, Tricia. 1994. Black Noise: Rap Music and Black Culture in Contemporary America. Hanover: Wesleyan University Press.

Rúa, La. 2005. *Una Noche de Abril*.

Ruiz, Alex. 2007. "La Chica Que Conocí." *El Joven del Ritmo*. Univision/Fonovisa 088353281-2.

Rumble, John W. N.d. "Charlotte Country: A Sixty Year Tradition." *History South*. Weblog. www.historysouth.org.

Russell, Tony. 1970. *Blacks, Whites, and Blues*. New York: Stein and Day.

Sacks, Karen, and Dorothy Remy. 1984. *My Troubles Are Going to Have Trouble with Me: Everyday Trials and Triumphs of Women Workers*. New Brunswick: Rutgers University Press.

Sagás, Ernesto. 2000. *Race and Politics in the Dominican Republic*. Gainesville: University Press of Florida.

Saguaro Seminar. N.d. "Social Capital Community Benchmark Survey: Executive Summary." John F. Kennedy School of Government, Harvard University, Cambridge, MA.

Santana, Carlos. 1969. "Evil Ways." Written by Clarence (Sonny) Henry. *Santana*. Columbia.

Sarig, Roni. 2007. *Third Coast: OutKast, Timbaland, and How Hip-Hop Became a Southern Thing*. Cambridge: Da Capo.

Sassen, Saskia. 1988. *The Mobility of Labor and Capital: A Study in International Investment and Labor Flow*. New York: Cambridge University Press.

———. 1991. *The Global City: New York, London, Tokyo*. Princeton: Princeton University Press.

Sawers, Larry, and William K. Tabb, eds. 1984. *Sunbelt/ Snowbelt: Urban Development and Regional Restructuring*. New York: Oxford University Press.

Schafer, R. Murray. 1993. *The Soundscape: Our Sonic Environment and the Tuning of the World*. Rochester, VT: Destiny Books.

Schneider, Jane, and Ida Susser, eds. 2003. *Wounded Cities: Deconstruction and Reconstruction in a Globalized World*. Oxford: Berg.

Schulman, Bruce. 1991. *From Cotton Belt to Sunbelt: Federal Policy, Economic Development, and the Transformation of the South, 1938–1980*. New York: Oxford University Press.

Scott, James C. 1987. *Weapons of the Weak: Everyday Forms of Peasant Resistance*. New Haven: Yale University Press.

Shearer, Toby, Hannah Levinson, and Armando Bellmas. 2013. *From the Back of the Line*. Film. Haberdashery Films.

Silverblatt, Irene. 2004. *Modern Inquisitions: Peru and the Colonial Origins of the Civilized World*. Durham: Duke University Press.

Silverstein, Paul A. 2005. "Immigrant Racialization and the New Savage Slot: Race, Migration, and Immigration in the New Europe." *Annual Review of Anthropology* 34:363–84.

Simmons, Merle. 1953. "Attitudes toward the U.S. Revealed in Mexican Corridos." *Hispania* 361:34–42.

Simon, Paul. 1986. *Graceland*. Warner Brothers.

Simonett, Helena. 2001. *Banda: Mexican Musical Life across Borders*. Middleton: Wesleyan University Press.

Smith, Harry, ed. 1997 *Anthology of American Folk Music*. Smithsonian Folkways B00001DJU.

Smith, Heather A., and Owen J. Furuseth, eds. 2006. *Latinos in the New South: Transformations of Place*. Burlington: Ashgate.

Smith, Michael P. 1994. "Behind the Lines: The Black Mardi Gras Indians and the New Orleans Second Line." *Black Music Research Journal* 14, no. 1 (Spring): 43–73.

Smith, Neil. 1992. "Geography, Difference and the Politics of Scale." In *Postmodernism and the Social Sciences*, edited by Joe Doherty, Elspeth Graham, and Mo Malek, 57–78. New York: Macmillan.

———. 2004. *American Empire: Roosevelt's Geographer and the Prelude to Globalization*. Berkeley: University of California Press.

Smith, Robert C. 2005. *Mexican New York: Transnational Lives of New Immigrants*. Berkeley: University of California Press.

Smith, Stephen Samuel. 2010. "Development and the Politics of School Desegregation and Resegregation." In *Charlotte, NC: The Global Evolution of a New South City*, edited by William Graves and Heather A. Smith, 189–219. Athens: University of Georgia Press.

Southern Poverty Law Center. 2009. "Under Siege: Life for Latinos in the South." Montgomery, AL.

———. 2012. "Alabama's Shame: HB 56 and the War on Immigrants." Montgomery, AL.

Spellman, A. B. 1966. *Four Lives in the Bebop Business*. New York: Pantheon.

Springfield, Dusty. 1963. "I Only Want to Be with You." Phillips Records.

Stack, Carol. 1996. *Call to Home: African Americans Reclaim the Rural South*. New York: Basic Books.

Stavans, Ilan. 1995. *The Hispanic Condition: Reflections on Culture and Identity in America*. New York: HarperCollins.

Steward, Julian. 1956. *The People of Puerto Rico: A Study in Social Anthropology.* Urbana: University of Illinois Press.

Stokes, Martin. 2004. "Music and the Global Order." *Annual Review of Anthropology* 33:47–72.

Striffler, Steve. 2005. *Chicken: The Dangerous Transformation of America's Favorite Food.* New Haven: Yale University Press.

Strimling, Jacobo. 2010. "Circulando, circulando . . . que ya llegó la maldita." *Mi Gente,* April 13, 31.

Sublette, Ned. 2004. *Cuba and Its Music: From the First Drums to the Mambo.* Chicago: Chicago Review Press.

Suro, Roberto, and Anthony Singer. 2002. "Latino Growth in Metropolitan America: Changing Patterns, New Locations." Brookings Institution, Washington, DC, July.

Susser, Ida. 1982. *Norman Street: Poverty and Politics in an Urban Neighborhood.* New York: Oxford University Press.

———. 2011a. *AIDS, Sex, and Culture: Global Politics and Survival in Southern Africa.* Malden, MA: Wiley-Blackwell.

———. 2011b. "Organic Intellectuals, Crossing Scales, and the Emergence of Social Movements with Respect to AIDS in South Africa." *American Ethnologist* 38:733–42.

Takaki, Ronald. 2000. *Iron Cages: Race and Culture in Nineteenth-Century America.* New York: Oxford University Press.

Telles, Edward E. 2004. *Race in Another America: The Significance of Skin Color in Brazil.* Princeton: Princeton University Press.

Thompson, E. P. 1963. *The Making of the English Working Class.* New York: Vintage.

Tigres del Norte, Los. 1988. *16 Super Exitos.* Fonovisa.

———. 1997. *Jefe de Jefes.* Fonovisa.

———. 2000. *De Paisano a Paisano.* Fonovisa.

Tilley, Virginia. 2002. "New Help or New Hegemony? The Transnational Indigenous Peoples' Movement and 'Being Indian' in El Salvador." *Journal of Latin American Studies* 34:525–54.

Tonnies, Ferdinand. 1887. *Gemeinschaft und Gesellschaft.* Leipzig: Fues's Verlag.

Touchet, Leo, and Vernel Bagneris. 1998. *Rejoice When You Die: The New Orleans Jazz Funerals.* Baton Rouge: Louisiana State University Press.

Tri, El. 2004. *35 Años: En Vivo desde el Auditorio Nacional.* WEA.

Tropic Culture. 2008. *Live to Love Love to Live.* B001DM3HD6.

———. 2010. *Dance Revolution.*

Trust for America's Health. 2011. "New Report: North Carolina Is 14th Most Obese State in Nation."

Tsing, Anna Lowenhaupt. 2005. *Friction: An Ethnography of Global Connection.* Princeton: Princeton University Press.

Tucanes de Tijuana, Los. 1995. "Mis Tres Animales." *14 Tucanazos Bien Pesados.* Alacran/EMI Latin.

Tullos, Allen. 1989. *Habits of Industry: White Culture and the Transformation of the Carolina Piedmont.* Chapel Hill: University of North Carolina Press.

Turner, Victor. 1969. *The Ritual Process: Structure and Anti-Structure*. Chicago: Aldine.

Twine, France Winddance. 1997. *Racism in a Racial Democracy: The Maintenance of White Supremacy in Brazil*. New Brunswick: Rutgers University Press.

U2. 1987. "I Still Haven't Found What I'm Looking For." *The Joshua Tree*. Island.

Urban Land Institute. 2007. "Eastland Mall, Charlotte, North Carolina: An Advisory Services Panel Report." March 5–8.

U.S. Census. 2000. "Charlotte Region: Race and Ethnicity." http://factfinder2.census.gov/faces/tableservices/jsf/pages/productview.xhtml?src=CF.

———. 2010. "Charlotte Region: Race and Ethnicity." http://factfinder2.census.gov/faces/tableservices/jsf/pages/productview.xhtml?src=bkmk.

Valdés, Bebo, and Diego "El Cigala." 2003. "Lágrimas Negras." *Lágrimas Negras*. Calle 54 Records.

Vasconcelos, José. 1997. *La raza cósmica*. Baltimore: Johns Hopkins University Press. First published 1925.

Vidales, Guadalupe, Kristen Day, and Michael Powe. 2009. "Police and Immigration Enforcement: Impacts on Latino(a) Residents' Perceptions of Police." *Policing: An International Journal of Police Strategies and Management* 32, no. 4: 631–53.

Vinson, Ben, III, and Bobby Vaughn. 2004. *Afroméxico*. México DF: Centro de Investigación y Docencia Económicas.

Wade, Stephen. 2012. *The Beautiful Music All around Us*. Urbana: University of Illinois Press.

Wainer, Andrew. 2006. "The New Latino South and the Challenge to American Public Education." *International Migration* 44, no. 5: 129–65.

Wald, Elijah. 2001. *Narcocorrido*. New York: HarperCollins.

Walser, Robert. 1993. *Running with the Devil: Power, Gender and Madness in Heavy Metal Music*. Hanover, NH: Wesleyan University Press.

Washburne, Chris. 2008. *Sounding Salsa: Performing Latin Music in New York City*. Philadelphia: Temple University Press.

Waxer, Lisa. 2002. *The City of Musical Memory: Salsa, Record Grooves and Popular Culture in Cali, Colombia*. Middletown, CT: Wesleyan University Press.

White, Bob W. 2008. *Rumba Rules: The Politics of Dance Music in Mobutu's Zaire*. Durham: Duke University Press.

Wilde, Oscar. 2008. *The Picture of Dorian Gray*. New York: Penguin. First published 1891.

Wilkerson, Isabel. 2010. *The Warmth of Other Suns: The Epic Story of America's Great Migration*. New York: Random House.

Wolf, Eric. 1984. "Culture: Panacea or Problem?" *American Antiquity* 49, no. 2: 393–400.

———. 1997. *Europe and the People without History*. Berkeley: University of California Press.

Wolfe, Thomas. 2011. *You Can't Go Home Again*. New York: Scribner.

Woodward, C. Vann. 1971. *Origins of the New South, 1877–1913*. Baton Rouge: Louisiana State University Press. First published 1951.

Zavella, Patricia. 2011. *I'm Neither Here nor There: Mexicans' Quotidian Struggles with Migration and Poverty*. Durham: Duke University Press.

———. 2012. "Beyond the Screams: Latino Punkeros Contest Nativist Discourses." *Latin American Perspectives* 39, no. 2 (March): 27–41.

Zolov, Eric. 1999. *Refried Elvis: The Rise of the Mexican Counterculture*. Berkeley: University of California Press.

Zúñiga, Víctor, and Rubén Hernández-León, eds. 2005. *New Destinations of Mexican Immigration in the United States: Community Formation, Local Responses and Inter-Group Relations*. New York: Russell Sage.

Zurdok. 1997. "El Gallito Inglés." *Antena*. Universal Music.

INDEX

ABOUT THE AUTHOR

Samuel K. Byrd is an anthropologist (Ph.D., City University of New York Graduate Center) and Adjunct Assistant Professor at Hunter College (CUNY). His research interests include music, urban life, immigration, and the U.S. South. He lives in Manhattan with his wife and two daughters.